Islam in An

SECOND EDITION

The Columbia Contemporary American Religion Series

Columbia Contemporary American Religion Series

The spiritual landscape of contemporary America is as varied and complex as that of any country in the world. The books in this series, written by leading scholars for students and general readers alike, fall into two categories: Some titles are portraits of the country's major religious groups. They describe and explain particular religious practices and rituals, beliefs, and major challenges facing a given community today. Others explore current themes and topics in American religion that cut across denominational lines. The texts are supplemented with carefully selected photographs and artwork, and annotated bibliographies.

Roman Catholicism in America
CHESTER GILLIS

Islam in America
JANE I. SMITH

Buddhism in America
RICHARD HUGHES SEAGER

Protestantism in America
RANDALL BALMER AND LAUREN F. WINNER

Judaism in America
MARC LEE RAPHAEL

The Quakers in America
THOMAS D. HAMM

New Age and Neopagan Religions in America
SARAH PIKE

Baptists in America
BILL J. LEONARD

Islam in America

SECOND EDITION

Jane I. Smith

COLUMBIA UNIVERSITY PRESS
NEW YORK

CONTENTS

INTRODUCTION

"Muslim Americans represent the most affluent, integrated, politically engaged Muslim community in the Western world," professed *Newsweek* magazine in sharing the results of a major survey conducted by the Pew Research Center in 2007.[1] Good news indeed. All seems well for American Islam, and indeed in many ways that is quite true. Muslims are as educated and as financially stable as other citizens in America. Yet the subtitle of the article gives the fuller picture: "Muslim Americans are one of this country's greatest strengths. But they're vulnerable as never before." Close to half of Americans feel that their country has too many immigrants from Muslim countries, the poll revealed, and a majority confess to being either somewhat or very worried about radicals in the American Muslim community.[2]

This book was first published in 1999, two years before the attacks on the twin towers in New York and on the Pentagon. The present version updates that material, taking into account many of the things that have happened to American Muslims in the past decade. Those parts of the book that continue to represent the realities of Islam in America as they were earlier described remain here with little revision. Many events have taken place, however, in the United States and in the Muslim community itself that have deeply affected the lives of Muslims in America. As much of that new material as possible has been included, both in the first seven chapters and in the conclusion, chapter 8, which is dedicated specifically to post-9/11 American Islam.

Where Is Islam?

It has become commonplace to note that in the West in general, and the United States in particular, Muslims no longer can be thought of as "over there." They have become a visible part of the fabric of Western society. Still, only recently have many Americans begun to grasp that Islam, along with Christianity and Judaism, is itself a "Western" religion. Most scholarly as well as popular writing continues to slip easily into the dichotomy of "Islam *and* (or, *over against*) the West." But information about American Islam and American Muslims is increasingly available through media accounts, in an enormous range of popular and scholarly books and articles, and of course on the Internet. It is also difficult not to notice the presence of Muslims in virtually all American cities and towns. The American public, however, knows little if anything about the religion itself. For the most part, Americans have no concept that approximately as many Muslims as Jews live in America and that they outnumber many of the mainline Protestant denominations. On one occasion before 9/11, after an introductory talk I gave on Muslim faith and practice, a woman asked me, "Where is Islam?" supposing it to be a country. Now, a decade later, those who know very little about Islam are more likely to ask, "Why do Muslims hate the West?"

Students of recent American history are well aware of the dramatic changes in the religious demography of the United States with the arrival of Muslims, Hindus, Buddhists, Sikhs, Jains, Zoroastrians, and many others to the urban and rural areas of America. One can now find Muslim communities across the continent, their citizens occupied as farmworkers and day laborers, as teachers and social workers, as physicians, engineers, and other highly successful professionals. Houses of worship range from storefront mosques in crowded urban areas to some of the striking new Islamic centers constructed in the last several decades. The sharp rise in scholarly studies in the field of American Islam, the addition of materials on U.S. Muslims in a number of university courses, the increased attention to Islamic religion and culture in high school curricula, and opportunities for Muslim children to talk about their holidays to their classmates at the grade-school level all make it unnecessary for those coming through the American educational system to ask, "Where is Islam?"

Unfortunately much of the post-9/11 media coverage of Islam has served not to help the American public really understand the faith but rather to foster and perpetuate negative images and stereotypes of malevolent figures unrecognizable as Muslims by their coreligionists in America. What is this religion whose presence in the United States is so visible, and so permanent, that many Muslims are asking for America to be called a Judeo-Christian and Muslim country? Is it simply a foreign faith transplanted onto Western soil, or is it emerging as a genuinely American phenomenon? Is it a frightening religion that still lives by the sword and denigrates women, or is it one to be appreciated, admired, and respected alongside Judaism and Christianity as an Abrahamic faith sharing the understanding of one true God?

The faith of Islam arose in seventh-century Arabia when, as Muslims believe, God chose a religious visionary named Muhammad to be the last prophet of the monotheistic religions. It spread rapidly throughout the greater Middle East, North Africa, and Southern Europe and within a century was a vital force in much of the known world. For most of their history, Muslims have been creative contributors to the development of science and art, literature and philosophy, technology and culture. Major Muslim empires ruled over vast areas of the world until the beginning of the twentieth century. Today there are well over a billion Muslims across the globe, in virtually every country, and Islam is considered one of the five or six "great world religions." Muslims understand the Qur'an, the holy book of Islam, to be the verbatim revelation of God to Muhammad, and it is now available in translation (Muslims would say "interpretation") in most of the world's languages.

The Deep Roots of Anti-Muslim Sentiment

Centuries of encounter between Islam and Western Christianity, including the dramatic growth and spread of the new religion that spilled over the frontiers of Christian territory, as well as the long, drawn-out battles and skirmishes of the Crusades, left on both sides a legacy of misunderstanding, fear, prejudice, and, in some cases, hatred. This legacy, along with current fears and concerns about "Islamic extremism," forms part of the context in which to understand the experience of Muslims in what has been a mainly Christian America. Non-Muslims in the United States are sometimes clear and vocal about their distrust of Islam, and negative images of the Prophet and his religion have been part of public rhetoric for quite a while. Sometimes, however, people do not even realize that they are the victims of a prejudice that they would be unable to name. Describing her first experience at an American women's conference in 1980, Leila Ahmed, an Egyptian scholar of women's studies who now teaches at Harvard, said she was "nearly speechless and certainly in shock at the combination of hostility and sheer ignorance that the Muslim panelists, myself included, almost invariably encountered."[3] Expecting to be joining a discussion in which women were asked to critique their various faiths, she found such strong anti-Muslim feelings that she felt instead as if she were being asked to give up her faith entirely.

Since that time, American sensitivities have become somewhat more sharply honed in relation to Islam, partly of course because more Americans are themselves now Muslims or from Muslim cultures. The ugliness of September 11 has led to a dreadful aftermath in many ways, although in some others it has served as a wake-up call to both Muslims and non-Muslims. Many citizens have recognized that it is their responsibility to learn something about this religion that gained their attention in such a sudden and unexpected way. Muslims have spoken endlessly about their faith, study groups have proliferated, and political action committees have been formed to ensure that Muslim American citizens will be protected should another such calamity occur. Americans are also working with Muslim groups to achieve a more fair presentation of Islam in the media, the classroom, and the common imagination.

As for Muslim Americans themselves, 9/11 seems in some ways to have shocked them out of a kind of complacency with which they were living and working in America but not yet coming to terms with the responsibilities of citizenship. For a major part of their history in America, many Muslims wanted to live somewhere on the margins, maintaining a degree of separation so as to devote their attention to preserving their Muslim identity in a Western culture. Since 9/11 that marginality has become much less viable. The fact that Muslims are now being challenged to seriously analyze Islam and its role in twenty-first-century America coincides with the passing of a generation of Muslim leadership and the rise of new young leaders—educational, religious, political—who seem ready to take on the task of thinking in new ways and creating incentives to encourage their fellow Muslims toward greater involvement in American life.

Much of the development of Islam in the twentieth and early twenty-first centuries, detailed in the last part of chapter 2, has been in reaction to what is perceived by Muslims as Western imperialism—in its political, economic, and even religious aspects. In recent decades a number of movements have arisen in different parts of the Muslim world calling for a renewed intentionality about the role of Islam in the running of the state and in the public lives as well as the private lives of Muslims. Unfortunately, recent years have also seen the rise of a reactionary kind of Islam that has often led to violence, the events of 9/11 being but one manifestation of that tendency. Many different kinds of responses are described by the single label *Islamic fundamentalism*, or *Islamic extremism*, though each is in fact a product of particular political, geographical, and economic circumstances. The challenge for American Muslims is to live and practice an Islam in which the values of justice, morality, and peaceful coexistence with people of other faiths and persuasions are able to overshadow the image of militant Islam that is so often publicized in the U.S. media.

Establishing Some Parameters

Three or four decades ago there were probably fewer than half a million Muslims in America, including immigrants and African Americans. Without question the numbers have increased, although to exactly what extent is difficult to determine. A number of factors make reasonable estimates difficult: (a) The U.S. census does not ask for religious affiliation. (b) Figures depend on who is doing the counting. Different groups have their own reasons for inflating or deflating the numbers. (c) It is not always clear who has the right to determine whether a person is really Muslim. Some groups and individuals claim Islamic identity, while others deny that identity for them. (d) Some people of Islamic heritage do not want to be actively identified as Muslims at this moment in history. A reasonable guess is that four to six million Muslims now live in America, though most Muslims would claim that the actual figure is higher and some non-Muslims would claim that it is lower.

Scholars used to talk about Muslims in the United States as being either immigrants or African Americans. With the passage of time and the establishment of more families who have lived in the country for several generations, however, the clearest distinction seems to be between foreign-born Muslims (first-generation immigrants) and American-born Muslims (those of immigrant heritage, African Americans, and other converts), remembering that a number of Muslims are always in the country in a sojourner capacity as students, government officials, business executives, and so on.

While again it is difficult to determine exact proportions, several studies have estimated that perhaps 40 percent of the Muslim community is African American. That number includes followers of the recently deceased Imam W. D. Mohammed, members of other Sunni organizations, and those who belong to heterodox groups that adhere to some interpretation of Islam. The largest representation of first-generation immigrants and those of longer-standing immigrant heritage is from South Asia, followed by Arab countries, Iran, sub-Saharan Africa, East Asia, and the former Soviet Union, with many other cultures also represented. By religious affiliation some 80 percent are Sunnis. Most of the rest represent Shi'ite groups, including Ithna 'Asharis or Twelvers from Iran, Iraq, Lebanon, East Africa, and the Indian subcontinent; Isma'ilis or Seveners, followers of Aga Khan, from the Indian subcontinent and West Africa; Zaidis or Fivers from Yemen and Algeria; and some 'Alawis and Druze from Syria and Lebanon.

The picture of American Islam is greatly complicated by the many sectarian movements that want to identify themselves as "Muslim," an identification often seriously challenged by other Muslims. American Muslims are deeply involved in formulating what it means to be part of the "*umma* (community) in the West," and through the development of Islamic organizations, increasing numbers of local and national meetings and conferences, and rapidly proliferating communications, they are in the process of determining the nature and authenticity of an indigenous American Islam. It is clear that the primary responsibility for making this determination is now in the hands of the new young adult generation of American Muslims.

What Is This Book About?

This volume provides a general introduction to the religion of Islam as American Muslims experience and practice it and to the range of communities and groups that are part of the faith. The opening chapters help the reader locate the experiences of American Muslims within the history of Muslim beliefs, institutions, and developments. Chapter 1 introduces the beliefs and rituals that have characterized the Islamic community from the time of the Prophet and that frame the religious life of American Muslims. It sets the five articles of Muslim faith and the five elements of formal religious practice within the context of community life and suggests some of the reasons why Muhammad continues to be a model for the faithful. "Following the Sunnah [way of the Prophet] does not mean just imitating the outward appearance of the Prophet, but it means creative learning from his character and example," says Muzammil Siddiqi, past president of the Islamic Society of North America. "He is our paradigm because he was closest to Allah in his relationship and lived his life fully and totally for the sake of Allah. That was the secret of his moral excellence and his life became a paradigm for this reason."[4]

Chapter 2 looks at the lives and personal experiences of people who have played significant roles in the past and recent history of Islam. It describes the swift and broad spread of the religion during the early years of its existence and the development of the main Islamic disciplines, including law, theology, philosophy, and mysticism. This section illustrates some of the ways in which the lives of individual Muslims, their influence, and their decisions about what Islam means and how to live ethically and religiously have shaped the faith and practice of those trying to determine what it means to be Muslim in today's Western society.

In chapters 3 and 4 we consider some of the many ways in which Islam has come to be a significant and highly visible part of American history and culture. Chapter 3 sketches the complex history of immigrant Islam in America. It traces the immigrant movements from the middle of the nineteenth century, primarily from the Middle East, through the several waves of immigration, to the present time, in which Muslims come from virtually everywhere in the world. Illustrating the broad range of cultural contexts represented by Muslim immigrants, this chapter describes their great variety of educational and professional levels, and the different ways in which they believe Islam should be practiced in America. Adding to this already complex scene is the phenomenon of growing numbers of converts to Islam from among the white, Hispanic, and Native American population, sometimes coming to the faith through affiliation with one of the many Sufi movements in the United States and Canada. Chapter 4 begins with the introduction of Muslim slaves to America and their (in most cases) forced conversion to Christianity. Their story includes a detailed discussion of the rise of African American Islam, from the early expressions of black nationalism through the appearance and development of the Nation of Islam to contemporary manifestations of both orthodox and heterodox Muslim movements.

The next three chapters look at some of the issues that confront Muslims who want to live faithfully in the context of America. Many Muslims in the West do not attend a mosque or participate in religious observances, considering themselves Muslim primarily by heritage or cultural affiliation. Others, especially since 9/11, are observant, practicing, and mosque-attending Muslims. These chapters describe the concerns that such Muslims face with respect to worship and religious life, family and personal matters, the role of women in American Islam, the raising and educating of children, care for the elderly and for those in the military and in prison, the use of Islamically acceptable products, appropriate dress and behavior, and many other issues related to life in a country in which Islam is misunderstood, unappreciated, and since 9/11 often feared.

Particular attention is paid to the development of mosques and American Islamic organizations, the propagation of the faith, and growing Muslim involvement in American political processes. The phenomenon of Islamic outreach activity is discussed in some detail, reflecting the intent of some Muslims to make America their mission field. "The Islamic vision endows North America with a new destiny worthy of it," said Isma'il al Faruqi, late Palestinian professor from Temple University. "For this renovation of itself, of its spirit, for its rediscovery of a God-given mission and self-dedication to its pursuit, the continent cannot but be grateful to the immigrant with Islamic vision. It cannot but interpret his advent on the shores except as a God-given gift, a timely divine favor and mercy."[5]

The final chapter concentrates on how the events of September 11, 2001, dramatically changed the lives of Muslims as well as the American public as a whole. It considers the consequences of the "war on terror" and the resulting attacks on Muslim civil rights, including government profiling of Muslims and curtailing of certain Muslim organizations. New Muslim leadership is calling for equal protection under the law, demanding the constitutional guarantees of freedom *of* religion and *from* repression. Vilification of Muslims is nothing new on the American scene, but since 9/11 it has taken on new dimensions with the rise of what is known as "Islamophobia," or fear of Islam, exemplified in anti-Muslim literature and videos, the demonizing of Islam by certain evangelical Christian clergy, and the implications of U.S. war propaganda. Muslims are working at the grassroots levels both to get elected to local public offices in order to effect change and to form political liaisons from the ground up. Affirming the democratic nature of Islam, they are learning how to respond to American foreign policy decisions.

Chapter 8 also considers some of the tensions that now exist within the Muslim community in America—between conservatives and liberals, Sunnis and Shi'ites, African Americans and Muslims of immigrant heritage, as well as the differing responses to foreign influences on American Islam such as the Wahhabis/Salafis, Shi'ite Ayatollahs, and international organizations that are suspected by the government of having ties to "terrorist" groups. The chapter considers the growth in literature about pluralism, dealing with questions of Islam and democracy, with Muslim responses to other Muslims and with attitudes toward other religions such as Christianity and Judaism. Members of the Muslim community have greatly expanded their interfaith outreach in the aftermath of 9/11, from holding mosque open houses to

health care and new forms of social service, community outreach, and the
initiation of interfaith dialogue.

Here, then, are some of the concerns facing Muslims in America—
immigrant, African American, and convert—as they look to the next
decades. The issues are those that Muslims themselves are raising in their
literature, conversations, and local and national meetings. The complexity of
the American Muslim scene is reflected in its racial-ethnic and cultural mix,
in the changes from early immigrants to those who are second-, third-, and
even fourth-generation Americans, in the ways in which Muslims are and
are not allowing themselves to be influenced by trends and movements overseas, and in the many different understandings of what it means to affirm
and maintain an Islamic identity in a context in which Islam is still a small
minority faith.

The matter at hand for the American Muslim community as a whole is
how to discern "American Islam" in the face of the many conflicting ethnic and cultural identities, languages, and interpretations of which it is composed, and how to ensure that the "moderate" Islam that emerges is defined
not by outsiders and not by the American government but by American
Muslims themselves.

The picture of American Islam changes each day as new people join the
community, new information becomes available from a range of resources,
and new interpretations are developed to help Muslims know more about
their faith and how it can be practiced in a pluralist society. "The time has
come for the American Muslim community to take full responsibility for
their affairs," insists one Muslim commentator. "We must lay the foundation
for our younger generation to live and prosper in this country as political
and economic equals."[ ] That task will be easier to the degree that Americans know more about, and can come to better appreciate, the religion of
Islam as a vital contributor to this country's religious landscape. This book is
intended as one way to facilitate that task.

Islam in America

SECOND EDITION

But while the surroundings are different, the ritual is the same—washing, standing, sitting, prostrating, reciting. Muslims take great pride in the fact that despite architectural and other kinds of variations, no matter where in the world one goes to worship, the essentials of the ritual will be the same. In some mosques non-Muslims are welcome to attend the service, although this is not true of all mosque communities, either in the United States or elsewhere. When the service in the mosque is over, the men may stay and talk with the imam and one another for a while, sometimes about the sermon but more often about community affairs. The women gather the children, greet and hug their neighbors, retrieve their shoes, and leave; they too are ready to get on with the business of the day.

How have rituals such as this become part of the fabric of Islam? What binds Muslims around the world in recognition of the importance of the ritual prayer, whether or not they actually participate in it regularly, and of the other elements of Islamic faith and practice? The answer that American Muslims will give to such questions is clear and direct. Muslims believe what they do, and practice as they do, because of the example of the Prophet Muhammad, who established his community in Mecca and Medina according to the directives he received from God. Before looking more specifically at those elements that make up Muslim faith and practice, it is important to get an idea of how central the figure of the Prophet is to Muslims, and why many American Muslims pattern their own lives as closely as possible on the model he set for all succeeding generations.

"By the star when it sets, your companion is not in error, nor is he deceived, nor does he speak out of his own desire. Truly this is a revelation revealed, taught to him by one who is strong and mighty in power. He was on the cusp of the uttermost horizon, then he drew near and approached until he was the distance of two bows' lengths or even closer. Thus did [God] reveal to His servant that which He revealed" (Sura 53:1–10).

With this stirring description of the appearance of the angel Gabriel to a man named Muhammad ibn (son of) Abdullah in the Arabian desert more than fourteen centuries ago, the Qur'an, the Holy Book of Islam, confirms that God himself chose to send his revelations to this, the last of his messengers and prophets. For a people who are accustomed to the regularity of nature, nothing is more sure than the setting of the morning star, and the chapter of the Qur'an in which this early meeting between Muhammad and Gabriel takes place bears the title "The Star." Muslims believe that as this daily event is utterly reliable, so is the affirmation made here that Muhammad himself, identified in the verse as the "companion," is truly the recipient of divine revelation.

CHAPTER ONE

Muslim Faith and Practice

On Friday shortly after noon in a small inner-city mosque, a converted storefront used primarily by African Americans, the worshipers slowly gather. A man who has volunteered to vacuum before each prayer service makes certain that the carpets are clean to receive the foreheads of those who will soon bow in prostration to God. Each person removes his or her shoes before entering the worship hall, placing them in a wooden rack near the front door. The carpets, which are really thin runners, are arranged so that those gathered for prayer will be facing in the direction of Mecca, indicated by a plaque at the front of the hall. The room is bare of furniture except for a lectern in the front and a few folding chairs in the back for those who are unable to sit on the floor. Arabic calligraphy on the wall proclaims the *basmalla*, or invocation, "In the name of God, the Merciful, the Compassionate." The vacuum stops. Worshipers, who have performed their ablutions in the basement before entering the prayer hall, individually prepare themselves for participation in the communal worship. A man rises, faces the front, puts his hands behind his ears, and chants the call that will begin the service: "Come to the prayer, come to the time of felicity. . . ." The imam steps forward, and the ritual begins.

For the Muslim, prayer is not simply a mental or spiritual attitude or even just a matter of thanksgiving of the mind and heart. It involves a total bodily response, both sitting and putting oneself through a series of physical prostrations. For that reason, mosques do not have chairs or pews. Each of the five daily prayers consists of a series of ritual bowings and prostrations (each set called a *raka'* accompanied by the appropriate prayers and invocations.

Standing shoulder to shoulder, the worshipers are arranged in rows facing the imam, or leader, of the prayer, men in the front and women in the back. Children, who are almost always present, remain more or less quietly with the women, the older ones learning the steps of the prayer ritual. Boys who are past early childhood sit with their fathers. Most of the men are wearing small woven or embroidered caps, and the women have long sleeves and skirts or pants, with their hair fully covered. Together they perform the several sets of prayer prostrations, which include standing, bowing at the waist with hands placed near the knees, and kneeling and placing one's forehead on the carpet in full supplication. "When you are in that position of complete vulnerability," explains the imam, "you really get a feel for what it means to submit yourself fully to God."

The ritual includes the common recitation of the Fatiha, the brief opening chapter of the Qur'an that functions for the Muslim much as the Lord's Prayer does for the Christian when it is said in unison. The imam renders the phrases of the ritual as much in Arabic as possible so that his congregants can become more familiar with the language. Because it is Friday, the service includes a sermon given by the imam, in English, generally on a topic related to living as faithful Muslims in America or, occasionally, learning to relate to people of other faiths. Listeners remain seated on the carpets during this homily. At the end of the prayer the worshipers say the *taslim*, or salutation, invoking peace, by which one both greets those who are worshiping around him or her and signals once more one's absolute submission to God. When the service is over, worshipers stand, greet one another, and file out to return to their daily activities.

Meanwhile, across the city, the same ritual is being carried out in another mosque, but under quite different circumstances. This mosque, whose congregation is made up mainly of professional immigrant Muslims, has been built on a classical Islamic model. A dome on top, mounted with a visible crescent, leaves no doubt that this is a Muslim house of worship. The prayer hall is large, and thick carpets cover its floor. Women come into the mosque through a separate entrance and worship on the second level in a kind of balcony, from which they can watch the imam and the men through a latticework railing. The presence of women in the mosque is, for the most part, an American adaptation. Children roam freely and feel less constraint to be quiet than when they are in the same room with the men and the imam. Most of the women participate in the prayer ritual, although some prefer to sit and talk quietly with one another in the corner. They too are dressed conservatively, sometimes in the traditional clothing of their country of origin.

Muslims praying on Madison Avenue in New York City before Muslim Day parade.
© JOLIE STAHL

Muslims accord the highest respect to Muhammad, seeing in him the prototype of spiritual guidance, wise leadership, and moral example for the best of human living, both communally and individually in relation to God. American Muslims are often particularly conscientious about adding the phrase "may the blessing and peace of God be upon him" whenever mentioning the name of the Prophet. And yet the three things specifically denied concerning the Prophet Muhammad in the Qur'an's "Star" chapter actually came to pass. Over the centuries he has been accused, especially by Christians, of being in gross error, of being led astray (deceived) by the powers of Satan, and of being so overcome with his own desires for power that he invented a false and diabolic religion with which to dupe his people. Some have even suggested that he must have suffered from epilepsy, citing the testimony that he was quite overcome with the early revelations he received from God through the angel.

Muslims in America today still find that these three accusations characterize the opinions most non-Muslims have about the Prophet. Was he well meaning but simply wrong? Somewhat less charitably, was he somehow in the grip of a kind of malignant power that led him to such erroneous claims?

Or worst of all, was he a self-aggrandizing seeker of personal glory who fabricated divine revelations to secure a position of political leadership?

While many Americans decry the negative assessments of Muhammad that have characterized Western judgments over the centuries, blatant examples still appear. AT&T WorldNet Service, the largest direct Internet service provider in the United States, in June 1998 removed a Web site that referred to Muhammad as a lecherous hypocrite who clearly was no man of God. Muslims in America and around the contemporary world expressed their hurt and anger in the so-called Cartoon Controversy of 2005, when journalists in Denmark published sketches of Muhammad in the *Jyllands-Posten* with a bomblike head and in other highly derogatory images. The cartoons were replicated in more than fifty newspapers.

Non-Muslims who are uncomfortable with viewing Muhammad as misguided, opportunistic, or simply wrong may with some hesitation admit to Muhammad's status as a prophet of God, although generally without the essential Islamic understanding that his was the last and final divine revelation, or without conceding that the message to Muhammad could in any way contravene the truth of the Bible. Muslims are saddened, puzzled, and even angry that non-Muslim Americans still seem to have so little understanding or appreciation that the founder of Islam exemplified the finest of human qualities. It is to him that Muslims continue to look as the recipient of the final and lasting word of God, and the exemplar for their own modes of public and private behavior, and it is to him that are credited the basics of Muslim belief and practice.

The Elements of Islamic Faith and Practice

The articles of belief and practice that structure the life of the faithful American Muslim today have been developed out of the experiences of the Prophet Muhammad (detailed in chapter 2) and drawn from the basic teachings of the Qur'an. Muslims understand that as there are five responsibilities that all the faithful are expected to perform, often referred to as the five "pillars" (*arkan*) of Islam, so there are five articles of faith that together constitute the Muslim affirmation of divine being and human responsibility. Many struggle to practice all of these duties as faithfully as possible and to make them evident in their daily life. Others may do none, or pick and choose, or even modify them when they feel it is appropriate to life in America.

The Five Elements of Faith

From an early age Muslim children learn from their parents and mosque schools that Islam is based on five specific beliefs:

I. BELIEF IN GOD Implicit in the Islamic understanding of God is the notion of an unqualified difference between divine and human. The very recognition of God is often expressed by the term *tawhid*, meaning both God's oneness and the human acknowledgment of that oneness. It presupposes that no other being is like God and that humans must not only testify to God's uniqueness but also reflect their belief through their own lives and actions. As God alone is Lord and Creator of the universe, so the Muslim acknowledges God's oneness by living a life of integratedness, integrity, and ethical and moral responsibility. In the Islamic understanding, the greatest sin a human being can commit is to impugn the oneness of God, to suggest by word or deed that anything else could share in that divine unity. This sin is called *shirk*, association or participation. Over history, orthodox Muslims have often felt that some mystics have come dangerously close to heresy in their affirmation of experiences of oneness with God.

Islam is the only major religion whose very name suggests a bidimensional focus of faith. On one axis it refers to the individual human response to God's oneness, and on the other it means the community of all of those who share that response. While pious people through the ages have been understood to be *muslims*, it was only with the official beginning of the community at the time of the Prophet that there arose a specific recognition that Muslims together form a group, an *umma* or community. The term *Islam* itself was not much used in that sense, however, until considerably later. The struggle to identify what *umma* means in the Western milieu and to determine if there can be a distinctively American Muslim community is one in which American Muslims are deeply immersed, as succeeding chapters will illustrate.

2. BELIEF IN THE REALITY OF ANGELS In the West, in the early twenty-first century, angels are the subject of much speculation. Their popularity seems to have experienced a considerable revival, as depictions of angels even embellish the covers of popular magazines. Muslims might find this somewhat amusing, since the conviction that angels exist and play an active role in human life has been part of their religious awareness from the earliest days of Muhammad's encounter with God through the angel Gabriel. Muslims believe that there are many angels, one of the most dramatic being Israfil, whose blowing of the mighty trumpet at the end of time will signal the coming of the Day of Resurrection and Judgment.

3. BELIEF IN GOD'S MESSENGERS Muslims understand that God has sent his revelation (*wahy*) through a series of communications to humanity in a variety of ways, through a variety of people. The recipients of these communications are referred to as both prophets and messengers. The distinction between prophet (*nabi*) and messenger (*rasul*) is that the words of the former are intended for specific communities of people, while those of the latter have universal significance. Thus all messengers are also prophets, though the reverse is not true. The Qur'an is full of references to those who are acknowledged to be prophets, many of whom Jews and Christians recognize for their role in Old Testament history. Only a limited number of prophets are also messengers, including Adam, Abraham, Moses, David, and Jesus. The final prophet and messenger was Muhammad, after whom there will be no more prophets. In recent times, relations among Muslims, Christians, and Jews in America are often cultivated under the rubric "Abrahamic religions," suggesting that the common ancestry of the three faiths may be a more productive basis for interfaith conversation than the rehearsing of theological differences. Jesus is considered to be the greatest of the prophets and messengers of Islam before Muhammad, although not a son of God or in any way divine. With the revelation to Muhammad, God is said to have concluded the process of revelation. Muhammad is thus referred to as the seal of the prophets. This doctrine is of such great importance in Islam that for anyone to claim for himself or for another the designation of prophet is considered heresy.

4. BELIEF IN THE HOLY BOOKS As the Qur'an makes quite explicit, God sent books, or complete revelations, to both the Jews and the Christians before the coming of Muhammad. The message contained in those books is essentially that contained in the Qur'an. Muslims believe that Jewish and Christian communities either purposely or inadvertently changed or distorted God's messages, with the result that the revelation needed to be sent one last time. The Qur'an is that final revelation. However, Christians and Jews have a special status in the Muslim community because they were chosen by God to be the recipients of his books, the Torah and the Gospel respectively. The Qur'an consistently refers to Jews and Christians as *ahl al-kitab*, the People of the Book. The Qur'an itself is often referred to simply as the Book, a term

relating it to the previous divine revelations and suggesting its own position
as the final word of God to humanity.

5. BELIEF IN THE DAY OF RESURRECTION AND JUDGMENT   The basic revelation
given to the Prophet Muhammad was the double message of God's oneness
and of a day of final assessment of human actions. In Islam, as the concept
of *tawhid* ties together God's oneness and human responsibility, so God will
gather together all people at the end of time for an accounting of how they
have lived their lives. The Qur'an makes it abundantly clear that this will
be a momentous occasion, signaled by the trumpet of the angel Israfil, the
most amazing cataclysmic events, and the resurrection of all bodies, which
will be joined with their souls for the judgment. Each person will be given
his or her "book of deeds." If the book is put into one's right hand, then the
reward will be the gardens of paradise near to God himself. If, however, the
book is received in the left hand, the unhappy sinner will face the eternal fires
of punishment. The coming Day of Judgment emphasizes the importance of
living an Islamic life. American Muslims often discuss conduct, dress, and
other issues in the context of God's final assessment of human actions.

These five articles of faith are all grounded in the message of the Qur'an
and are non-negotiable for Muslims. They are elaborated upon in the literature available to the Muslim community in America and, according to the
ability of the child to absorb them, are part of the religious education that is
increasingly taking place in mosques and Islamic centers across the country.

The Five Pillars

Even before learning about these articles of faith, however, young Muslims
are taught the essentials of living a good and responsible life by performing
the ritual duties commanded by God. These essentials are expressed in the
five pillars, which form the essence of the individual Muslim's personal piety
(*taqwa*). Muslims actively working for the propagation of Islam in America
understand that one of its most appealing aspects is the simplicity and clarity
of the responsibilities that frame the Muslim life.

I. TESTIMONY CONCERNING GOD AND HIS PROPHET MUHAMMAD   "I give testimony that there is no God but God and that Muhammad is the Prophet of
God." While all of the five pillars, or responsibilities, are incumbent on every
Muslim, the *shahada* is basic. Failure to believe in and articulate the oneness
of God and the prophethood of Muhammad means that one is outside the

Pages from a manuscript of the Holy Qur'an dating from the twelfth century.
NEW YORK PUBLIC LIBRARY PICTURE COLLECTION

community of Islam. Those who wish to affiliate themselves with Islam in America, or anywhere else, need only pronounce the *shahada* three times in a formal setting to be henceforth effectively and legally Muslims. Many buildings in the United States and Canada have been converted to function as mosques, and often they specify that new status by putting up some kind of calligraphic rendering of the two affirmations of the *shahada* painted on the walls or hung as a sign or banner in the front.

2. PERFORMANCE OF THE RITUAL PRAYER Formal prayer was part of the expectation of the Prophet for the members of his community from the beginning, based on the injunctions of the Qur'an. "Worship at fixed hours has been enjoined on the believers . . ." (Sura 90:103); "Establish worship at the two ends of the day and in some watches of the night . . ." (Sura 11:114). At first, Muhammad ordered believers to face Jerusalem in their prayer orientation, but sometime after the *hijra* he directed that orientation to Mecca. All mosques contain what is called a *qibla*, or indicator of the exact direction for the worshiper to face when performing the prayer. In America as in other non-Muslim countries, if a building has not been built specifically to serve

Calligraphic rendering of a Qur'an verse that reads: "Over every knowledgeable being is One more knowing." COURTESY MOHAMED ZAKARIYA

as a mosque, the direction of prayer will most likely not coincide with the "front" of that building. Travelers can make use of small mechanical devices to help orient them toward Mecca. Many hotels in Islamic cities provide indicators of the prayer direction in the rooms.

Ritual prayer, *salat*, is not a casual thing for the Muslim but assumes a regularity and discipline. God is said to have prescribed to Muhammad the daily ritual of five formal prayers for every believer, although the Qur'an itself does not specify that demand. The exact times of day for performing the *salat* are clearly established in the *hadith*, or traditions taken from the life and practice of the Prophet, and have been codified in the law. Specifically, they are the *salat al-fajr* at dawn before the rise of the sun, the *salat al-ẓuhr* after the sun passes its highest point, the *salat al-'asr* in the late part of the afternoon, the *salat al-maghrib* just after the setting of the sun, and the *salat al-'isha* sometime between sunset and midnight. If one is ill or on a journey, combining the noon and afternoon prayers, or the sunset and evening prayers, is acceptable. Muslims have some difference in opinion as to what to do if one's workplace does not permit prayer at the appropriate time. Some Muslims who find the prayers difficult to perform in the workplace may combine the noon and afternoon prayers. Occasionally, and now more frequently, students in public schools will ask for the right to pray. "My cousin and I were the only two Muslims in the school, and the school did not want to give us permission to leave the room to pray," recalls a Palestinian woman. "I told my teacher that if he wouldn't let me pray, I was going to walk out of class and do so anyway. Finally, they backed down and let us go."[1] Some Muslim students are finding common cause with Christian students who want prayer in the public schools, working around the law by organizing prayer clubs after classroom hours.

Visitors to the Muslim world over the centuries have seldom failed to be struck, sometimes enchanted, by the call to prayer (adhan: literally, "proclamation" or "announcement"), through which the faithful are reminded to interrupt their daily routines to remember God. So important is the ritual prayer in Islam that the one to give that call to prayer, called the mu'adhdhin, has been said to be worthy of special merit in many of the traditions of the Prophet. Throughout the centuries, the call to prayer has been sung from atop a minaret, or tower, of the mosque. While the adhan in some senses parallels such reminders in other traditions, as, for example, the shofar (ram's horn) in Judaism or the ringing of bells in Christianity, it is unique in its reliance on the human voice. The mu'adhdhin receives careful training as to proper intonation and vocalization, and his craft has been seen as one of the great arts of Islam. At the specified time he (and it is always a man who performs this function) ascends to his place on the minaret, or to some other appropriate spot, turns toward Mecca, and begins his invitation to prayer. In recent times, particularly in the major Islamic cities, the noises of traffic and industry have necessitated replacing the live human voice with a recording played over a loudspeaker. Some American cities have seen great controversy about whether the call to prayer should be allowed to "disturb" the other residents of the neighborhood in which a mosque is located. Different communities have come to terms with this problem in different ways. Most often in American mosques the call is given inside the prayer hall rather than outside, serving not so much as a reminder to the faithful to pray as a kind of beginning to the prayer ritual. Shi'ites sometimes add to the prayer a phrase of special respect for 'Ali (see chapter 3 for further discussion of Shi'ites).

The salat cannot be performed without careful preparation on the part of the worshiper, including entering into a state of ritual purity, which involves both the cleansing of the body and the purification and readying of the mind and heart. Ritual washing (*wudu'*) is performed outside or inside the mosque and includes wiping water over the head, ears, neck, and feet. American buildings that have been adapted as mosques have had to designate this pur‐pose, normally with separate washing places for men and women. During prayer a man's body should be covered at least from his waist to his knees, and by most interpretations a woman should have only her face and hands uncovered. After washing, one declares the *niyya*, or intention, which serves as the transition from ordinary daily activity to the special state of prayer‐ful attention.

Ritualized prayer can take place in the mosque, at home, or in any other place that is clean and appropriate. The congregational prayer is tradition‐ally held on Friday, attended by men and sometimes by women. In America this communal ritual is often (also) observed on Sunday because of the dif‐ficulty some worshipers have in getting away from their work on Fridays. Muslims also practice a private, personal, and non-ritualized form of prayer called *du'a*, in which the worshiper addresses God in praise and supplication. *Du'a* can be spoken at any time.

Many articles stressing the importance of prayer are available online today. "What Good Is Salat (Prayer)?" asks Khalid Baig in a 2007 online article,[2] reiterating a classical theme that prayer is the key to paradise while neglecting the *salat* is the key to hell. The author argues that one cannot plead ignorance of the prayer because it is constantly being called some‐where around the globe, what he calls a massive and continuous universal call. Other sites such as YouTube give regular advice to new converts as to how to perform the various elements of the ritual prayer.

3. ALMSGIVING In a number of places the Qur'an specifically enjoins the believer to pay the alms tax (*zakat*, sometimes rendered *zakah*). "Truly those who recite God's book, perform the *salat*, and spend privately and publicly from what We have provided to them, are engaged in an enterprise that never fails" (Sura 35:29). From the earliest days the Prophet preached that those who call themselves Muslims have a responsibility to care for the less fortunate among them. The Qur'an particularly identifies the poor, widows, and orphans as needing attention. The responsibility of giving away a por‐tion of one's personal property on a regular basis has served a number of purposes in the structure of the Islamic *umma*, not all of them, of course, functioning perfectly in all instances. In theory, however, it does indeed give support for the needy and assures a more equitable distribution of wealth.

Place for performing *wudu'* or ritualized washing before the prayer in the Islamic Center of Cleveland, Ohio. COURTESY ISLAMIC CENTER OF CLEVELAND, OHIO

Zakat provides support for the maintenance of the Islamic community and it is a means of thanking God for the blessings he has bestowed. The word *zakat* itself suggests both piety and purity, underscoring the relationship of financial responsibility to righteous living. Like all Islamic requirements, its observance helps assure the giver of a better chance for a felicitous reward in the hereafter.

For Sunnis, *zakat* is a tax of 2.5 percent of what is estimated to be the sum value of all of one's possessions. It is not, therefore, an income tax as such but takes into consideration the totality of a person's holdings. In the early centuries the central authorities kept the monies collected through *zakat* and distributed them to run the state. *Zakat* earnings were used not only for charitable purposes but for education, the ransom of captives, and other purposes deemed important for the welfare of the community. Non-Muslims, specifically Jews and Christians who had "protected" status as People of the Book, had to pay a poll tax instead, although those who were needy were also supported by *zakat* money. The administration of *zakat* is considerably more difficult now than in earlier days, particularly since so many countries in which Muslims reside have a mandatory income tax. Muslims are strongly encouraged to understand regularized giving to worthy causes to be part of their religious responsibilities and an expression of their piety and righteousness. A few Muslim countries insist on the right of the government to levy a *zakat* tax on its citizens. In most of the Islamic world, the government runs and financially subsidizes the mosques. In America, of course, this is not the case, and the American Muslim community has had much discussion about how to understand and employ *zakat* to build and maintain mosques.

Increasingly, *zakat* is also being understood as a means of providing some kind of service to members of the community. Such service can be handled by organizations and Islamic centers, small private groups, or even individuals. A Kansas high school senior talks about the work she and her friends do in hospitals, soup kitchens, and retirement homes: "Our youth group . . . visits these places and helps people. Many of them are very lonely, and they enjoy and appreciate having someone to talk to. Since many of them have never met Muslims before, we talk to them about our religion and tell them what we believe and why we dress the way we do. . . . It makes us feel good to do something."[3]

Since 9/11 the American government has been vigilant in scrutinizing certain common recipients of *zakat* contributions, most notably the Holy Land Foundation, on the grounds that they may serve as training and support groups for potential terrorists. Resources on the web and in other source materials have tried to help Muslims know what and who are appropriate recipients for their money. For example, a July 2008 web article titled "Does CAIR Qualify to Receive Zakat?"[4] argues that the Council on American-Islamic Relations, on the basis of the services it has provided for Muslims as well as its professionalism and integrity, is indeed a worthy recipient of *zakat* contributions. A 2008 book titled *The Zakat Handbook* is now available online through the Zakat Foundation of America,[5] designed to answer questions that American Muslims have about how to pay their *zakat* monies. Some commentators have argued that by raising questions about international agencies that in the past have received such contributions the U.S. government is in fact aiding the American community by keeping its monies invested in American services and agencies.

4. FASTING DURING THE MONTH OF RAMADAN While the Qur'an contains a number of references, some direct and some oblique, to the other four pillars, in only one place does it specifically enjoin fasting during the month of Ramadan: "O you faithful, fasting is ordained for you in the same way that it was ordained for those who came before you, so that you may fear God. . . . It was during the month of Ramadan that the Qur'an was sent down as a guidance for humanity. . . . Whoever among you sees the moon, then he should fast, but the one who is sick or on a journey, [can fast] an equal number of other days" (Sura 2:183–185). Specifically, this passage means that everyone of an appropriate age (generally recognized to be past puberty) and not too elderly or infirm is expected to refrain from food, drink, tobacco, and sexual relations during the daylight hours of this month. In a kind of subsidiary fashion, Muslims are also expected to follow the strictest ethical codes during this time, being especially careful to be honest, thoughtful, and sensitive to the needs of others and to refrain not only from eating and drinking but also from using foul language and untruthful words. The Prophet is frequently cited as having said: "God does not need the fast of a person who does not abandon false speech or acting according to his false speech."

Like many of the duties required of Muslims, fasting has both physical and spiritual dimensions. As prayer and pilgrimage involve the body as well as the mind and heart, fasting and the breaking of the fast engage the totality of one's faculties. To fast each day from first morning light to dusk requires intense mental, emotional, and bodily discipline. The act of eating at the end of the day, when one smells and tastes the first fruits and sweets, involves the heart in thanksgiving and the senses in the enjoyment of food. In Islamic understanding, God has constructed the universe according to a balance (*mizan*, the same word used for the balance that will weigh one's deeds on the Day of Judgment). Thus each of the five responsibilities balances and supports the others, and all of the constituent elements that go to make up the human person work together in balance and harmony.

"When I was growing up in Pakistan, we never thought of Ramadan as a month of spiritual reawakening. It was more a kind of cultural festival. It is good that our youth here are challenging the old customs and thinking about Ramadan from a fresh perspective," says a Muslim mother who lives in Chicago, when asked about the time of fasting. "Ramadan should be a time not only for focusing on our own obligations or even our own spiritual needs. We should use it as the occasion to introduce Islam to others, and even to organize special food drives for the homeless and poor," remarks a youth from Washington, D.C. "I eagerly wait for this month. I love being in the mosque every day listening to the divine message. I rediscover myself in this month. I think I grow in every aspect of my personality each year," says a young Muslim girl in Southern California.[6] These comments suggest

Advertisement from the Islamic Circle of North America suggesting how Muslims might spend their *zakat*, or alms tax. Courtesy ICNA Relief

some of the ways in which Muslims experience the month of Ramadan in the American context.

Only recently have the American media realized that many Muslims in this country do something noteworthy during one month of the year. It comes as a refreshing change from the concentration of the press on so-called Islamic extremism to find some thoughtful and even appreciative coverage of this important time in the life of the Muslim community. Muslims themselves are devoting increasing attention in their journals, periodicals, and Web sites to sharing with one another the importance of this month-long event, and in particular to hearing the responses of the youth of the community to the experience of participating in it.

The rigorous and demanding discipline of the fast is exacerbated for American Muslims because of the lack of ready facilities for its support or understanding on the part of most non-Muslims about its purpose. Not all Muslims in the United States participate fully, or even at all, in this stringent exercise, although many of those who choose not to fast express the wish that they had either the discipline or the support to be able to do so. Those who do fast clearly believe that the rewards fully justify the rigors. "All of a sudden my sleeping and work habits change," insists a teenaged Muslim boy who has only recently practiced the full fast. "I sleep early and wake up early. I feel an urge to read the Qur'an and think about what it means. I really look forward to the breaking of the fast every day not so much because I am hungry, although of course I am, but because it is really the only time of the year when we are sure that the whole family will sit around one table sharing food." "I do fast," says a young woman. "It used to be that I would stop eating some meals, and in between I would smoke or drink a Coke or something. But since then I have begun coming to the mosque, and I realize that fasting really means a commitment to God. Now Ramadan is not just another month for me but a special time for developing self-control."[7]

The months of the Islamic lunar calendar, which are slightly shorter than solar months, in effect rotate around the Western calendar. Thus Ramadan may fall at any time of the year and "moves forward" ten days each year. Fasting in the winter is generally less arduous because the days are shorter, while strict observance during the summer can be particularly difficult. "I used to work in the lumber yards all day," comments an Arab student who used to live in the Pacific Northwest. "It takes a lot of energy, and particularly in the summer when the days are long and hot it is really hard not to even have any water. My boss sort of understood what I was doing, but not enough to let me take any time to rest like I would have been able to do back home."

The month of Ramadan ends with 'eid al-fitr, a greatly anticipated time at which families and communities gather together to celebrate the breaking of the fast and people dress in their finest clothes. Traditionally an animal—lamb, chicken, camel, or whatever is available—is slaughtered for the occasion and people eat their fill. Mosques in some urban areas have determined that the meat (or food in general) left over from the sacrificed animal is to be shared in thirds by the members of the family, the poor of the Muslim community, and the needy among non-Muslims.

The many Muslim theologians and commentators who have thought, spoken, and written about the fast of Ramadan over the centuries have suggested that it leads to a number of beneficial ends. Considered both a physical and a spiritual regimen, fasting brings a greater appreciation for the blessings of God, which are so easily taken for granted; it ensures that one will reflect on what it means to live in obedience to the commands of God; it reminds one that life is truly in God's hands; and it serves to unite in fellowship all of those who are participating in this observance. The month of the fast is also traditionally the time in which the faithful extend special forgiveness to anyone who might have offended them. That it may also be a time of reaching out to people outside the Islamic community, while not unknown to Muslims in other times and places, is a particular contribution of those who are living in America. Recognizing that fasting is a part of Jewish and Christian practice, some commentators have suggested that this month is a special time for the promotion of better interfaith understanding. The Council on American-Islamic Relations (CAIR) posts on the Internet detailed suggestions for publicizing the meaning of and the events related to Ramadan, including proposals for contacting newspapers, television and radio stations, schools, libraries, and hospitals, as well as ideas for organizing daily *iftar* (breaking the fast) meals for the homeless and food drives for the needy.

Leaders of the various American Muslim communities currently are giving a good deal of attention to the importance of Ramadan as a time of charitable outreach. Some of these events are national in scope. In the last several years CAIR has hosted Ramadan fund-raising events that have topped $1 million in revenue. Others are locally initiated. Particular efforts at outreach during Ramadan might include having young people from an Islamic center go to an orphanage to give out clothes and toys and talk with the children about Islam and the meaning of a month's fasting. With the growing numbers of Muslims in prison, the observance of Ramadan for the incarcerated is drawing increasing attention. Muslims are taking this special time to visit prisons to speak to Muslim inmates about the faith and about the significance of fasting. Some even stay to participate in the special prayers and Qur'an recitation, which in some prisons may last all night.

The literature of Islam pays increasing attention to ways of sharing this important time with non-Muslims and to using this opportunity to present Islam as a religion of piety rather than one of violence and extremism. On some university campuses Muslim students invite non-Muslims to join them in a one-day "fastathon," with the money saved by not buying lunches going to charity. The Council on American-Islamic Relations sends out information relating to Ramadan to its non-Muslim constituency as well as to Muslim friends. Local mosques and Islamic centers generally hold open houses, public lectures on Ramadan, and interfaith *iftars*. Muslim American organizations also sometimes use the occasion of Ramadan to put advertisements on TV as reminders that Muslims play an integral role in American society. Since the early 1990s the president has issued happy Ramadan greetings to Muslims around the world, and on several occasions has hosted Muslims at the White House for the *iftar*.

5. PERFORMING THE PILGRIMAGE TO THE HOLY CITY OF MECCA ONCE DURING ONE'S LIFETIME The Qur'an contains several references to the necessity of visiting Mecca on pilgrimage, as in the following: "Fulfill the pilgrimage and the visitation unto God" (Sura 2:196–197). Although the Prophet moved his community to Medina at the time of the *hijra*, Mecca has always remained primary in the worship life of Muslims. It was the place of his birth and the home of the Ka'ba, the most sacred shrine of Islam with its venerated Black Stone reportedly given by the angel Gabriel to Abraham. When Muhammad returned to Mecca, he cleansed it of all impurity from having housed idols. The Ka'ba became the symbol of the victory of the Islamic community and regained its status as the central sanctuary for those who worship the one true God. It is the responsibility of each Muslim to make at least one ritual visit (*hajj*) to Mecca at least once in a lifetime, and many choose to return more than once to experience the thrill of joining literally millions of fellow worshipers in the adoration of the one God. The official time for the pilgrimage is during the month named Dhu al-Hijja, the last month in the lunar calendar. One may also choose to make an individual pilgrimage at any other time of the year, a visit that is called not *hajj* but *'umra* and is known as the "lesser pilgrimage."

Those who have reported their experiences on the *hajj* generally attest to its enormous significance in their personal religious lives. "How was I to know this would be the journey of a lifetime," muses a female Muslim from Philadelphia. "Tears poured down my face like a fresh spring shower. The air left a sweet taste in my mouth, as if I had eaten the most succulent piece of fruit. I am here, really here. My eyes scanned this canvas of buoyant faces, effervescent smiles and nodding heads affirming the peace felt in their hearts. The serenade of voices from many tongues, this a cornucopia of Allah's servants, made a soothing welcome. . . . My Hajj experience served as my vehicle for the placating of my soul. This excursion took me up the paths and down the trails of the human spirit. The internal strength I gained induced a genuine love of Allah."[8] The gathering of so many people in what is considered to be the most holy spot on earth—up to two million may be there at one time—is literally quite overwhelming. Some have expressed their awe as akin to a combination of intense reverence mingled with fear of both the power of the occasion and the practical reality of moving within such giant circles of humanity.

Because of the sheer numbers, however, the experience that is supposed to engender such great joy can also be rather intimidating for some. A Pakistani Muslim who teaches high school in Denver, Colorado, relates that she made her first pilgrimage when she was only sixteen. "Even though I clung tightly to the hands of my parents," she said, "I was terrified that I might get swept away from them just because there were such great throngs of people. When I went again in my twenties I was better able to cope and appreciate the experience for its enormous awe and beauty."

It is often said that during the pilgrimage the true idea of an egalitarian Islam is realized. All male worshipers, whatever their status or position in everyday life, don the same simple white cloth to symbolize a state of ritual purity and participate in the same set of ceremonial rituals. Women are allowed more flexibility in their dress.

The process of the pilgrimage begins when the pilgrim states his or her intention, *niyya*, and greets the city of Mecca with the cry "Here I am, Lord, here I am!" During the days of the *hajj* pilgrims circumambulate the Ka'ba, kiss the Black Stone, and reenact Hagar's legendary search for water to give her infant son, Ishmael. Toward the end of the pilgrimage, which lasts some ten days, pilgrims journey through Mina to the plain of 'Arafat, where the worshiper recalls the struggle of the patriarch Abraham against idolatry. Back in Mina, pilgrims throw seven stones at a small pillar in the main square said to symbolize the recalcitrant Satan. The last act of the pilgrimage is the sacrificing of an animal with its head facing Mecca. Some of the meat is eaten and the rest distributed to the needy. At this point the (male) pilgrim's head is shaved, and he begins the process of desacralization. Throughout the *hajj* ritual the worshiper says many prayers and listens to many sermons to help orient himself or herself to the proper attitude and response. Some pilgrims choose to visit the tomb of the Prophet in Medina, although that is not a formal part of the pilgrimage. Passengers on international airlines at the conclusion of the pilgrimage sometimes see returning pilgrims carrying large plastic bottles of water from the well of Zamzam, a lifegiving source said to have been provided by God for Hagar and Ishmael. These waters are believed to retain their restorative powers.

American Muslims have made successful businesses out of helping Muslims get ready for the pilgrimage. Software engineer Omar Bellal, for example, for several years has been leading a *hajj* class at his mosque in Freemont, California, preparing them to join some twelve thousand other Americans who will be taking the trip. Using PowerPoint slides he shows them how to get as close as possible to the Ka'ba, both to make the circuits shorter and to give them a chance to actually kiss the Black Stone.

The Saudi state goes to enormous lengths to provide for the safety and welfare of pilgrims. Huge tent cities are erected to house them, millions of meals are prepared, and transportation to the outlying areas is provided for those who cannot walk. While accidents do occasionally happen, there is generally remarkably little illness or other problems, given the massive numbers of people who must be accommodated. The "miracle" of the undertaking, however, is said to pale in significance compared with the personal "miracle" experienced by the individual worshipers during this ritual that is truly the event of a lifetime. Because non-Muslims are not allowed in Mecca, careful procedures are maintained to ensure that those who participate are genuine Muslims, sincere in their *shahada*. The man or woman who has completed the pilgrimage is known, respectively, as a *hajji* or *hajja* and is accorded special respect by the members of his or her family and community.

In recent years, a number of books and films have chronicled the events of the *hajj*, providing access for both Muslims and non-Muslims to the events and emotions of the experience. Michael Wolfe, for example, in his book *The Hadj: An American's Pilgrimage to Mecca*, takes the reader through each stage and experience of the pilgrimage. It is recommended for those planning to make the pilgrimage themselves, as well as those who as outsiders can never have the experience but can benefit from the candid perspectives of this American Muslim.[9] As more educational material about the beliefs and practices of Islam becomes available to the American public, and as the media provide more coverage of the ritual observances of Islam, Muslims hope that other Americans can see Islam as a faith of beauty, rigor, and ethical responsibility rather than as the vehicle of terror and the inspiration of "Islamic bombs."

Travel industry experts note a new trend among American Muslims—namely, making the pilgrimage at a young age rather than waiting until one's family has matured and one is at a later stage in life. Many young Americans are affluent as a result of technological developments and have the money to travel easily. Why not go while they are still free from the responsibilities of family, they say, and still physically able to take the best advantage of this challenging experience?

While most Americans return from the *hajj* feeling that their lives have been changed by this dramatic and spiritually moving act of faith, the experience is not without its difficult aspects. Some say that fellow *hajjis* from other parts of the world retain certain feelings of hostility toward Americans because of the government's Middle East policies and may even question their right to be in the holy places of Islam. On the other side, they say, some fellow Americans may not understand why Muslims need to do this "strange thing," especially if it means taking time off work or leaving families to cope without them for several weeks. As in all things, they say, education is working slowly to facilitate better understanding on all sides.

In the decade since 9/11 many American institutions have made accommodations in order to allow Muslims to practice their faith with greater ease and convenience. Muslim watchdog institutions are helping Muslims realize their legal rights to the free practice of religion. Some American Muslims are critical of their fellows who do not observe the five ritual practices as diligently as they might, particularly those who have recently come from conservative cultures. A practicing physician who writes about his understanding of the right way to practice Islam, for example, refers to those whom he views as too casual about their faith as "Supermarket Muslims."[10] Others, however, are clear that the decision about how and when to practice in this Western culture is up to them as individuals, and many are writing publicly about their right to respond to the demands of their religion in ways that reflect their own faith and understanding. The question of who has the authority to determine the genuine practice of Islam in the American context is one of the most important issues facing the American Muslim community today, and one to which it will continue to turn its attention in the coming decades.

CHAPTER TWO

Contributors to the Development of Islam

What is Islam? For American Muslims, it means many different things, although the most immediate answer is that it consists of the revelation of the Qur'an, the experiences of its Prophet, and its requirements of faith and practice. This is Islam in its essential meaning. However, the many individuals who over the centuries have identified as Muslim have shaped and developed Islam as a living faith. In the same way, the decisions that American Muslims make about how to understand and practice the faith in a Western context will significantly define Islam in the next century. In this chapter we will learn about the development of the religion over the fourteen centuries of its existence as illustrated in the lives of people recognized to have helped mold Islam into its present reality. Included here are many of the men and women whose particular contributions to faithful living, understanding, and interpretation have molded and determined the kinds of Islam to which American Muslims today adhere.

The Prophet Muhammad and the Revelation of the Qur'an

For the Muslim today, as has been true over the centuries, Muhammad is understood to have been fully human, in no way sharing in the divinity that is God's alone. Indeed, he had humble origins and was raised as an orphan by his uncle Abu Talib. While Muhammad was still in his early teens, it is said, a Christian monk recognized in him signs of prophecy. Another narrative relates that when a stone fell from a wall of the Ka'ba, the tribes of Mecca quarreled as to which one should have the honor of replacing it. The young Muhammad is said to have solved the problem by placing the stone on a cloth that representatives of all the tribes could lift up together. By the age of twenty-five he was employed in the lucrative camel trade of a well-to-do merchant woman named Khadija, whom he ultimately married. Muhammad and Khadija's marriage was apparently a warm and close one, and until her death his wife was his strongest supporter. She is considered the first to accept the call to Islam. They had four daughters, of whom the best known is Fatima. All of their three sons died as infants, complicating the matter of community leadership when the Prophet himself died in 632.

Mecca, where Muhammad lived and first preached, was a well-developed commercial town at the crossroads of major trade routes connecting Africa to the Far East. It was also the center of a pilgrimage route, providing a lucrative business for many of its inhabitants, business they did not wish to see disrupted by any new preaching. The century or so before the time of the Prophet, who received his first revelations circa 610 C.E., is generally known as the *jahiliyya*, or time of ignorance, a term highlighting the fact that worship of idols in and around the local shrine was the religious practice of the day. The shrine itself, the Ka'ba, still visited by Muslims on pilgrimage and considered the holiest of shrines, is believed by Muslims to have been built by the Prophet Abraham with the assistance of his son Ishmael. The Prophet transformed the ancient practice of pilgrimage from a time of idolatrous adoration to the *hajj* described in chapter 1.

Arabia at the time of Muhammad's youth had a vague concept of a kind of supreme creator God called Allah (literally, Al-Lah, "The God"), but three goddesses, or "daughters" of Allah, named Al-Lat, Manat, and Al-'Uzza, along with a male god called Hubal, held sway. Among the many reasons why Muslims all over the world accused the notorious Salman Rushdie of blasphemy was his portrayal of the Prophet Muhammad in his novel *The Satanic Verses* as having acknowledged the existence of one of those goddesses on his deathbed.

> "Who's there?" [Muhammad] called out. "Is it Thou, Azraeel [the angel of death]?" But Ayesha ['A'isha] heard a terrible, sweet voice, that was a woman's, make reply: "No, Messenger of Al-Lah, it is not Azraeel." And the lamp blew out; and in the darkness [Muhammad] asked: "Is this sickness then thy doing, O Al-Lat?" And she said, "It is my revenge upon you, and I am satisfied."[1]

Tradition affirms that while Muhammad was on a retreat in a cave near Mecca, he was stunned to hear a voice commanding him to recite in the name of the Lord. The year was 610, and Muhammad was forty years old. The words of God to the trembling Muhammad, mediated through the angel Gabriel, are recorded in chapter 96 of the Qur'an, generally conceded to be the first of the divine revelations: "Recite in the name of your Lord who created man from a clot of blood. Recite, for truly your Lord is the most generous. He taught by the pen, taught man that which he did not know." A man with no pretensions to having achieved such a high state of contemplation as to have induced this experience, Muhammad was understandably terrified. It was on his descent from the mountain that he saw the figure of the angel Gabriel filling the horizon and heard the voice declaring that he, Muhammad, was the Messenger of God. Covering himself with his cloak in fear, he ran home as fast as he could, begging his wife to protect him. Again according to tradition, she wisely encouraged him to heed the voice of God. Because the Arabic word for "recite" is the same as the word for "read," the response given by Muhammad in Arabic to God's first command at once serves to express the question "What shall I recite?" and the statement "I cannot read."

This response, found not in the Qur'an but in later traditions, served as the basis for the dogma that the Prophet was unlettered. While it may seem difficult to support in light of his association with the caravan trade, it is important in portraying him as a pure recipient of divine revelation. Because he was illiterate, goes the argument, he could not have read and copied anything from other sacred writings circulating around Arabia at the time. He received the first revelation from God through the angel Gabriel during the month of Ramadan, on what is referred to as the "Night of Power." Coming near the end of the month, it is generally marked by special observances in the mosques of America.

With Khadija's support, and with the arrival of subsequent messages that he recognized as coming from God, Muhammad began to fulfill the vocation to which the angel had charged him. He was to receive many more direct communications from God over the next twenty-two years. In the earlier days these were generally mediated through Gabriel, on the understanding that direct communication between human and divine is too overwhelming to be borne without training and experience. Later, as the Prophet grew in spiritual strength and wisdom, such mediation was no longer necessary.

The earliest revelations to the Prophet contained two messages that were foreign to the citizens of Arabia at that time. First, Muhammad preached that there is only one God, that the many deities and especially the daughters of God are a fiction, and that human beings have the responsibility to acknowledge God's oneness by their own submission. Second, he tried to convince his listeners that, contrary to their current beliefs, life does not end with death, that immortality is not only through progeny but all will be resurrected and judged at the end of time. From the earliest days of his receiving these messages from God, he understood that one of his most important roles was to warn the heedless that they would ultimately be called to accountability for their actions.

Muhammad found few who were ready to appreciate his preaching. His own tribe, called the Quraish, opposed him at every turn, ridiculing his claim to prophecy. The death of his beloved wife, Khadija, and the loss of his uncle and protector, Abu Talib, made the Prophet's task even more difficult. Muslims today accord special honor to Muhammad for his faith and singleness of purpose in preaching the message of God during these dark and seemingly hopeless days. For years he was unable to persuade more than a small handful of believers of the essential truth of his teachings. In addition, the stringent moral content of the divine revelation required believers to help the needy, to care for the hungry and the orphans, and to offer hospitality to all. While these values were not unknown in pre-Islamic society, they represented a new kind of social order, which constituted one more threat to an established and comfortable way of life in the community of Mecca.

Despite the extreme difficulties that attended the first decade of Muhammad's Meccan preaching, a small band of followers gradually formed. Others after Khadija came to acknowledge the truth of his teachings, including his cousin 'Ali and Abu Bakr, who was to be the first caliph, or leader, of the community after Muhammad's death.

Then came an event that would change his fortunes dramatically. A delegation from a city several hundred miles north of Mecca invited him to arbitrate a matter deeply contested among its tribes. It is clear that the Prophet's reputation as a wise statesman was beginning to spread. Determining that the antagonism toward him personally as well as the opposition to his message was so great in Mecca as to make the propagation of the revelation virtually impossible, Muhammad took the opportunity to migrate with his small band of followers to the new location. The city was Yathrib, later to be known as Madinat al-Nabi (the city of the Messenger) or Medina, and to become the second holiest city in Islam and Muhammad's final resting place. The year of this *hijra*, or migration, was 622, and it signals the formal beginning of the community (*umma*) of Islam as such. The Islamic calendar, which is based on lunar rather than solar cycles and consists of 354 days, starts at the moment of the *hijra*.

Those attempting to provide an appropriate historical antecedent for the Muslim community as a minority in America frequently invoke the example of the *hijra*. As the Prophet and his small band of followers were able to find a home in Medina and to establish a vibrant Islamic community, so Muslims today emigrating from their homelands see the *hijra* as a model for living together responsibly as Muslims in the new and often alien context of America.

The story of the growth and spread of Islam from this base in Medina is well known. Muhammad established himself as the true Prophet-statesman, the religious leader who continued to share with his community the revelations that came regularly from God, and the political leader who gradually consolidated power over the whole of Arabia. Most of the tribes of Arabia came either to acknowledge the truth of his message, converting to Islam in faith, or to recognize his rising political power, converting out of expediency and a desire to throw in their lot with the victor.

Meanwhile, the revelations from God continued to arrive. Although those he received while struggling in Mecca were generally short and focused, Medinan revelations were longer and more concerned with the particular issues that the Prophet was facing as he moved to consolidate his community. During this time much of the legislation that was to become the basis for the establishment of the Islamic law, or *shari'a*, was set down. At the same time that the Prophet was advancing the political fortunes of Islam, he was also developing a structure for the religious and social life of his followers. He himself exhibited the virtues, many of which were extensions of the values of pre-Islamic Arabia, that have come to characterize the righteous Muslim. Among these are honesty, generosity, hospitality, charity, fairness, and modesty. It is on these qualities that many American Muslims seek to pattern their lives.

During the consolidation of the community at Medina the basic relationship between male and female followers of Muhammad was established. There is little doubt that women were considered full members of the *umma*, that they participated in its public as well as its private life, and that they shared in both the developing set of religious obligations and worship activities. Many Muslim women in America today look to the time of the Prophet as one in which women's rights were fully acknowledged and implemented and in which women were encouraged to assume positions of leadership in the community. They challenge any of their coreligionists who want to continue excluding women from public spheres, pointing to the egalitarian practices of the Prophet and the example of many of his wives, who held positions of economic, political, and even religious leadership. The traditions of Islam insist that Muhammad extended every possible effort to treat his wives fairly and equally, although it seems clear that he most deeply loved his first spouse, Khadija, and his youngest wife, 'A'isha. It was in Medina that the regulations for marriage and divorce were established. It was also there that he received the revelation advising that, to protect their privacy, his wives should stay hidden by a partition when he was visited by delegations of men. Some have argued that it was this verse, mistakenly extrapolated to apply to all other women, that has served as the impetus for the seclusion and exclusion of women from public life that was to characterize many later centuries of Islam.

Two years before his death Muhammad succeeded in subduing Mecca, the city of his ancestry. Following his policy of charity whenever possible, the Prophet granted amnesty to all its inhabitants, despite their years of opposition to him and his message.

One of the last official acts of the Prophet was to take his followers on a final pilgrimage to the Holy City of Mecca. On the way, God revealed to him the following message, which is now found in chapter 5, verse 3 of the Qur'an: "Today I have completed for you your religion and have fulfilled My favor to you, and have chosen for you al-islam as your religion." The Arabic word for "I have completed" (akmaltu) is also the word for "I have perfected," and Muslims see in these definitions the affirmation that Islam is both complete and perfect, the best and most appropriate way in which to acknowledge and worship the one God and to live in right relationship with one's fellows. Much contemporary Islamic apologetics turns to this verse as the final proof that Islam is indeed the right and true religion for all humankind.

In 632, after a brief illness, the Prophet of God succumbed. By then he had managed to consolidate virtually all of the Arabian Peninsula under Islam and set the stage for what was to be the quick and remarkable spread of the faith across much of the known world.

Pioneers of Early Islam

Muslims in America today look for inspiration not only to the Prophet as the exemplar of right and faithful living but also to many of Muhammad's family members, companions, and associates. Though these people lived at the beginning of the history of Islam, they are held up as models by those in positions of authority today. Both men and women who are adopting the faith of Islam look to these early pioneers as they select Muslim names, and Muslims continue to refer to the early days of the community for guidance in their relationships with one another as well as with God.

When his beloved wife Khadija died, the Prophet suffered an enormous personal loss. Although for political reasons he later married a number of wives, he was never to find another who played quite the same role for him as had Khadija. It is said, however, that it was the daughter of Abu Bakr, 'A'isha, who captured his heart and held it to the end of his life. 'A'isha's most important religious role was as collector and recorder of traditions from and about Muhammad. By virtue of her position as the wife closest to Muhammad, her memories are particularly important to Sunnis. It is said that more than twelve hundred traditions are credited directly to her. Among recorded instances of women leading prayers for other women in the early community, 'A'isha is the most often mentioned. She was at the Prophet's side when he died, and she herself was buried a quarter of a century later in Medina. Of all the names taken by American women who convert to Islam, 'A'isha is one of the most popular.

Among the very earliest of the supporters of the Prophet, in the days when support was very difficult to come by, was 'A'isha's father, Abu Bakr. Although Muhammad was three years his senior, Abu Bakr was to become his father-in-law. Abu Bakr was one of the small group to accompany the Prophet in the *hijra* to Medina. Known for his wisdom and piety, he had been selected by Muhammad to perform the important function of leading the prayer when he himself was unable.

As the Prophet recited each revelation he received from God, one of the companions recorded it on whatever material was available. When Muhammad died, those fragments were gathered into various collections. A few minor variations in these collections appeared, and soon it became clear that some kind of official version was necessary. Abu Bakr is said to have initiated the production of a standard version, although it was officially completed under the rule of the third caliph, 'Uthman b. 'Affan, some twenty years after the Prophet's death.

When Muhammad died, there was consternation in the young community not only at the loss of its beloved leader but also at the lack of a clearly established policy for determining future leadership. Blood succession through a son was not a possibility, as Muhammad's own son died in infancy. The Prophet's companions gathered to make a decision, reassuring the followers that there would indeed be an orderly and wise transfer of authority. Because of his reputation for faith and piety, the companions chose Abu Bakr to assume official leadership as the *khalifa*, or caliph, of the young Muslim community. Abu Bakr was followed in succession by 'Umar, 'Uthman, and 'Ali.

Despite successes in the growth and spread of Islam externally, there were serious internal tensions. Both 'Umar and 'Uthman died by the knife. The community chose 'Ali to be the fourth caliph, but he faced serious challenge, from both 'A'isha and the forces of a Damascene governor named Mu'awiya. In what has been called the "Battle of the Camel," 'A'isha rode out with a small army to oppose 'Ali. It must have been a somewhat bizarre scene as the beloved wife of the Prophet engaged in battle against his also beloved cousin and son-in-law. Many men died defending 'A'isha, but in the end 'Ali was the victor. This incident, marking the first time that Muslim forces fought against one another, has served the designs of commentators who argue that a woman's place is not on the battlefield, in the political arena, or anywhere else outside the home.

All during the early days of Islam a number of Muslims felt that succession through the natural bloodline of the Prophet, not popular acclaim or election, should determine the leadership of the community. Thus they felt that the legitimate first leader should have been 'Ali rather than Abu Bakr, by virtue of his blood relationship as cousin to Muhammad. Muslims became irreconcilably split as supporters of 'Ali broke away to form what has become known as the party of 'Ali, or Shi'ites. Thus came into being the two major divisions of Islam, Sunnis (those who followed the Sunna, or way, of the Prophet and accepted the authority of the line of caliphs) and Shi'ites. Unlike the Sunnis, Shi'ites have always believed that Prophet Muhammad designated 'Ali to be the leader of the *umma* after his death and that the first three caliphs were able leaders but not true spiritual guides.

Despite these internal divisions, all Muslims acknowledge the significance of 'Ali in the life of the early Islamic community. It is said that, after Khadija, either he or Abu Bakr was the first to recognize the prophethood of Muhammad. 'Ali was instrumental in facilitating Muhammad's flight to Medina, providing a ruse to cover his departure. In fact, it was 'Ali who later suggested that the *hijra* mark the beginning of the Muslim calendar. The Sunnis say that 'Ali was the transmitter of many traditions of the Prophet and a significant religious authority. The Shi'ites consider him the preeminent holy person of Islam after the Prophet, the first Imam, and the most saintly servant of God.

In the year 661 'Ali was to meet his end with the same violence that had done in his two predecessors. Entering a mosque for prayer, he was struck by a poisoned sword. The violence that claimed the lives of three of the four "rightly guided caliphs" has been manifested all too often throughout the history of Islam and has stood in stark and unhappy contrast to the ideals of peace and communal support that are at the heart of the Islamic message. Despite the political turmoil and bloodshed that characterized their rule, Sunnis refer to the first four rulers as the "rightly guided caliphs," and their period in Sunni Islam (632–661) is often idealized as a time of near-perfection.

The largest number of Shi'ites believe that twelve Imams succeeded Muhammad, the last of whom disappeared in 873 at the age of four for reasons of political persecution. He remains alive but hidden even today, guiding the affairs of his community through his designated leaders. This branch of Shi'ites is known as the Ithna 'Ashariyya or Twelver Shi'ites. They live in hope of the return of the hidden Imam to serve as the deliverer, under whom there will be a final rule of justice and peace.

Another group of Shi'ites split from the main body in 765 over the issue of which son of the sixth Imam, Ja'far al-Sadiq, should be considered the legitimate successor. The Twelvers believe that the one designated was the second son, Musa al-Kazim, while others are convinced that the legitimate leader should have been the first son, Isma'il. The latter are thereby known as the Isma'ilis, or more colloquially and in contrast to the Ithna 'Ashariyya, the Seveners. Twelver and Sevener Shi'ites together form about one-fifth of the American Muslim community.

While the Shi'ites have experienced various splits and divisions over their long history, they are united in their conviction that the greatest of injustices was done in the early days of Islam when Husayn, 'Ali and Fatima's son and the grandson of the Prophet, was gruesomely massacred in the fields of Karbala in Iraq. Sunni Muslims as well as Shi'ites have lamented the Karbala event, but it is among the latter that the most regularized practices of remembrance and participation in the suffering of Husayn have become established. This event is memorialized in the observance of Muharram, one of the most important of holy days for American Shi'ites.

The Early Development of the Islamic Community

The community of Muslims in Medina established its presence and extended its domain first through a series of marauding expeditions, then through more serious and carefully planned encounters. Although Abu Bakr's rule as caliph lasted only two years, under the leadership of a talented commander of the armed forces he was able to see the lands of Islam begin their expansion. First, rebellions in Arabia were quelled, and Islam began to move into Palestine, Persia, and Byzantium. The final advance of the Muslim East into the Christian West came when Muslim armies crossed the Pyrenees from Spain into France. The northward spread of Islam was stopped at last in 632 when the legendary Charles Martel repelled Muslim forces outside Poitiers. By the beginning of the ninth century, however, the West had virtually lost control of the Mediterranean as a result of the expansion of Islam.

A little more than a century after the death of the Prophet, dramatic changes also came to the heartland of Islam. The Umayyad Caliphate, which had ruled since the death of 'Ali, gave way to the beginning of 'Abbasid rule in 750. This political change prompted a young Umayyad prince to flee westward and establish a separate caliphate in Spain. The Umayyads ruled the Iberian Peninsula for the next two centuries, and were succeeded by other Islamic rulers for several centuries. The 'Abbasids moved the capital from Umayyad Damascus to the newly created Baghdad, in Arabic called "the City of Peace." With this, the *umma* of Islam was to turn into an empire of enormous political power, great opulence, economic prosperity, and cultural achievement such as has scarcely been rivaled. Muslims in the West today take pride in recalling the glory of the 'Abbasid days, especially its accomplishments in the arts, sciences, philosophy, mathematics, and medicine, seeing such achievements as integral to the meaning and structure of Islam. The 'Abbasids called great attention to their support of religion and were active in the construction of new mosques and religious schools. The state supported the religious scholars, *ulama* (literally, "the learned ones"), as a professional elite with great prestige and power. Those trained in the Qur'an, the law, and other religious disciplines controlled many aspects of life in 'Abbasid society. Arabic was becoming a truly international language, and massive projects of translation were undertaken, especially by Christians employed at the caliphal court.

Soon after the death of the Prophet, the community began assembling narratives of what the Prophet had said and done during his lifetime, as collected by his close companions and confidants. This task involved determining the authenticity of each individual narrative (*hadith*) and arranging an enormous number of reports into categories of clearly authentic, probably reliable, and unsubstantiated. They were then gathered into six main collections of traditions, which are still of great importance to Muslims. These traditions constitute the Sunna, or way, of the Prophet, which many American Muslims continue to cite as their most important guide for conduct.

The term *hadith* can refer to both a single narrative and the whole body of accounts. Along with the verses of the Qur'an that describe proper modes of action and social intercourse, these narratives were to become the basis for the development of Islamic law, or *shari'a*. In the early days, the law varied considerably from place to place as the Islamic empire expanded into different geographic and cultural areas. By the eighth century, dissatisfaction with these legal variations led to the attempt to standardize the law. Four legal scholars who lived and worked in the eighth and ninth centuries have come to be known as the founders of the major Sunni schools of law. Abu Hanifa (d. 767) is the founder of the Hanafite school, Malik ibn Anas (d. 796) of the Maliki tradition, and Ahmad ibn Hanbal (d. 855) of the Hanbali interpretation. Muhammad al-Shafi'i was the fourth of these legal giants whose influence continues so strongly today, and he is often referred to as the architect of Islamic law. A fifth school is the Ja'fari school of Shi'ite law. America, of course, with immigrants from around the world, represents a mix of them all.

Perhaps because he had traveled and been exposed to many different areas of the Islamic world, al-Shafi'i has been known as somewhat of an eclectic. While he emphasized strict adherence to the Qur'an and Sunna, which he saw as the foremost legitimate bases of the *shari'a*, he is nonetheless considered an advocate of an intermediate position between rigid traditionalism and too free rational interpretation of the law. To the Qur'an and Sunna (the one divinely revealed and the other, according to him, divinely inspired) he added, when necessary, two subsidiary sources of legal opinion. These are the consensus (*ijma'*) of those who are qualified to render judgment and the use of analogical reasoning (*qiyas*) in very specific circumstances. In his emphasis on consensus he moved the focus away from individual interpretation to the importance of the community as a whole, asserting that God will not allow his community to agree on anything erroneous. His famous work, titled the *Risala*, stands as a monument to legal construction and has earned him the title of founder of the discipline of *usul al-fiqh*, literally meaning "the foundations of the law." Today the Shafi'i school of law predominates in Southeast Asia, East Africa, and the southern part of Arabia. Muslims in America, like those in many other parts of the world, understand the importance of the Qur'an and Sunna as articulated by al-Shafi'i, and many attempt to live in as close accord as possible with the way of the Prophet. Some others, although still minority voices, hold that the traditions of the Prophet, while normative for behavior, need not necessarily be considered binding.

Meanwhile, as the forces of Islam were marching and gathering more lands and more wealth for the caliphal coffers, and the scholars and legists were struggling to find ways in which to adjudicate the lives of Muslims, some people found themselves restless with the directions in which the *umma* of Islam seemed to be moving. These pious men and women of the early community were becoming concerned that the acquisition of territories and wealth was leading Muslims far from the simple ideals propounded by Prophet Muhammad and practiced in the first days of Islam. They heeded the Qur'anic warning about the fires of eternal damnation for those who do not lead responsible lives and became increasingly concerned that such a fate awaited them, as well as those in leadership positions.

With this heightened awareness of the Day of Judgment, some of these pious souls began to express a repugnance even for the good things of the earth itself, a rejection that does not reflect the world-affirming nature of the Qur'an. This rejection manifested itself in intense self-denial and asceticism. Some chose to wear scratchy wool clothing, reminiscent of Christian hair shirts, to enhance their own discomfort. After the Arabic word for wool, *suf*, these folks came to be known as *Sufis*, a term that stuck. *Sufism* is the generic name for the ascetic/mystical movement that has played a significant role in the history of Islam. Sufism has also served as the vehicle through which many Americans have come to Islam, and a number of different Sufi orders are now growing in popularity in the United States.

Many American women are attracted to the spiritual and communal dimensions of Sufism. Among the most famous of the women mystics of Islam, a person greatly revered for her piety and extreme God-consciousness as well as her strict ascetic practices, was Rabi'a al-'Adawiyya, renowned as a lover of the divine. While she is one of the few women ascetics whose name has been recorded in history, a number of women found the pietistic-mystical path to God more congenial than strict adherence to the dictates of the emerging law. Rabi'a, born around 717, is said to have lived alone in the most humble of circumstances, for a while remaining a recluse in a small cell. Many stories circulate about her spending days with no more than a morsel of bread and a few sips of water, so dedicated was she to the contemplation and adoration of God and so persuaded that he would provide for her basic needs. While some of the other early ascetics lived in fear of the fires of punishment, Rabi'a professed to be so overcome with God-consciousness that she had no time to consider either this world or the next. Asked once if she loved the Prophet, she replied that yes, of course, she did, but in fact her whole consciousness was so devoted to the reality of God that she really did not have time to think about the Prophet.

One of the issues illustrated by Rabi'a, as well as by others who believed that they had a kind of direct access to God, was that of possible antinomianism, or the tendency to circumvent the legal prescriptions. As we have seen, Rabi'a lived at a time when great attention was being paid to the importance of law in binding the community. While there is little evidence that she necessarily ignored the formal responsibilities of Islam, clearly they were of less importance to her than the direct love of God. Rabi'a was one of the first to espouse the kind of love-mysticism that often leads to a coming together of lover and beloved, human and divine, in ways that threaten the sanctity of *tawhid*, or the affirmation of God's unicity (uniqueness). Later Sufism developed two schools of approach to God, sometimes called the "sober Sufis" and the "intoxicated Sufis," the latter in their extreme proclamations of intimate association with the divine often earning the severe disapprobation of the orthodox.

In the centuries after Rabi'a lived, despite the misgivings of orthodoxy, Sufism developed as a highly significant movement within the faith of Islam. It came to represent a kind of parallel to the *shari'a*, or law (which is often known as the external path to God) in its emphasis on the internal path, called the *tariqa*. This term applied to both the journey of the individual mystic in his or her quest to draw near to God and the different orders that ultimately developed as distinguished Sufis gathered disciples and formalized their teachings. These movements grew up in all the Islamic lands and found adherents among every social and economic class. After some four centuries a number of Sufi orders were permanently established, their followers still maintaining affiliation with them today.

The *tariqa* is understood to provide a practical way in which an individual aspirant learns how to gain heightened God-consciousness. A spiritual master, a *pir* or *murshid* claiming lineage from the Prophet Muhammad, heads each order, and each has its own set of particular teachings, involving a series of states and stages in the spiritual quest along which the master guides the disciple. In later centuries Sufism came to be an important vehicle for the teaching of Islam, and the orders included not only those dedicated to pursuing the mystical path but also followers who wanted Islamic training and the collegiality of the congregation.

The Development of Philosophy, Theology, and Mysticism

As the first several centuries of Islam passed, the community moved into a new phase of its existence. The immediate expansion was completed, the

Qur'an was gathered and authorized, the *hadith* collections were determined, and the law was becoming formulated. Islamic civilization was moving toward the height of its glory, with new developments in the arts and sciences illustrating a wide range of intellectual and artistic creativity. The third and fourth centuries of Islam saw amazing developments not only in the specifically religious sciences but in mathematics, art and architecture, medicine, literature, and philosophy as Islam absorbed, assimilated, and developed the many concepts it encountered through its rapid geographical spread.

One of the signal achievements of this period was the flourishing of Islamic philosophical sciences. Most of the works of Plato and Aristotle were known to Arab Muslims, and it has long been recognized that the medieval Muslim world made a lasting contribution to Christendom by providing Western scholars with access to the great classics of Greece and Rome through Arabic translations, from which they were rendered into European languages. In addition, Muslim philosophers used the tools of Greek philosophical thought to develop their own reflections, sometimes supporting the dogmas of orthodoxy and at other times providing serious challenge and engaging in significant debate and even controversy. Into this scene came Ibn Sina, known to the West as Avicenna, one of the great intellectual giants of Islamic philosophy and science.

Ibn Sina is said to have early exhibited those qualities of intellectual curiosity and achievement that were to serve him so well through his distinguished career. By the time he was ten years old he had memorized the entire Qur'an and was well on his way with the study of grammar, logic, and mathematics. By sixteen he had taught himself physics, metaphysics, and medicine and was already well known as a philosopher, astronomer, and physician, as well as one well versed in the law. For a number of years he wandered through Persia, meeting and engaging with mystics, philosophers, and men of letters. He finally settled in the magnificent city of Isphahan, where during a long period of relative peace he wrote some of his most important works. He died in 1037 in Hamadan, and there modern travelers may visit his tomb.

Ibn Sina's writings cover a great range of subjects. A devout Muslim, he understood his own philosophy as supporting rather than contradicting the central doctrines of Islam. One important exception was his denial of the notion that physical bodies will be resurrected at the end of time and be subject to a final judgment. He argued instead for the immortality of the soul, one of the primary areas of disagreement between Islamic philosophers and theologians. Later scholars have noted the relationship of his philosophy-theology to his own mystical leanings, and his writings always insist that the first reality is God and it is on him that the existence of all other creatures and things depends. If the genius of Islamic civilization at its height was indeed the flowering of arts and sciences and their integration into a common body of knowledge, surely Ibn Sina was the quintessential representative of both that range and that integration. Still acknowledged as an intellectual and philosophical giant in the development of Islam, he occupies as great a place of respect and veneration in the West as any figure in the history of the Muslim community. As Muslims in America continue to move increasingly into positions of professional leadership, they may well look to Ibn Sina as a model of scientific as well as artistic creativity and range.

Some half a century after Ibn Sina, another extremely influential figure appeared, who was to serve as the great "integrator"—or perhaps more appropriately "reconciler"—in the history of Islamic thought. That person is the renowned theologian, philosopher, and mystic Abu Hamid al-Ghazali. As al-Shafi'i had provided a kind of middle way between the legal extremes in his day, and Ibn Sina in his very person brought together a range of disciplines, so al-Ghazali served as a reminder to the sometimes fractured Islamic *umma* that true Islam both integrates and reconciles and that the umbrella of the faith has room for a range of interpretations. Like many others in the history of Islam, al-Ghazali was considered a *mujaddid*, or renewer of the faith, who, according to tradition, appears once in every century to restore the faith of the community.

Al-Ghazali was born in the Iranian city of Tus in the year 1058, three years after the Turkish Seljuks had taken over as rulers of Baghdad. By this time the rapid growth of the faith and the incorporation of such a range of peoples and cultures into the *umma* had made the ideal of unity difficult to achieve. The caliphate had fallen on difficult days, and the 'Abbasid ruler in Baghdad was virtually powerless. Isma'ili Shi'ites were seriously challenging Sunni leadership of the Islamic community. Differences between philosophers and theologians were driving a notable wedge between the religious and intellectual leaders of the community. Those who followed an esoteric Sufi path were, by the time of al-Ghazali, finding themselves often at dangerous odds with those who espoused a more "orthodox" interpretation of the faith. Into this complex set of communal tensions came this young scholar and theologian, who took it upon himself to bring as much harmony as possible through example and intellectual endeavor.

By al-Ghazali's time, Islamic theologians had resolved some of the more sticky issues, though not without some attending violence. Several centuries earlier a philosophical-theological school called the Mu'tazila had tried unsuccessfully to defend the notion of human free will, on the grounds that divine justice must necessitate human choice and agency. The orthodox conclusion was that while humans have responsibility, only God creates; thus God is the author of human actions. Al-Ghazali himself was part of what was known as the Ash'arite school of theology, after the name of one who tried to reconcile human responsibility with divine authority and knowledge. Interestingly, much twentieth-century Islamic theological reflection finds itself in sympathy with Mu'tazili presuppositions.

If he was a theologian, al-Ghazali was also a philosopher, and it was his particular genius to incorporate the philosophical sciences into the study of theology in a way that really had not previously been done. Then in 1095 al-Ghazali went through a spiritual crisis that changed his life. Through his teaching and writing he had achieved great fame as one of the outstanding theologians of the time. But his dissatisfactions ran deep, and as he relates in a later autobiography, God ultimately forced him to take stock of his life in a completely new way. In a final moment of crisis, God actually froze his tongue so that he was unable to do what he did best: lecture in a public forum in his classroom. Suddenly he saw his teaching as insignificant, his motives insincere, and his whole life apparently leading to disaster. "I saw for certain that I was on the brink of a crumbling bank of sand and in imminent danger of hell-fire unless I set about to mend my ways," he wrote in his autobiography. "Worldly desires were striving to keep me by their chains just where I was, while the voice of faith was calling, 'To the road! To the road! What is left of life is but little. . . . If you do not prepare *now* for eternal life, when will you prepare? If you do not now sever these attachments, when will you sever them?'"[2]

With this unavoidable challenge, Abu Hamid al-Ghazali began serious engagement in the practices of Sufism. Gradually, he became persuaded that it is through neither the mind nor the senses that truth is to be obtained, but in the realization of God's presence in one's life and heart achieved through careful training and disciplined spiritual activity. During this period of his life al-Ghazali wrote what was to be his most enduring and significant work, titled *The Revivification of the Religious Sciences*. He brought law and theology together with philosophy so as to give each a place in the fabric of Islam, all through the lens of a deeply mystical faith. Perhaps most important, he demonstrated how Sufi practices responsibly observed were not dangerous or antithetical to orthodoxy but provided a base of religious experience through which the living breath of God could truly enliven the heart of the believer. Conflicts between "intoxicated" Sufis and sober theologians never fully abated, but al-Ghazali had given assurance of a way in which to understand all these strands of religion as integrated into the full fabric of Islamic faith. Significant as al-Ghazali's mystical reflections are, his greatest gift was in fact the coordination of the intellect with the heart and the presentation of this integration in a rigorous and persuasive set of treatises.

Other mystics, however, gave themselves completely to highly poetic utterances that told of their intimate experiences with the divine Lord. The literature of Islamic mysticism is replete with Sufi love poetry, from Egypt to Persia to India and beyond. Many of these poets have captured the imagination of readers and pious aspirants to the Sufi path, and they continue to be read today in many versions and translations. Probably none has fired the hearts of those with religious sensibility and a longing for communication with the divine in quite the same way as the famous mystic of Anatolia, Jalal al-Din Rumi.

Rumi, who lived about a century after al-Ghazali, came originally from the area of Balkh in Khorasan, a melting pot of many cultures and forms of religious expression. Probably because of the threat of Mongol invasions from the East, his father fled with his family through such famed Islamic cities as Baghdad and Mecca, and finally into Asia Minor. They settled in the ancient city of Konya, which today lies in the central part of the modern state of Turkey. Like al-Ghazali, Rumi became extremely popular as a teacher, gathering large numbers of disciples and followers. The most stunning event of Rumi's life was his encounter with the enigmatic and charismatic Shams al-Din of Tabriz. A Sufi of great spiritual discipline who normally shunned social contact, Shams, it is said, swept into Konya seemingly from nowhere and quite overwhelmed Rumi with the power of his presence. In later years Rumi was to write of Shams as both his beloved teacher and his spiritual confidant. His relationship with Shams symbolized that between lover and beloved, the divine aspirant and the Lord who is the object of adoration, and engendered some of the most beautiful mystical love poetry ever written. Though their relationship lasted only a few short years, its impact on Rumi was so intense that he was able to draw on it for inspiration and spiritual power throughout his life. It is said that he received death with the joy of knowing that he would at last be in the presence of his beloved Lord. His tomb in Konya is a place of great importance as a pilgrimage site and is revered as the spiritual center of Turkey.

Rumi's poetry has a rhythmic character that easily allows it to be put to music, as when the haunting melody of the flute portrays the reed-soul.

Although the use of music and dance has raised the hackles of the orthodox over the centuries as a too-easy method of God-intoxication, it has continued as an important mode of mystical expression in many orders. None, perhaps, is more famous than that adopted by the order of Mevlevis founded by Jalal al-Din Rumi, often referred to as the "whirling dervishes." While the word *whirling* would seem to connote a kind of frantic spinning, in fact the participants, who are dressed in long skirts and conical hats, turn slowly and gracefully, their motion intended to reflect the movement of the planets around the axis of the universe. This spiritual dance has continued to attract devotees and is gradually being attempted by groups of Sufis in America, although in many cases its resemblance to the Mevlevi dance might well be questioned. Rumi himself remains one of the most beloved figures of Islamic mystical piety, with his poetry and teaching reflecting the most profound aspects of the divine-human relationship.

The Intervening Years

Over the ensuing centuries, many developments too complex to detail here took place in the vast lands of Islam. The Mongols did, in fact, arrive, and in 1258 Baghdad was destroyed and the 'Abbasid caliphate with it. The year 1492 saw not only the venture of Christopher Columbus to America but also the fall of Granada, the last bastion of Islam in Iberia, and the beginning of the Christian Inquisition in Spain and the death or expulsion of its Muslim citizens. The Crusades, an ill-fated adventure of the West to reconquer Jerusalem that resulted in terrible slaughter and carnage, staggered to an end by the middle of the second millennium. Succeeding centuries of Muslims would long remember what they now label as the first of a long series of Western imperialist ventures into Muslim lands. The accusation of Western "Crusader mentality" has been commonly raised in post-9/11 Islamist literature.

After occupying Baghdad, the Seljuk Turks, who had adopted Islam as their religion, moved gradually to establish control over all of Anatolia. In 1453 Western Europe, weakened by the Crusades, saw one of its worst fears realized when Turkish Muslim forces seized and occupied the ancient city of Constantinople, establishing the Ottoman Empire, which was to continue until the end of World War I. Under Sulayman the Magnificent, Constantinople, then called Istanbul, became one of the glorious cities of the world with its Blue Mosque and other monuments to Islam, a place of fascination for Westerners who were becoming increasingly intrigued by Muslim

"Whirling dervishes" of the Sufi order of Jalal al-Din Rumi at Konya, Turkey.
COURTESY TURKISH TOURIST OFFICE

culture. In the early 1500s, with the ascension of Babur as the first Moghul emperor of India, Islam became a permanent feature of the Indian subcontinent. His successors continued the construction of Islamic edifices, the most notable being that great masterpiece of Islamic architecture the Taj Mahal.

As early as the thirteenth century, merchants from the southeastern coast of Arabia established trade routes across the Indian Ocean into the lands of Indonesia, where they brought the word of Islam and intermarried with the women of that country. The spread of Sufism also played a major role in the introduction of Islam to the area, and Indonesia was to become what is today the largest Islamic country in the world. Malaysia and other parts of Southeast Asia also became major centers of Islamic life, with the first Southeast Asian Islamic state established in the early 1600s. Under the Safavid Kingdom in Persia in the sixteenth and seventeenth centuries, the great Islamic sciences, still strikingly evident today in the glorious art and architecture of the city of Isphahan, flourished.

Islam, of course, had established itself across North Africa soon after the death of the Prophet. Many centuries of exploration, trade, and wandering Sufi teachers and preachers to the lands of Africa also brought Islam to a number of areas of the sub-Saharan continent. All of these areas into which

Richard the Lion-Hearted and his Christian troops watch as Muslims are massacred at Acre during the Fourth Crusade. Bibliothèque Nationale

Muslim faith and culture spread are represented today in the many faces of American Islam.

At the beginning of the Western colonialist venture, three huge Muslim empires controlled a significant portion of the world: the Ottoman in much of the Middle East, the Safavid in Persia, and the Moghul in India. Starting perhaps with Napoleon's invasion of Egypt in 1798, the West entered into an unfortunate phase of its collective history in which economics and the desire for expansion of territorial control combined with a strikingly parochial sense of manifest destiny. The West convinced itself of its mission to civilize and educate much of the rest of the world, particularly those areas under Muslim control, a venture that took the form of military, political, and Christian missionary interventions. Over the course of the nineteenth century the British took India and Malaysia, the Dutch occupied Indonesia, and the Russians moved into Turkestan. In 1830 France seized Algeria and from there extended control over the central Sahara and much of the Islamic West and equatorial Africa, and in 1881 took Tunisia. Egypt fell to Britain in 1882, and by the end of the century British control extended up the Nile into the Sudan. Spain, Germany, and Belgium also participated in the feast, although with fewer obvious results. Italy's largest conquest was that of Libya in 1911. At the same time the Ottoman Empire was being dismantled, with Eastern European lands one by one taken away by the West. Even the Middle East came heavily under Western influence.

By the end of World War I the Ottoman Empire was history. Arabs who had thrown their support to the West against their Turkish coreligionists, believing promises of an independent Arab state, found to their horror that Britain and France had no intention of keeping such a promise and, in fact, had agreed in secret to divide the Middle East into their own separate spheres of influence. Britain, which was still in control of Egypt and India, took Iraq, Palestine, and Transjordan. France, in addition to its North African territories, moved into Lebanon and Syria. These arrangements were called "mandates," sanctioned by the newly created League of Nations. Turkey itself was divided into a number of areas under different forms of Western control, with only a fraction of its former empire still in Muslim hands. Iran, which had tried to be neutral in the war only to find itself violated by a number of Western forces, was unstable, with Britain the most significant presence there, as in much of the rest of the Middle East. To add to the humiliation and disillusionment of Muslims came another blow to the Islamic world: the Balfour Declaration, which provided for the establishment of a homeland for Jews in the heart of primarily Muslim Palestine.

It would be difficult to overestimate the devastating effects that these Western incursions into the lands of Islam had on the deep sense of pride that Muslims held in their faith and culture. While during the nineteenth century the responsibility for what is seen as unqualified Western imperialism lay mainly with Europe, primarily Britain and France, in the twentieth century the burden shifted to the United States. Throughout the century European powers relinquished their political control of Muslim countries one by one, although the boundaries drawn around many of them remain those arbitrarily set at the end of World War I. The United States, however, through its support of the state of Israel, its collaboration with Muslim rulers considered to be working against the interests of true Islam, its economic exploitation, and its Christian missionary endeavors that seem to be aimed at the extermination of Islam, became the target of great criticism on the part of many Muslim leaders. Since 9/11 and what is perceived in the Muslim world as the American invasion of Iraq and Afghanistan, many Muslims see America as the model of imperialist venture. Muslims emigrating to America, therefore, often find themselves caught between the political or economic need to make a new home here and the psychological burden of coming to a place they have perceived as the cause of much exploitation and pain.

Framers of Twentieth-Century Islam

Muslim leaders throughout the twentieth century struggled to recover pride in their religion as a faith and a cultural foundation. The many movements they initiated, influential among both American Muslims and Muslims who have trained in America and then returned home, are too numerous and complex to detail here. They can be extrapolated, however, from the lives of a few of the people who have significantly contributed to the formation of modern Islam.

At the end of World War I the Muslims of Turkey were forced to abandon all thoughts of an empire and concentrate on rebuilding their state. They did this under the exceptional leadership of Mustafa Kemal, later called Ataturk, who has been considered the founder of the modern state of Turkey. Many Muslims, and many Turks, felt strongly that the appropriate leadership of the Islamic community was still the caliphate. Mustafa Kemal came quickly to realize that the future of Turkey lay not in an antiquated institution but in the swift identification of itself as a national entity with power and influence. When the Turkish Republic was officially formed in 1923, Mustafa Kemal proclaimed that it was to be governed by a president elected by the National Assembly. Not surprisingly, Ataturk himself was the first to hold the office. In 1924, despite strong urgings to the contrary by other world Muslim leaders, the assembly ratified Ataturk's proposals for a completely secular state and officially abolished the caliphate. While the office of caliph had long since lost the authority originally invested in it after the death of the Prophet, it had remained as a symbol of pan-Islamic governance and authority. That it came to such an end deeply shocked much of the Islamic world and has had a lasting effect on Muslim political thought.

Ataturk did not believe that he was abandoning Islam. His goal was to further the state as such, and religion was seen as one highly significant force in that process. But religion was to be a moral rather than a political force. Kemal is notable not only for his success in establishing Turkey as a major player in the twentieth century but also for being a major proponent of restricting religion to private life. Muslims in America watch with great interest as Turkey struggles to legitimate itself as a member of the European assembly of powers at the same time that some of its leadership and much of its population refuse to relinquish what identifies it as a state in which Islam continues to play a role of great significance.

Among those who expressed concern over Ataturk's secularism and the abolition of the caliphate were several prominent Muslim leaders in India. From the late nineteenth century through all of the twentieth, Indian (and later Pakistani) Muslims have been among the most articulate of those attempting to design a proper course for a modern Islam. Some were strongly influenced by the West and European rationalism, while religious leaders who were more traditional objected strongly to such Western leanings. By the middle of the twentieth century a number of strong currents in Islamic thought were to contribute to the creation of the state of Pakistan in 1947.

Muhammad Iqbal is the name most commonly associated with the idea of forming a separate state in which Islam would be the official religion. That he died nearly a decade before the realization of that vision in 1947 does not detract from his influence. It was Muhammad 'Ali Jinnah who, in fact, was the architect of the new state, though he lived only long enough to see its creation. Jinnah became so convinced by Iqbal's arguments that as leader of the Muslim League Party, he led the way to the founding of a new nation, despite the desperate pleas from many of his countrymen, including Mahatma Gandhi, that India not be divided.

While events of extreme significance for the future of Islam were occurring in Turkey and the Indian subcontinent during the first half of the century, other areas were experiencing the tension as well as the excitement of new and creative thinking. One of the most fertile grounds for this kind of regenerative theological adventure was Egypt. The most prominent pioneer of reform in the early 1900s was Muhammad 'Abduh. 'Abduh was a practical reformer who chose to work through the evolutionary process that he hoped would bring about steady change. He fostered a series of reforms in religious education at the traditional al-Azhar University, worked as the *mufti*, or chief legal official, of Egypt to bring about the new developments he advocated, and with Rashid Rida authored a commentary on the Qur'an that is still foundational for understanding Islam in the twenty-first century.

As the early decades of the century unfolded in Egypt, however, 'Abduh's legacy (he died in 1905) came to be challenged by some who saw him as too progressive, too accommodating to Western ideas, or too unwilling to advocate a more radical solution to the problems of a somewhat dormant Islam. One of those who proposed a quite different approach was Hasan al-Banna. His insistence on dramatic change led to the formation of the still very powerful Muslim Brotherhood, an organization that is influential in many segments of American Islam today. He saw in Egyptian society not the steady change that 'Abduh had hoped for but increasing secularism, a disregard for the heritage of Islamic law and tradition, and the development of an upper middle class that was thoroughly enchanted with Western culture. In the late 1920s al-Banna and several associates began the Muslim Brotherhood as a call to return to a God-centered political and social life. Largely an urban movement, it appealed to both the masses and a large segment of educated and socially mobile professionals. While not a political party, at least in the early days, it quickly earned the disfavor of the ruling parties. In 1949 the Egyptian government had Hasan al-Banna assassinated after the Brotherhood mounted a public challenge for the establishment of an Islamic state. In 1954, after an attempt on President Nasser's life, the Brotherhood was outlawed, although it continued to be active. One of its most influential contributors was Sayyid Qutb, also executed by the Nasser government, whose writings form the basis of much post-9/11 radical Islamic ideology. The Brotherhood's fortunes have risen and fallen over the decades, while its political philosophy remains attractive to many contemporary Muslims.

Developing as a kind of parallel to the Muslim Brotherhood in Egypt is a movement called the Jama'at-i-Islami (literally, "the Islamic Society") in Pakistan. Like the Brotherhood, it has looked to a conservative interpretation of Islam for a social framework in which religion and the state are unified under the *shari'a*. Also like the Brotherhood, it has considerable influence on American Islam, and the writings and ideas of its founder, Abu'l-'Ala al-Mawdudi, are more easily accessible to Western audiences because they are available in English.

Al-Mawdudi was born in 1903 in India into the Sufi order of the Chistiyya, which claims a lineage of descent through the Prophet's daughter Fatima. Known as a strong Indian nationalist, Mawdudi began to speculate on the nature of a true Islamic state, which, as in Brotherhood ideology, would look to the community of the Prophet as a model. Invited by Iqbal to move to Lahore, he there founded the Jama'at-i-Islami organization in 1941. Like the Brotherhood, the Jama'at saw itself not as a political party but as an ideological fraternity with a growing network of branches and cells. Its members were committed to religious training and to the development of a range of social projects designed for a new generation of young people dedicated to Islamic morality.

Mawdudi became increasingly convinced that Western influences endangered Islam and that the best hope for Pakistan was a sound religious basis. He criticized both modernists and conservative traditionalists who paid more attention to their own legal deductions than to the true sources of Islam, the Qur'an and the Sunna of the Prophet. His ideas became extremely popu-

Mustafa Kemal Ataturk, founder of the modern state of Turkey. ARCHIVE PHOTOS

lar, and the Jamaʻat spread rapidly across Pakistan. Unlike the more popu-list Brotherhood, it was basically an elitist movement designed to train new leadership for an Islamic state and society. In many ways Mawdudi is the father of Islamic revivalism, the set of movements that became so influential in the Islamic world in the last part of the twentieth century and that the Western media erroneously label "Islamic fundamentalism." He envisioned Islam as invigorated, pure, and unwilling to compromise with the forces of Westernization or secularization or with those who stressed Indian national-ism over Islamic identity. Politically, the Jamaʻat often opposed official gov-ernment policies and, again like the Brotherhood, was suppressed and finally officially banned, its activists sometimes imprisoned.

Although al-Mawdudi died in 1979, his international influence and the popularity of his ideas have not flagged. His many writings are internationally consumed and in the American context provide a significant model for Islamic living in the contemporary world. Many find him too conservative, while others perceive his urgings to return to the Qur'an and Sunna to be extremely persuasive. Mosques and Islamic centers in the United States regularly feature his books and pamphlets, as do Islamic bookstores, grocery and convenience stores, and other establishments selling and distributing Islamic materials. Al-Mawdudi's call for what many interpret as the virtual seclusion of women has appealed to some and outraged others. For conservative Muslim communities in America, both immigrant and African American, it is clear that the prescriptions of Abu'l-'Ala al-Mawdudi will be influential for some time to come.

Among the most significant events in the Islamic world in the latter part of the twentieth century, and one that resulted in the migration of many Muslims to the United States, was the Iranian revolution of 1979, which brought to power the Ayatollah Ruhollah al-Musavi Khomeini. In many ways the revolution served to give credibility to the aspirations of Islamic revivalists in Egypt, Pakistan, and many other places in the modern world. While the original hope of some of Khomeini's supporters that he might be the returned Imam so long expected by Twelver Shi'ites was not fulfilled, he became a symbol of great pride to Shi'ite and Sunni Muslims everywhere for having established an Islamic state and, perhaps especially, for having done so in the face of strong American opposition.

Khomeini was born in central Iran two years after the turn of the century. After studying in several centers of Islamic learning, he was accepted as a *mujtahid*, one credited with determining a methodology for legal interpretation. Later, he was to achieve the status of *ayatollah* (literally, *ayat Allah*, "sign of God"), the highest and most learned authority over the religious, social, and political life of Shi'ite Islam. By the 1960s Khomeini had emerged as one of the most articulate spokesmen in opposition to the policies of Mohammed Reza Pahlavi Shah. During the Shi'ite holy month of Muharram in 1963, Khomeini went so far as to compare the shah with the murderer of 'Ali's son Husayn at Karbala, triggering massive demonstrations against the shah in Tehran. Such activities led to Khomeini's arrest and exile to Turkey, then to Iraq and Paris. He became a hero to leftist youth movements opposed to the shah as he advocated the authority of the jurist as the appropriate rule for the state.

From exile, his messages continued to be transmitted to his public in Iran through illegal pamphlets and cassettes. Growing in popularity, Khomeini became the personification of opposition to the shah. In 1979 he returned

Ayatollah Ruhollah al-Musavi Khomeini, supreme leader
of Iran, 1979–1989.   ARCHIVE PHOTOS

triumphant to Iran, sent the shah into exile, and founded the conservative
Islamic Republic, whose clerical rule continues today. America had never
imagined that its "island of security in the Middle East" could fall. The
holding of American hostages for 444 days by the revolutionary "students"
added to American revulsion, reinforced by Ayatollah Khomeini's claims,
still repeated today, if more rhetorically, that America is the embodiment of
Satan. Tensions today between the United States and Iran continue to rise as
the West accuses the Iranian state of secretly developing nuclear capability
for other than peaceful purposes.

Iranian Americans evidence extremely mixed feelings about their home
country. Some, uprooted from a land they loved, rue the day that Khomeini
came to power and sincerely believe that his austere rule, mitigated only

somewhat by his successors, does justice neither to Islam nor to the heritage of Iranian leadership in all of the great sciences and arts of Islam. Others applaud the ability of a committed Muslim leader to challenge the power of what they perceived as an American-supported dictatorship, though regretting the repression that still makes the lives of many Iranians difficult. Still others look with increasing pride at the new thinking and interpretation that they see evidenced in the works of Iranian intellectuals, both men and women, as they struggle to balance support for an Islamic state with the need to survive both ideologically and economically in the contemporary world.

These, then, are some of the people and movements that influenced the shaping of twentieth-century Islam and whose heritage continues to influence the lives of Muslims in America. As we shall see later, the influence is often two-way, as Muslim students, diplomats, and businesspeople bring American Islamic influences back to their home countries. Those who then return to the West, often in positions of national leadership, add through their international connections yet another dimension to the formation of American Islam.

What is that Islam—or, perhaps more accurately, what are the many forms of Islam—that have come to characterize the American scene? To that diversity and complexity we now turn.

CHAPTER THREE

Islam Comes to America

The First Muslims

Commentators on the emergence of Islam in the North American scene have looked for the most part to the middle and latter part of the nineteenth century as signaling the first real arrival of Muslims in the United States. Indeed, at this time the first Muslim immigrants, primarily from the Middle East, began to come to North America in hopes of earning some kind of fortune, large or small, and then returning to their homelands. We will return to their story shortly. Going back considerably further, some Muslim scholars currently argue that for nearly two centuries before the time of Christopher Columbus's venture in 1492, Muslims sailed from Spain and parts of the northwestern coast of Africa to both South and North America and were among the members of Columbus's own crew. African Muslim explorers are said to have penetrated much of the Americas, relating to and sometimes intermarrying with Native Americans. Some hypothesize that Muslims set up trading posts and even introduced some arts and crafts in the Americas. Evidence to support such claims, cited from artifacts, inscriptions, and reports of eyewitness accounts, is still sufficiently vague that the thesis remains somewhat hypothetical.[1]

The date 1492 is of historical significance not only because of the Columbian exploits. It also signals the official end of the presence of Islam as a power in the Iberian Peninsula, now known as Spain and Portugal. After having enjoyed a glorious rule in the ninth and tenth centuries in Cordoba, and a more checkered North African rule in the succeeding centuries,

Muslims saw their fortunes decline rapidly. In 1474 the husband-and-wife team of Fernando of Aragon and Isabella of Seville succeeded to conjoint but separate thrones. Known as the "Catholic monarchs" for their dedication to reuniting all of Spain under Christendom, they captured the last stronghold of Muslim occupation in Granada in 1492. By the turn of the fifteenth century, Muslims (generally referred to in Western literature as Moors) throughout the peninsula were forced to choose among the unfortunate alternatives of conversion to Christianity, emigration, or death. A few who chose the first continued to practice their faith in secret, maintaining a hidden enclave of Islam for centuries. Others tried openly to rebel and were subsequently expelled from the land that only a few centuries earlier had been one of the few historical examples of Christian and Muslim (and Jewish) cultural harmony.

Evidence is coming to light indicating that some of the Moors who were forced to leave Spain managed to make their way to the Caribbean islands, with a few even getting as far as the southern part of the present United States. As scholars representing a variety of disciplines continue to explore these theories, some American Muslims see in them proof that Islam played a role in the early history of this country. The possibility of such connections with Spanish cultures is particularly appealing to U.S. Hispanics who are attracted by Islamic teachings.

Muslim Immigrants in the American Context

With this combination of evidence and conjecture in mind, let us turn to the well-documented history of immigrant Muslims. Migrations occurred in a series of distinguishable periods. The first was between 1875 and 1912, from rural areas of what was then called Greater Syria under the rule of the Ottoman Empire, currently comprising Syria, Jordan, Palestine, and Lebanon. The majority of immigrants from the Middle East at that time were Christian, often somewhat knowledgeable about America because of training in missionary schools. A small percentage was made up of Sunni, Shi'i 'Alawi, and Druze Muslims. By the latter half of the twentieth century that ratio was to be reversed. For the most part these early arrivals remain nameless to us, with occasional exceptions such as one Hajj Ali (rendered by Americans as "Hi Jolly"), brought by the U.S. cavalry to the deserts of Arizona and California in 1856 to help breed camels. This experiment failed, but Ali is said to have stayed in California to look for gold.

When the Ottoman Empire, which had controlled most of the Muslim Middle East, came to its demise at the end of World War I, more Muslims headed to America. Many were relatives of Muslims who had already emigrated and established themselves to some degree in this country. U.S. immigration laws passed in 1921 and 1924 imposed quota systems for particular nations, which significantly curtailed the numbers of Muslims who were allowed to enter the country. Throughout most of the 1930s, immigration was open specifically and only to relatives of people already living in America. The actual numbers of Muslims allowed to settle here were limited and did not rise until after World War II.

The postwar period, from 1945 to around 1960, saw considerable expansion in the sources of immigration. Each country had an annual quota of immigrants. Because that quota was based on population percentages in the United States at the end of the nineteenth century, however, most of the immigrants allowed to enter the country were from Eastern Europe. Still, the trickle of Muslims continued, coming now not only from the Middle East but also from many other parts of the world, including India (after the partitioning of the subcontinent in 1947), Eastern Europe (mainly from Albania and Yugoslavia), and the Soviet Union. Most of these arrivals settled in large cities such as Chicago and New York. Unlike their earlier counterparts, many of these immigrants were urban in background and well educated, and some were members of the families of former ruling elites. Often already quite Westernized in their attitudes, they came to the United States in hopes of continuing their education or receiving advanced technical training. The creation of Israel in 1948 began a movement of Palestinians to America that increased after the disastrous and humiliating defeat of Arab troops at the hands of Israel in 1967. The exodus of Palestinians heading for the West has continued, although it was curtailed by 2001.

Perhaps the most significant event for immigrants to America in the twentieth century was the signing of an immigration act in 1965 by President Lyndon Johnson in which he repealed the quotas based on national diversity within the United States. For the first time since the early part of the century a person's right to enter the country was not specifically dependent on his or her national or ethnic origin. Immigration from Europe thus declined, while that from the Middle East and Asia increased dramatically, particularly of course for those who collaborated with or were sympathetic toward the West.

Over the last several decades, political turmoil in many countries of the Muslim world has occasioned increased emigration. The 1979 revolution in Iran and the ascent to power of Ayatollah Khomeini forced many Iranians to flee their country, and a number of them decided to come to America. Civil strife in Pakistan and the breaking away of East Pakistan to form Bangladesh, anti-Muslim pogroms in India, the military coup in Afghanistan, the repressive regime of Idi Amin in Uganda, and the Lebanese civil war all contributed to the Muslim presence in America. Civil wars in Somalia and Afghanistan, the tightening of the military regime in Sudan, and ethnic cleansing in Bosnia also swelled the numbers of immigrant Muslims. Most recently, American invasion and occupation of Iraq and Afghanistan have resulted in the exodus of more Muslims, many arriving in Europe and the United States.

Today the largest ethnic Muslim group in America is from the subcontinent of South Asia, including Pakistanis, Indians, and Bangladeshis. A few arrived as early as 1895, but the numbers did not increase significantly until the 1970s and 1980s. Muslims from the subcontinent today number more than a million, and have become increasingly important in the development of Muslim political groups in America. Immigrants from Indonesia and Malaysia also make up a significant proportion of the American Muslim population. Some estimates place the number of Iranians at close to a million (including Eastern Christians, Jews, Zoroastrians, and Baha'is), with Muslims from Arab countries of the Middle East, Turks, and Eastern Europeans close behind. Muslims also come from a large number of African nations, including Ghana, Kenya, Senegal, Uganda, Cameroon, Guinea, Sierra Leone, Liberia, Tanzania, and many others.

Naturally, these immigrants represent a great range of Islamic languages, cultures, movements, and ideologies. They are Sunnis and Shi'ites, Sufis and members of sectarian groups, religious and secular people, political Islamists and those who espouse no religious or political agenda. Many have come from circumstances in which Islam is the majority religion and find their new minority status in America difficult to adjust to. Others already know what it means to be a member of a minority religious group and come with their coping skills well honed. With each new arrival the picture of Islam in America becomes increasingly complex.

Lives of the Early Muslim Immigrants

Let us return, then, to the America of the late nineteenth century. The young, relatively unskilled Muslim men coming primarily from Syria and Lebanon left home for a number of reasons. Some were fleeing conscription into the

Turkish army, which they saw as little connected to their own national identities. Others had known Christians from their homeland who returned from the United States with considerable wealth, and despite their reluctance to go to a setting in which they would be surrounded by non-Muslims, they were tempted to try their luck.

Generally single, or at least traveling without their wives, they looked upon their time in America as only temporary, hoping that they could earn money to return and establish homes and families. Their dreams were hard to realize, however, as jobs were not easy to find in America, and often they were unable to compete for those that were available because of insufficient knowledge of English or inadequate educational preparation. Many were forced into menial work such as migrant labor, petty merchandising, or mining. One of the most common occupations was peddling, which required little capital, language skills, or training. Working at first along the Atlantic seacoast, peddlers traveled into the South and the West, often facing severe weather, thievery, and local hostility. Other Muslim immigrants served as cheap laborers on work gangs, as, for example, those contributing to the construction of railroads in the Seattle area. The women who gradually began to arrive as marriage partners for the men sometimes found employment in mills and factories, where they worked long hours under extremely difficult conditions. The lack of language skills, poverty, loneliness, and the absence of coreligionists all contributed to the isolation and unhappiness of Muslims in America in the early days. Compounding these difficulties was the fact that Americans of those decades certainly had little enthusiasm for foreigners, especially those whose customs seemed strange and whose religion was not Christian.

These early groups of Muslim immigrants tried to maintain a community of believers in an alien context, without institutional support. The religious training available to their children and grandchildren was minimal. They recalled that in their home countries, young people grew up with their Muslim holidays, festivals, prayers, and observances a constant part of the environment. America presented a different context, in which maintaining even an awareness, let alone regular observance, of the faith was obviously difficult. Neither schools nor businesses had any facilities for, or interest in, providing opportunities for daily prayer. Those who wanted to fast during the month of Ramadan could expect no special accommodation in the workplace. Extended families to provide support and instruction were not available, and economic circumstances generally did not allow families to visit home for reinforcement of the larger familial context. Since so much of the practice of Islam is communal as well as personal, it was difficult to observe the prayers, holidays, and other Islamic occasions. The pioneer families thus had to struggle to maintain their religion and identity in a society that had been built on the backs of immigrants but that, paradoxically, had never appreciated the differences in culture that the immigrants brought with them.

Muslim Communities Across the American Continent

As the immigrants' visions of becoming rich quickly began to fade, so did their hopes of an imminent return to their homes and relatives overseas. Inevitably, they were forced to adapt to a new life in their adopted land. Young men, eager to marry and establish families, found it difficult if not impossible to locate available young Muslim women in this country. Some went back home for brief visits to take a bride; others had their relatives arrange marriages with girls from their home countries. In any case, traditional patterns of courtship gave way to speed and expediency. Others married outside the faith, such as Arab Muslim men marrying Arab Christian women, although the pressure from other Muslims not to succumb to marriage with "nonbelievers" was great. That concern, of course, continues today in the American Muslim community.

Immigrants looked for more permanent kinds of employment, often successfully establishing their own small businesses. Many turned to their native cuisine as a source of revenue, founding coffeehouses, restaurants, bakeries, and small grocery stores. Initially, these were for their compatriots so that Muslims could at least enjoy their own food in a culture in which so much was alien to their tastes and traditions. Gradually, other Americans learned to appreciate Arab cooking, and in most cities today one can enjoy Arab cuisine at everything from gourmet restaurants to fast-food joints featuring such treats as *shawarma* (spicy meat cooked on a rotating spit and stuffed into Syrian bread), *hummoz* (chickpea dip), and *tabouli* (chopped salad with tomatoes, onions, and parsley).

In the early twentieth century many Muslim families found themselves, especially their young people, drifting away from the faith and attempting to hide or do away with those things that marked them as different from their American colleagues. Those whose skin was darker than that of the average American discovered, especially in the South, that they were treated as "colored" by local populations and were refused access to public facilities reserved for "whites only." Stereotypes of Arab Muslims as people with large black eyes, big noses and mustaches, and ill-fitting clothes were commonplace. It became very difficult to maintain the use of Arabic as the youth resisted speaking a tongue that sounded strange to their peers. Their refusal to even learn the mother tongue was doubly painful for their families, as Arabic was not only their cultural but their liturgical language. Muslims began to choose American names for their children or to allow the use of nicknames. Muhammad became Mike, Ya'qub was changed to Jack, Nasreen to Nancy. Arab and, to some extent, Muslim identity began to be something of the past rather than the present and the future as new generations of young people struggled to be part of the culture of their current homeland rather than of their heritage. When these young people matured and began to look to marriage, they turned increasingly to non-Muslim partners, and intermarriage rates rose with each generation.

At the same time, however, and to some extent in response to concerns about acculturation and secularization, in a number of places across America Muslims began to organize into communities in which they affirmed their identity. Following are just a few examples of Muslim life in America.

The Midwest

Among the first of these groupings were those located in the Midwest. North Dakota was home to one of the earliest documented Muslim groups in America. In the small town of Ross, Lebanese Muslims organized for prayers in the early 1900s, and around 1930 they decided to build a mosque. The main structure was low in design to withstand the winds of North Dakota, and for warmth the prayers were held in the basement. Most of those who attended were eventually buried in the adjacent cemetery. By the 1940s few people were using the mosque, some having converted to Christianity. By the 1970s the offspring of the early community voted to tear it down. A new mosque now stands on the site, made of concrete and topped with a bronze dome. Four minarets are inside waiting to be placed on the corners of the building. The second mosque to be built in America after this one in Ross was erected in Rapid City, Iowa. It is a simple white-frame building with a green dome, set in the midst of a residential community.

In Michigan City, Indiana, an Islamic center of sorts was established as early as 1914, its members primarily Syrians and Lebanese who worked in the mercantile trade. They soon began to attract other Muslims from around the area and in 1924 reorganized as the Modern Age Arabian Islamic Society.

Cedar Rapids, Iowa, has had a long history of housing a Muslim community. Its members were peddlers turned shopkeepers, providing goods needed for daily life among the farmers of the region. The first continuing mosque in America was begun there in 1920 in a rented hall, and a mosque building was completed in 1934. It has periodically been refurbished and extended, with a minaret added in 1980. Because it is believed to be the oldest standing mosque in the United States it is often called the "Mother Mosque of America." It was registered as a historical site by the State of Iowa and the National Historical Society in 1960. Recently it was badly damaged by floods in the Midwest, and some of its documents dating back to the late 1800s were seriously damaged. Volunteers worked through the summer of 2008 to restore the building.[2]

New York

Islam has been a presence in the New York City area from the late nineteenth century on, and its history there has been rich and complex. Always a hub of immigrant activity, the city was home to a variety of different racial-ethnic groups, and its Muslim population included merchant seamen, itinerant tradesmen, and those who chose to settle and establish businesses. The American Mohammedan Society was founded in Brooklyn in 1907 by immigrants from Poland, Russia, and Lithuania, who eventually purchased a building to use as a mosque in the early 1930s. By the 1950s the society claimed to have some four hundred members. It has struggled but remains active today as the Moslem Mosque, a name adopted in the 1960s.

In the 1930s a Moroccan immigrant began New York's second real mosque, called the Islamic Mission of America for the Propagation of Islam and the Defense of the Faith and the Faithful. Located near a significant settlement of Middle Eastern Muslims, the mission is still an important institution in the city. Over the past several decades, as the population of greater New York City has mushroomed, so has the construction of mosques and Islamic centers. Some are rebuilt houses, others refurbished office buildings and plants, and still others newly built structures. "Internally driven by the desire to obey and observe Islamic law and externally motivated by what many of them perceive to be a hostile environment, New York City's Muslims have labored to ensure that Islam will evolve into a significant social force within the five boroughs."[3] Today the five boroughs of New York City include some seventy-five mosques.

Because of the size and heterogeneity of its population, New York City provides perhaps a unique locus for the gathering of Muslims from virtually all parts of the world. While many of the Islamic associations of the city are characterized by particular ethnic identities, others are consciously attempting to use this very diversity to emphasize the potential unity of the Muslim *umma* and are making particular efforts to bring together immigrant and indigenous Muslims as well as Sunnis and Shi'ites. One such group is the Islamic Cultural Center of New York, the first mosque to be built in Manhattan, and it is noticeably Islamic in style, with a traditional minaret and dome. The Islamic Center has made significant efforts to attract both immigrant and African American Muslims. National Islamic organizations find the city a particularly fruitful place to extend their activities, and a large number of elementary and upper-level Islamic schools, as well as Muslim stores and businesses, are springing up all over the city. Mosques representing virtually every Muslim culture, ethnicity, and orientation can be found somewhere in greater New York City, and it is an especially popular meeting place for national Islamic organizations.

Chicago

Another of the major cities of America to become home quickly to immigrant Muslims was Chicago. The first Muslims arrived before the turn of the century, primarily from Syria and Palestine. Some claim that Chicago had more Muslims than any other American city in the early 1900s. Like other early arrivals, they had intended not to stay but to earn as much money as possible and then return to their home countries. When they did settle, they did so generally on the south side of Chicago, near the African American district. They too found that their associations with other Muslims were more for cultural identity and support than religious interaction. Yet as they became concerned about the possibility of their children's becoming Christian, they gradually began to take steps to provide some kind of Islamic education for them. After World War I, following the pattern of immigrant waves, more Muslims came to settle in Chicago, especially Arabs holding Turkish passports. The Communist revolution in Russia brought some Muslims from Central Asia to the Chicago area, as did the later partition of the subcontinent of India.

As in other major American cities, Chicago's Muslim population comprises people from a great range of cultural, racial-ethnic, and socioeconomic backgrounds. Chicago boasts the largest group of Muslims from

India, including Hyderabad, Gujarat, and Maharashtra. It is the home of the African American civic and religious leader Warith Deen Mohammed's organization, as well as being the base city for the work of Louis Farrakhan and the Nation of Islam (see chapter 4). Chicago's Kazi Publications, edited by Laleh Bakhtiar, is one of the major producers of both popular and classical Islamic materials. Among the longtime activists and scholars of Islam is DePaul University's Aminah McCloud, a major voice in articulating the relationship of African American and immigrant Islam.

Muslims in Chicago are active in promoting their faith, in providing a range of services to the Islamic community, and in interacting with one another and non-Muslims to foster good interfaith relations. More than forty mosques and Islamic centers have been established to work with the different Muslim groups in greater Chicago, the oldest and largest being the Muslim Community Center, established in 1969. Other mosques, centers, and schools are now located in the outlying suburban areas. "It is fair to say that the Muslim community of Chicago is religiously vibrant, financially sound, educated, and active," said a recent commentator. "It plays a significant role in the development and prosperity of the city of Chicago."[4]

One of the most interesting Muslim agencies operating out of Chicago is called the Inner-City Muslim Action Network (IMAN, an acronym that corresponds to the Arabic word for faith, *iman*). A community-based nonprofit organization that works for social justice, IMAN delivers a range of social services and cultivates the arts in urban communities. Formed in 1995 and incorporated in 1997 by Muslim students along with community residents and leaders, the organization combines spiritual ideals and human compassion with goals of social justice to respond to the needs of those abandoned to inner-city poverty. Though IMAN is led by Muslims, the organization has sought to work for and alongside community residents of all ethnic, cultural, and religious backgrounds.

California

Moving westward, we find that as early as 1895 Muslims from the Indian subcontinent began to arrive in the coastal area. Mainly farm laborers and unskilled workers from the Punjab, they settled in California, Oregon, Washington, and western Canada. Because the early Punjabi immigrants included both Muslims and Sikhs, Americans tended to lump them into the only category they knew appropriate for India and simply called them Hindus.[5] Soon California became a destination for other Muslim immigrants, with significant numbers from the subcontinent of India arriving after the partition of 1947. California today is a center for Muslims from most areas of the world, especially the Middle East, Iran, and South Asia. Recently a number of Afghanis have arrived, along with refugees from Somalia and other areas of Africa.

California as a whole experienced a notable rise in its Islamic population in the 1990s, and areas such as Los Angeles and San Francisco have become vibrant centers of Muslim life, providing much of the leadership of national Muslim organizations. The Islamic Center of Southern California in Los Angeles, for example, is one of the largest Muslim centers in the United States. It has a well-trained staff led by Egyptian brothers Hasan and Maher Hathout, widely known for their writings and community leadership, and a physical plant with mosque, media center, school, publications office, and numerous meeting rooms. More than a thousand people normally attend Friday prayers, representing a wide range of racial-ethnic backgrounds. The center provides a range of services, including counseling on anything from divorce to drugs, to teens, young adults, and families. The large staff conducts a range of activities, including publication of the widely read journal *The Minaret*.

Southern Californians Salam al-Mariati of the Muslim Public Affairs Council and Agha Saeed, founder of the Muslim Political Action Committee have been active in working on issues such as Muslim civil rights and political participation. Muslims in California have been among the most visible in the nation in helping to articulate a moderate Islam in contrast to the image of Islamic extremism often projected by the media.

The United States is home to the largest number of Iranians outside of Tehran. Los Angeles is often called "Tehrangeles" for its population of more than a third of the Iranians living in America. Southern California's Iranians are largely secular, but the population also includes Muslims, Jews, Baha'is, and Armenians.

Dearborn, Michigan

Originally home to small numbers of Sunnis in the early years of the twentieth century, Dearborn has continued to attract both Muslim and Christian Arab immigrants. Today it has one of the largest concentrations of Islamic communities in the nation, with sizable groups of Lebanese, Yemeni, and Palestinian Muslims.

In 1919 a Sunni mosque was built in nearby Highland Park, but it enjoyed only a short life. However, when the Ford Motor Company moved its plant to Dearborn in the late 1920s, providing sustainable sources of revenue for immigrant workers as well as for blacks from the South, a significant Arab community began to form. The pay was only five dollars a day, and working conditions were bad, but English was not required, and many Muslim immigrants welcomed the steady employment. Palestinian Muslims augmented the early Lebanese immigrant group in the late 1940s. A few Yemenis came down from the St. Lawrence Seaway to the Detroit area as early as 1910, but for the most part Yemenis have arrived since the middle of the century, mainly from Sana. Most recent arrivals have been Arabs fleeing the wars in south Lebanon and Beirut, as well as those immigrating from other towns and villages in Lebanon and Palestine.

In 1938 the Sunnis built a mosque, followed by the construction of the Shi'i Hashemite Hall in 1940. Today the Arab Muslim community, Sunnis and Shi'a together, are a close-knit group with numbers of coffeehouses, stores, and businesses that continue to attract immigrants. One can walk for blocks in some areas and find only Arabic signs in grocery stores and other businesses. Five active mosques or Islamic centers in the Dearborn area, two Sunni and three Shi'ite, summon worshipers to prayer five times each day. Dearborn is the home of the first of its kind Arab American museum, helping to make Dearborn a center for the study of Arab or Muslim Americans.

One of the oldest mosques in America is the Shi'ite congregation called "the Mosque of America." Predominantly Lebanese, it is located in Detroit but is expanding to Dearborn. The building will cost $8 million to $10 million and will be able to accommodate a thousand worshipers.

Shi'ite Islam in America

Since the mid- to late nineteenth century, Muslim immigrants to the United States and Canada have included both Sunnis and Shi'ites, as well as members of other smaller sectarian groups. Of the more than one billion Muslims in the world today, approximately one-tenth are Shi'ite. They constitute almost all of the population of Iran and more than half that of Iraq and Lebanon, and are present in various communities in Africa, India, and Pakistan.

Precise information as to the earliest movements of Shi'ites to this country is difficult to come by. We do know that soon after the arrival of Lebanese Shi'ites in the late nineteenth and early twentieth centuries, others from India came to settle here. Later they were joined by Shi'ites from Iraq and Iran. By the 1950s small groups of Shi'ite families were beginning to be found in some of the major cities of America. While in recent years the community has been represented by well-educated professionals and members of the middle and upper-middle classes, such was not true of the earlier immigrants. Shi'ites have always been among the less advantaged, both economically and educationally, and early Lebanese Shi'ite immigrants to America reflected that status.

It is estimated that today approximately one-fifth of American Muslims belong to Shi'a sects. Many are from Iran, coming originally as students during the reign of the Shah and returning after the revolution of 1979. The second-largest group of Shi'ites comes from Iraq, especially since the American invasion of their country, with smatterings of others from different global areas such as Lebanon, India, and Pakistan. In the larger urban centers they tend to have separate centers and places of worship, although in smaller cities and towns they often participate in already established Sunni mosques.

For the most part, when it is possible, Twelvers from Iran and those from the Indian subcontinent choose to keep their communities separate in America because of both language and cultural differences.[6] The latter are eager not to be associated with the Iranians, partly to avoid sharing in the American prejudices concerning Iranian Shi'ite "fundamentalists." The notoriety of events in places like Iran and Lebanon, in fact, has had a double influence on Shi'ites in America. On the one hand, it has heightened feelings of distrust on the part of other Americans. On the other, it has served to encourage greater efforts on the part of Shi'ites to promote understanding of their faith as a distinguishable entity within the complex of American Islam. Shi'ites in America, like other immigrant Muslims, are in the process of determining how to adapt their own Islamic practice, often heavily associated with particular cultural expressions, to the new environment. In this process they need to consider where their highest priorities lie—with Islam as a whole, with Shi'ism in general, or with their own particular sectarian affiliation.

Ithna 'Ashari (Twelver) Shi'ites

All Shi'ites believe that Muhammad's cousin and son-in-law 'Ali was the rightful first leader of the community after the death of the Prophet, and that leadership should continue by the direct descendants of Muhammad. The theological difference between the Seveners and the Twelvers lies in how the chain of leadership is interpreted. Twelver Shi'ites believe that the twelfth and last leader of the Prophet's line, al-Askari, went into hiding in

873. He continues to guide the community through esoteric means, and will return to restore justice on earth at some unknown time.

In the absence of a living Imam within the Shi'ite community, leadership for Iranian Twelvers has come from men designated as *mujtahids*, educated deputies of the hidden imam. They are organized into a central authority, independent of government control, that is supported by the payment of a religious tax called *al-khums*, a 20 percent levy required of all Twelvers. This system has extended to the United States, where *khums* money has provided for the building of Islamic centers and for the salaries of religious teachers and leaders. Shi'i scholars report considerable competition for *khums* money among the different Shi'i groups in America. The Kho'i Foundation in New York, despite the death of the Iranian Imam Kho'i, still continues to collect monies from a number of Shi'ites in the United States. Thus American Ithna 'Asharis, while still looking to the Middle East for leadership and guidance, are able to maintain an essentially autonomous position as they struggle to preserve and redefine their identity in this country.[7]

The civil war in Lebanon brought a large number of Shi'ite refugees to Dearborn. That event, the Iranian revolution, and the continuing war in Iraq have had a significant effect on the lives of these Shi'ites, who have had to defend themselves against the prejudice of the American public. This, too, has added to their sense of solidarity and identity apart from the Sunnis of the area.

The Shi'ite mosques in Dearborn, which loosely reflect ethnic particularities, differ primarily in the degree to which they adhere to Islamic law. Those that are stricter require women to be properly covered, follow Islamic dietary laws with care, and are in general reluctant to make any compromises with American society. Others argue, through their leaders, that to be too strict is to run the risk of alienating members, especially the youth, and that new times and new places do indeed encourage new understandings and interpretations. The late anthropologist Linda Walbridge tells the story of a woman asking one of the Muslim leaders if wearing makeup is permissible for women. "Knowing full well that it was hopeless to ask this woman to throw away her mascara and eyeliner completely," she says, "he instead opted to encourage her to pray and to follow the rules that forbid wearing makeup while at prayer. In this way he did not alienate her, yet gave her sound religious advice."[8]

Like many American Muslims, Shi'ites in Dearborn have had to make accommodations to their new environment. While Friday mosque services continue to be held, they are attended only by men. On Sundays, however, far more people come to the Islamic Center of America, including women and children, where they hear sermons that traditionally would have been delivered only on Fridays.

Isma'ili (Sevener) Shi'ites

The two main groups of Seveners are known generally as the Nizaris and the Mustalis, or Boharas. In the United States the Boharas are the smaller of these groups, with centers in major urban areas such as Chicago, New York, San Francisco, and Detroit. Boharas in America, while concerned for the unity of Islam, place a high priority on community preservation and generally associate both religiously and socially only with members of their own group. Intermarriage among these groups and others within the Muslim community is rare.

Nizari Isma'ili Shi'ites are a larger and faster-growing segment of American Islam. While firm about maintaining their distinct identity, they are much more assimilated than the Boharas. Nizaris are united in allegiance to their religious leader, Imam Prince Karim Aga Khan, who is considered a direct descendant of the Prophet Muhammad and 'Ali. The Imam gives both spiritual guidance and advice as to the general welfare of his community.

When the first Nizaris came to America, the group was small in number and had to gather informally for prayer, with their religious life taking place primarily at home. Since the increased immigration of Nizaris after 1972, worship life has become much more organized, with prayer halls and centers springing up in many cities. These structures serve as the loci of particular commemorative days, such as the birthday of the Prophet and the Imamate Day, honoring the time when the present Imam assumed his position.

Members of the community select the religious leader of the local mosque, and the Imam confirms the selection. The leader is generally not paid for his services, and he does not serve as a spiritual guide to the other members. He performs certain ceremonial functions at the prayer hall and on public occasions.

As always, it is difficult to determine exact percentages, but estimates are that Nizari Isma'ilis constitute some 10 percent of the American Shi'ite community. Since the middle of the century, the Aga Khan has made strong efforts to reconcile and integrate his followers into the Muslim community as a whole. The current Aga Khan is a well-known public figure who in America often addresses academic audiences.

Converts to Islam

Anglo Converts

While the great majority of Muslims in America are either African American or of immigrant identity or heritage, a growing but significant number of other Americans are choosing to adopt Islam as their religion and way of life. Estimates of the number of Anglo Muslims in the United States range from twenty thousand to fifty thousand, but as always it is difficult to determine anything close to exact figures. Some of these are Anglo women who have married Muslim men. Islamic law, as we have seen, permits Muslim males to marry women from among the People of the Book, namely Christians or Jews. While there is no compulsion for such women to convert, because the children will be raised according to the religion of the father, a number of them do choose to adopt Islam. A woman's conversion may occur because her husband is eager for her to accept Islam, or she is persuaded that Islam is the right religion for her, or she wants her children raised in a monolithic home. Probably more than half of the marriages between immigrant Muslim males and non-Muslim American females end in the wife's conversion to Islam, although it should be noted that surveys of female converts indicate that in many cases their adoption of Islam came before marriage to a Muslim man. Children are also raised in the religion of the father if a Muslim woman should marry a Christian or Jewish man. Although such marriages are not legally condoned, they do happen occasionally, putting great pressure on the husband to convert.

Other Anglo Americans choose to convert to Islam for a variety of reasons. One of the earliest on record is a white diplomat turned propagandist named Alexander Russell Webb, who established the first documented Islamic institution in New York, the American Moslem Brotherhood, in 1893. A native New Yorker, Webb was named U.S. consul to Manila in the Philippines in 1887. He became fascinated with the religion of Islam as practiced by believers in the East, and on returning home he authored a number of books and a journal called the *Moslem World*,[9] intended to introduce Americans to Islam. In the long run his results were meager, but Muslims today acknowledge him as the pioneer of *da'wa* to white America.

Some American converts find the intellectual appeal of a great civilization of scholarly, scientific, and cultural achievements a refreshing antidote to the often anti-intellectual and secularist climate of the contemporary West. One of the reasons for the spread of Islam in various parts of the world over the centuries has been the straightforward simplicity of the declaration of faith and the responsibilities that an observant Muslim is expected to carry out. For some Americans this directness is an appealing alternative to what they may find to be confusing Christological doctrines and Trinitarian affirmations espoused by the Christian church. Whites, like blacks, may find Islam an antidote to the continuing white racism of American society. Some Anglos without intimate personal relationships or close family connections hope that in a religion so explicitly community oriented they may find solace from loneliness. Unfortunately that is not always the result, as Muslims orient their communities not only to the commonality of Islam but also and often to the particularity of national and ethnic identities.

The zeal of the new convert to any faith or ideology is notoriously high and certainly not less so in the case of Americans who decide to adopt Islam. Generally conservative in religious belief and in dress, for reasons of personal conviction and perhaps with the hope of persuading themselves and their families of the rightness of their decision, converts are articulate and enthusiastic spokespeople for a clear and sometimes rather inflexible interpretation of their new faith. Rising in popularity is the inclination of converts to speak of themselves as "re-verts," those who are going back to their essential identity as Muslim. Those who adopt Islam tend to view their change of religion as a gradual realization of their true faith and identity. This understanding reflects a strong movement in intellectual apologetics that affirms the essential and basic nature of each human being as Muslim. The Qur'an 1:172 says that while we were all nascent in the loins of Adam, God appeared to us and said, "Am I not your Lord?" And in that primordial time we all answered, "Yes, we do testify." That, Muslims affirm, is proof that all people are really submitters (muslims, at least in their personal response to God). Such basic human submission, Muslims say, has characterized pious people since Adam.

It is not always easy to be a new convert. Pressures may come from family, the workplace, and the culture in general. How long do you have to be given your shahada, some ask, before you are considered by others to be a "real Muslim"? Some of the current literature discusses the loneliness that Anglo converts may feel after their conversion, especially those who are not married to Muslims. They share in neither the specific cultures often represented by immigrants and their descendants (an identity that naturally diminishes with changing generations) nor the ethnic identity of African Americans. Some resent what they view as the unnecessary monitoring of their progress as Muslims by conservative coreligionists. "Sometimes the questions can become pretty intimidating," writes one convert. "For example, if you are approached by a *salafi* [conservative] group, Beware! They will test your knowledge of Islam. . . . Don't get nervous. Don't panic. Remain calm."[10] Some Anglo converts have formed support groups to help one another in the transition to a new faith and identity.

On the other hand, it is also the case that Anglo converts are the most articulate spokespersons for an explanation of Islam as moderate, reasonable, rational, and viable in the American context. Americans who are troubled by the growing numbers of Muslims in the United States may find it easier to understand the religion when it is presented by someone who "speaks American" and can share a common idiom.

Hispanic and Native American Converts

A good deal of attention is currently being given, especially in the press, to the importance of the fact that small but growing numbers of Latinos/ Latinas are converting to Islam in America. Enthusiasts are quick to point to the natural affiliation of Islam with many parts of Hispanic culture, begun with its movement into the Iberian Peninsula in 711. Throughout the years of Muslim presence in Spain until Muslims were expelled after 1492, Islam and Spanish culture were deeply intertwined. Whether such historic affiliation really influences the decision of some Hispanic Americans to adopt Islam is questionable, however, especially given the fact that many who convert prefer to ignore their Hispanic heritage and refrain from speaking Spanish in the attempt to be part of the American Muslim "scene."

Islam first appeared in the barrios of the American Northeast in the early 1970s. Mainly first-generation Puerto Ricans from New York, many of these converts entered Islam by affiliating with African American mosques. Since then, immigrant Muslims have tried to organize missionary movements among the Latino populations, with the goal of integrating them into established Sunni mosque communities. Latinos/Latinas have found much in Islamic culture that is akin to their own cultural heritage, especially the importance of the family structure and specifically defined roles for men and women. Some Latinos/Latinas think that they are reclaiming their lost Muslim and African heritage. Many are of Roman Catholic heritage, believing that the Church today does not do enough to defend their rights for equality. They are also attracted by what they see as Islam's simplicity and directness to God as compared with the complexity of the Catholic hierarchy. Divorce, which has been growing in

American Hispanic communities, is noticeably much lower among Latino Muslim couples.

Muslims are slowly waking to the reality that the Hispanic community in America is a ripe source for new converts. "Olé to Allah!" reads the cover page of an issue of *The Message* devoted to articles about American Latino Muslims.[11] Increasing attention is being paid in Muslim journals to the fact that American Latinos/Latinas have been virtually ignored as a community in need of *da'wa*, and many are arguing for increased efforts at providing basic Islamic instruction in Spanish. A particular need has been identified for accurate Spanish translations of the Qur'an. The few Hispanic Muslims who actively teach members of their communities about Islam lament that so little is available on the history, traditions, doctrines, and practices of the faith for those whose first language is Spanish. Some works suffer from having been written first in an Asian language, then translated into English, and finally rendered in Spanish.

Latino/Latina Muslim presence is particularly evident on the east and west coasts of America. One illustration of the growth of Latino Islam is PIEDAD (Propagación Islámica para la Educación y Devoción de Ala'el Divino), a missionary effort in New York City. A Puerto Rican convert began PIE-DAD in 1987, and it has focused particularly on Latinas who are married to Muslims as well as on Latinos who are incarcerated. Another Islamic Latino organization in the El Barrio area of New York City, called Alianza Islámica, began some fifteen years ago as an outgrowth of the Darul Islam movement (see chapter 4), illustrating the close association between Hispanic converts and African American Islam. Operating out of a small storefront, it provides a number of social services for the surrounding community as part of its outreach program. Members do after-school tutoring, plan summer recreation, offer drug and alcohol as well as marriage counseling, and provide diploma instruction for kids who have dropped out of school. Alianza has served to bring wayward Muslims back into the fold, as well as to attract new members from the Hispanic community. The Latino-American Dawa Organization (LADO) works to increase learning about Islam among Latino Americans and to educate the American public about Islam.

In California the recently formed Asociación Latina de Musulmanes en las Américas (ALMA) seeks to spread Islam among Spanish-speaking people, educating them about the contribution of Islam to their society and culture, with the hope of bringing them back to their ancestors' way of life. ALMA is currently planning to begin publication of the first Spanish Islamic magazine for distribution in the United States, Canada, and Latin America.

The Islamic Society of North America (ISNA) features an annual conference for Latino/Latina Muslims, and recently established a Latino coordinating committee.

While their numbers are still very small, a few Native Americans are also becoming more vocal about their identification with Islam and are reminding other Muslims of the long association of Indians and Muslims on the North American continent. Some Seminoles in Florida claim that they are descendants of African slaves who before emancipation managed to escape and mingle with them, even converting some of the Seminoles to Islam. The Algonquian and Pima languages are said to contain words with Arabic roots. Cherokees claim that a number of Muslims joined their ranks and say that the chief of the Cherokees in 1866 was a Muslim named Ramadhan Ibn Wati.

Some Muslims are now recognizing significant commonalities between Native American and Qur'anic worldviews, such as a deep reverence for nature and obedience to God's laws for the created world and the acknowledgment that people of all races and colors must be treated equally. Native American understanding of a kind of original divine instruction for humankind parallels the Qur'anic concept of the *din al-fitra*, or natural inherent religious response basic to all people. Native American awareness of divine presence in all the four directions is compared with the Qur'anic assurance that wherever one should turn, there is the face of God. Native American traditions pay much attention to the importance of sacred sites and pilgrimage, which balances the Islamic duty of *hajj* to Mecca and pilgrimages to the tombs of saints. The current concern of American Muslims for what they see as the excesses of modernism and secularism in the West resonates in much of Native American tradition. As Muslims and Native Americans both struggle to clarify and maintain their identities in the American context, it may well be that their ties, both historical and philosophical, will be strengthened.

American Converts to Sufism

Another reason for a number of Americans to consider themselves Muslim is their association with Sufi groups in this country. As indicated in chapter 2, Sufism is a complex part of the history of Islam, sometimes greatly appreciated and at other times rejected as a deviation from the true faith. To the extent to which Sufi groups in America associate themselves with one of the established and recognized Sufi orders, they must be counted as part of what has emerged as a genuine American Islam. Some U.S. groups that choose to adopt the name Sufi as part of the New Age movement do little more than combine body movements with stylistic meditative practices and have no Islamic theological understanding of Sufism.

Particularly attractive to some Americans are forms of Sufi dancing. Normally, these dances are done with a leader in the center along with a musician, while the participants are grouped in a circle or circles moving in rhythm. Sometimes the movements are accompanied by group chanting. Such chanting and dancing have often been suspect to orthodox Islam. In some special cases, such as the "whirling dervishes" of the Mevlevi order of Jalal al-Din Rumi, the long, slow, rhythmic dance performed by highly trained members of the order has become a recognized and honored part of the tradition.

Muslims associated with long-established and internationally recognized orders have little patience for the "silliness" of Americans eager to adopt new fads of so-called spirituality, and they are quick to point out that pseudo-Islamic Sufi groups have no legitimate role in American Islam. Many immigrant Muslims of a traditional orientation find it difficult to acknowledge the legitimacy of any American Sufi groups. Muslim organizations that are supported financially by Saudi Arabia refuse to allow the participation of Sufi groups.

While those who actually "convert" to Islam via Sufism are relatively few, there seems to be a growing interest in Sufism as both a spiritual/psychological discipline and, in the American orders, a locus of fellowship and communal identification. In general, Americans find Sufi movements open, accessible, tolerant, and supportive of individual needs and concerns.

Two of the most popular Sufi personages in the West in the twentieth century, Hazrat Inayat Khan and Idries Shah, both saw Sufism as a phenomenon distinguishable from the formal religious structure of Islam. The writings of these two teachers, with their emphasis on the inner life over the outer forms of religion, have been voluminous and influential, especially on young American "seekers."

Hazrat Inayat Khan, who was initiated into the Nizami branch of the Chistiyya order in India, studied with both Muslim and Hindu masters. His philosophy blended Advaita Vedanta and the "unity of being" philosophy of the school of the Andalusian mystic Ibn 'Arabi. Commissioned by his teacher to bring harmony to East and West, he devoted his life to introducing Sufism to America. He was one of the first to teach Sufi doctrines in the West, lecturing and traveling across America from 1910 to 1927, initiating a number of disciples, and founding the Sufi order in the West. Many of his teachings are contained in a multivolume series titled *The Sufi Message of Hazrat Inayat Khan.*[12]

When Inayat died in 1927, his son Vilayat Khan, still a boy, inherited leadership of the order. By the 1960s, a time of growing appeal of Sufism in America, the European-educated Pir Vilayat emerged as the effective leader of the Sufi order in the West, and the movement grew rapidly. The classically trained Pir is said to have felt somewhat distanced by some of his new hippie followers. He was particularly distressed when his disciples wanted to use drugs to induce a spiritual state. The Sufi order in the West is still under Vilayat's guidance, although it has expanded to include a variety of teaching and experiential modes. The order continues to stress spiritual awakening, but it also does work in social services, education, and health. It is active in a number of major cities and sponsors retreats, psychotherapy and healing seminars, work camps, and musical presentations.

Idries Shah, a popular writer and teacher who emphasizes the psychological aspects of Sufism, has been influential in America since the 1960s. An Indian of Afghani lineage, Shah spent most of his time in the West in England, although his writings have been on the shelves of American bookstores from the beginning. Particularly popular are his folktales imparting Sufi wisdom through anecdote and example. Shah, whose followers constitute the Society for Sufi Studies, has been especially critical of those who perpetuate old forms and practices of Sufism that are not relevant to the modern Western world. Shah's works, such as the early and still popular *The Sufis*, conspicuously lack terminology that would specifically identify his interpretation of Sufism with traditional Islam.

Since the 1970s, Sufi groups that have clearly been formed and adapted to fit American culture and demand have been joined by others whose members are immigrants well familiar with Sufi lineage and the practices of a specific *tariqa*, or path, of which they were members in their home countries. These people tend to be more traditional than the earlier practitioners of Sufism in America and more committed to stressing the continuity of Sufism with Islam. Americans are increasingly drawn to these teachers, attracted by the mystical and pietistic form of Islam represented by their orders.

One group that illustrates a blend of New Age influences with the more institutional tradition-based Islamic orders is the Bawa Muhaiyaddeen Fellowship, located in Philadelphia. Its members are both immigrants and American converts from a range of ethnic and religious backgrounds. Born in Sri Lanka, Bawa was a member of the Qadiriyya order and is said to have so embodied the principles of love and charity in his own person and life that simply being in his presence was spiritually uplifting. He considered himself, and was considered by his followers, to be their *shaykh*, or spiritual leader. Bawa was eager to keep abreast of the latest technological developments, and his use of television and video equipment in the propagation of his message added to the sense that, despite his lineage, the Bawa Muhaiyaddeen Fellowship was a genuine American order, constantly adapting to new developments.

Bawa's death in 1986 did not mean the dissolution of the fellowship, and in fact the group has not only continued relatively unchanged in Philadelphia but has also added member branches in several other cities, such as Boston. His death did, however, raise the question of what it means to be an American Sufi group. By what means can another *shaykh* emerge to guide the community, and will such a person come from overseas or be an American-born convert to Islam? Because of the training prerequisites for a Sufi leader in a traditional order such as the Qadiriyya, the question of what constitutes the leadership of American Islam may be sharper for Sufis than for other Muslims. The Bawa Muhaiyaddeen Fellowship is only one such Sufi group to face these questions.[13]

Some Sufi groups combine holistic health, music, dance, poetry, and other aesthetic forms with traditional Sufi meditation. Many have become active in the *da'wa*, or missionary movement, of Islam in America. Members of the new generation of Muslims born in America to immigrant parents are joining white converts to Sufi movements. For many men and women, Sufism seems to breathe the possibility of life and activity into religion in a way that they have not known before, at the same time that one's relationship both to the *shaykh* and to God gives new meaning to the very word *islam*, submission. Sufism also seems to provide a way of cutting across the racial, ethnic, and cultural definitions of so many American Muslim groups, which despite the egalitarian appeal of Islam often continue to segregate themselves along lines of particular identity. In recent years Americans who have studied with Sufi masters abroad have returned and written numerous works to distill the Sufi message into a distinctly Western idiom.

Sufism particularly interests some American women, who find in it an appealing alternative to the Christianity or Judaism, or the agnostic environment, in which they may have been raised. Particularly attractive are those orders more lenient in their restrictions on, for example, the mixing of women and men during worship time. Sometimes practitioners may be seated in a circle, with men forming one half and women the other. Those Sufi groups unconcerned about separation of the sexes generally pay little attention to any affiliation with the tradition of Islam. As in the Muslim community as a whole, there is both considerable discussion about the appropriateness of women's assuming leadership roles in Sufi organizations and increasing examples of such leadership. The Naqshbandiyya, a "sober" Sufi order founded in the Indian subcontinent in the fourteenth century by Baha' al-Din al-Naqshbandi, is particularly popular in the United States and Canada and has provided a context in which significant numbers of women have felt comfortable participating.

Until recently, heads of traditional orders in the United States have been foreign born and educated. Now a group of American-born sheikhs is starting to appear, trained abroad and working with communities both in the United States and in other countries. Typical of this new genre of Sufi leaders is Sheikh Nuh Ha Mim Keller, born and raised in the American Northwest of America. He was educated at the University of Chicago, the University of California, and also at al-Azhar in Cairo, and in 1977 he converted to Islam. Keller was authorized as a sheikh in the Shadhili Sufi *tariqa* (order) by a direct descendant of the founder of the order, and now he teaches Sufism and holds retreats in the United States and Canada as well as countries in the Middle East and Southeast Asia.

Several Shi'ite Sufi orders exist in America, one of the most evident being the Nimatullahi order of Sufis founded and led by Dr. Javad Nurbakhsh, former head of the department of psychiatry at Tehran University in Iran. The order was established in America with his arrival in the 1970s. Located first in California, it maintains centers in a number of American cities, including San Francisco, New York, Washington, D.C., and Boston. Nurbakhsh, who himself now lives in England, stresses a Sufism concerned with doing and seeing rather than thinking and talking, one whose aim is the realization of truth through love and devotion. The writings of this prolific leader include works on Sufi poetry, psychology, and spiritualism, Jesus in the eyes of Sufis, and Sufi women. He is perhaps best known for *In the Paradise of the Sufis*.[14] Other Iranian Shi'ite Sufi orders have grown up across the country in the past several decades. Generally, they emphasize the connection of Sufis with the mystical movements of Islam above the beliefs and practices that would set these groups off as distinctively Shi'ite.

As interesting American communal-living experiment cast in a decidedly Sufi mold is the Dar al-Islam community located in Abiquiu, New Mexico (to be distinguished from the African American Dar al-Islam described in chapter 4). The community was begun in 1980, with the support of Saudi Muslims, as an attempt to model the lifestyle of the early Islamic community of the Prophet Muhammad. Located on more than eight thousand acres of land northwest of Albuquerque, the community includes a school, a library complex, elaborate prayer rooms, and living quarters. The showpiece of the community is an adobe brick mosque designed by the late and famed Egyptian architect Hasan Fathi. With the original goal of bringing together Muslims of all backgrounds from across America as well as from Europe and the Middle East, the community stresses the interracial and interethnic nature of Islam assured by God in the Qur'an: "We have made you tribes and nations so that you might know one another" (Sura 49:13). Members try as much as possible to lead a life of quiet piety exemplifying the Islamic virtues. The Abiquiu experiment never reached its goal of becoming a large and Islamically organized living community. Never more than twenty-five families at most, the membership in residence has dwindled and much of the original land has been sold. The Dar al-Islam, nonetheless, performs an important service for American Islam through its Institute of Traditional Islamic Studies for Muslims and Non-Muslims, as well as sponsorship of a number of Muslim youth camps.

The Ahmadiyya Community of North America

While the classification of Islamic individuals and associations in America into immigrant, African American, and convert is generally useful, some groups do not fall neatly into these categories. Immigrants who are converting to classical Sufism in the United States are one such exception. Another is the Ahmadiyya community, originally a Pakistani missionary movement, which has been a presence in North America for many decades. Its members have worked since the early part of the twentieth century for the conversion of Americans to Islam. Many, but certainly not all, of those converts have been African American. This group is one of the most active within the Islamic fold (if, indeed, it is within, an identification that is challenged by many Muslims) in the work of da'wa, calling or recruiting new members to its understanding of the faith of Islam. Ahmadis have worked particularly on translating and providing copies of the Qur'an to Muslim communities around the world. Claiming more than ten million followers in more than one hundred countries, they have recruited many thousands in North America.

The founder of the Ahmadiyya movement, Hazrat Mirza Ghulam Ahmad, was born in 1835 in Qadian in India's Punjab. An enormously

prolific writer, he claims to have received divine revelations or signs legitimating his role as an Islamic leader. Then in 1889 he announced that he was
the *mahdi*, or savior, whose coming Muslims have long expected. Critics
have charged that he actually appropriated the status of prophet, an accusation that his followers have explicitly denied. Around the turn of the century the movement began to move beyond India. Of its two branches, only
the group called the Qadiani Jamaat has been influential on the American
scene. Sunni Muslims have denounced the Ahmadiyya movement as a deviation from the true teachings of Islam, both because of its founder's claims
about his own status and because Ahmadis believe that Jesus was not taken
up to heaven at the crucifixion but continued his work on earth, ending up in
Kashmir, in India.

The first Ahmadi missionary to the United States was Mufti Muhammad
Sadiq in 1920. He began a society for the preservation of American Islam
and in 1921 started publication of the periodical *Moslem Sunrise* (changed
in 1959 to *Muslim Sunrise*). Chicago became the official headquarters of the
American Ahmadiyya movement and the site of its first mosque. Ahmadi
missionaries played a significant role in the early decades of the century in
attacking what they saw as the blatant racism of American society. By 1940
there were said to be between five and ten thousand converts in the United
States. In 1950 the Ahmadiyya headquarters moved to the American Fazl
Mosque in northwest Washington, D.C. This continues to serve as the center
for the educational and propaganda mission of the movement. Copies of its
publications are distributed to members of Congress and other government
officials, foreign diplomats, the press, and so on. At present Ahmadi centers
can be found in more than fifty cities in the United States and Canada.

In their Western missionary work, Ahmadis have been particularly
attuned to the necessity of maintaining a strict Islamic faith in the face of
Western secularism and materialism. Ahmadi women have played and continue to play important roles in the American Ahmadi mission. Like many
other Muslims, Ahmadis worry about appropriate education for their children, especially girls, and often choose to develop their own schools. Members of the community bear the special burden of affirming their Islamic
identity both within a culture that does not appreciate it and as part of Sunni
Islam, which does not accept it.

Clearly, the picture of American Islam is growing increasingly complex.
Stories of immigrant and African American Islam in this country for a long
time were quite distinct and separate, and relations between blacks and

immigrants were generally quite rare. Now, however, those stories are coming to be interrelated, and new generations of "American-born" Muslims work to obliterate the old categories. Added to this fascinating blend are the whites, Hispanics, and Native Americans who are converting to Islam. These groups are still small but are significant both for their actual presence and for the impetus they give to the *da'wa*, or mission movement, within Islam. They are also of great importance to those who want to gain political capital from the fact that American Islam is multiracial, multi-ethnic, and growing. Let us turn now to the story of African Americans and the many ways in which they have played and continue to play a crucial role in the development of American Islam.

CHAPTER FOUR

Islam in the African American Community

Students of black religion in America are now increasingly aware that voluntary immigration was only one of the ways in which Muslims arrived on the shores of "the promised land." Others came against their will, finding America a land not of promise but of bondage. These were the Muslims brought in the slave trade of colonial and postcolonial America. Scholars generally agree that a significant number of the black Africans who were brought to North America during the antebellum slave trade were Muslim, although numbers are impossible to determine. These men and women seized into slavery came from a variety of areas in sub-Saharan Africa from Senegal to Nigeria. A few were highly literate and educated in their religion, while others were more humble practitioners. Some individuals, such as the well-documented Prince Ayub Ibn Sulayman Diallo, who was abducted in 1731, even came from the ruling elements of their societies.

Most of these African Muslims had never had any contact with whites before being taken into slavery. The account of one of them, Kunta Kinte of Senegambia, is documented in Alex Haley's popular novel *Roots*,[1] also broadcast in a series specially made for television. The novel sets the scene of Kinte's Islamic heritage from page 1, on which Haley describes the Muslim early-morning call to prayer, which, as he says, had been offered up as long as any living person there could remember. Haley records other occasions attesting to Kinte's faith, as when he prays to Allah while chained in the bottom of a "Christian" slave ship.

Unfortunately for those who would have wished to practice their Muslim faith during the harsh circumstances of slavery in America, their

Christian overlords rarely permitted it. "When I was a Mohammedan I prayed thus: 'Thanks be to God, Lord of all [the] Worlds, the Merciful the Gracious. . . .' But now I pray for 'Our Father . . .' in the words of our Lord Jesus the Messiah."[2] While most of these black Africans did indeed become Christians, documents indicate that at least a few managed to maintain their Islamic faith, continuing as practicing Muslims until the early part of the twentieth century. Generally, they had to maintain their practice in secret. Some records indicate that a few even risked ridicule and harsh punishment by continuing to pray publicly, as they understood it to be their Qur'anic obligation to do. According to one account, a Muslim slave while pretending to write the Lord's Prayer in Arabic was actually writing out the Fatiha, the first chapter of the Qur'an. A few documents left behind have added to our understanding of who these people really were, their experiences recording more than a century of trade in human life.

A number of families now living on the coast of Georgia are descendants of slaves, some of them reportedly Muslim. Best known, perhaps, is one Bilali Mahomet, who was probably taken into slavery around 1725. His *Bilali Diary*, written in a West African Arabic script, is now located in the rare books library of the University of Georgia. Grant records from South Carolina contain reports of slaves who refused to eat pork and who prayed to a god named Allah. For many African American Muslims today, the presence of these Muslims in early American history, and their achievements both before being taken into slavery and while in bondage, have added a great deal to the sense of pride in being Muslim and of sharing in the long struggle for freedom that has characterized the black experience in America from its earliest days. "The Afro-American people have Islam in their hearts," says a female convert. "This was the culture that was stripped from us, along with the language and religion. Most critically, the religion of Islam was taken from us through slavery."[3]

As we have already seen, the question of who is and who is not a Muslim in the American context is sometimes straightforward and other times difficult to ascertain. While some individuals and groups consider themselves to be under the umbrella of Islam, or at least identify with elements of Islamic faith and practice, those very individuals and groups may be denied Islamic affiliation by others who accuse them of marginality, sectarianism, or even heresy. The history of African American groups who have looked to Islam for their identity is replete with illustrations of this kind of disputed identity. One of the earliest examples is that of the Moorish Americans at the beginning of the twentieth century.

Noble Drew Ali and the Moorish Science Temple of America

The early decades of the twentieth century were a time of social displacement, economic deprivation, and yearning for some kind of national identity for American blacks. A series of movements arose at that time geared to helping blacks find their identity. Among them were those that sought an identity outside of the American context, like Marcus Garvey's Universal Negro Improvement Association (UNIA), which advocated a return to Liberia in the African motherland. Garvey's movement strongly influenced several black leaders who, in the early decades of this century, associated themselves with Islam. One of these was Noble Drew Ali, born Timothy Drew in 1886 in North Carolina. He worked his way north, where he settled in New Jersey and began to preach a message that led to the development of his community, founded as the Moorish National and Divine Movement. The name was later changed to the Moorish Science Temple of America. Drew's community centered on five principles: love, truth, peace, freedom, and justice. The scripture he provided for Moorish Americans was titled *The Holy Koran of the Moorish Science Temple of America* but in fact has nothing in common with the Holy Qur'an of Islam.

The primary message of his teachings was that salvation can be achieved only if blacks discard the various identities forced on them by whites in America, such as Negro or colored person, and understand that their true origin is Asiatic. Drew Ali was convinced that he was a prophet of Allah, the last in a long line, and that it was his destiny to serve as a warner to the Asiatics of America, as Muhammad had been a warner to the Arabs of his day. Slave names should be dropped and new names adopted to reflect the pride and dignity of their heritage. Ali's message was appealing to little-educated blacks who were suffering from economic deprivation, bitter about their lot in American society, and desperate to find an identity that separated them from white oppression.

The first Moorish temple was established in Newark in 1913. By 1916 the community was divided into two groups. One remained in New Jersey, with its name changed to the Holy Moabite Temple; and the other moved with Noble Drew Ali to Chicago. By 1928, the year of the first Moorish National Convention, temples had also been established in Pittsburgh and Detroit. The various communities focused on achieving economic independence by setting up grocery stores, restaurants, and other small businesses. "We shall be secure in nothing until we have economic power," said Noble Drew Ali.

"A beggar people cannot develop the highest in them, nor can they attain to a genuine enjoyment of the spiritualities of life."[4] As pride in their black identity grew, so did tensions between members and the white community. In 1929 Ali was arrested and jailed, and shortly after being released he mysteriously died. Various claimants immediately arose to challenge one another for leadership, but as is so often the case, none was ever able to capture the admiration and devotion that had been accorded their original leader. Despite problems, however, the Moorish American movement has continued in a number of urban areas of the eastern and midwestern United States. W. D. Fard and Elijah Muhammad of the Nation of Islam are both said to have been Moorish Temple members.

The Moorish Science Temple, now a small association, is open to any people who consider themselves Asiatic, although its membership is essentially African American. The national office is currently located in Chicago, and meetings are held annually, although some local temples operate independently. Leaders are known as grand sheikhs or sheikhesses, members as brothers and sisters. Affiliates generally assume the name "El" or "Bey" after their given names. Appropriate dress is considered important, with men traditionally wearing fezzes and women turbans and long dresses, particularly in the temple. Members are strongly encouraged to avoid alcohol and drugs, sometimes even caffeine. The Moorish Science Temple community has received civic recognition for its achievements in promoting the social, economic, and moral advancement of Americans of African descent.

Elijah Muhammad and the Nation of Islam

Marcus Garvey was sent into exile in 1927, after which his movement was effectively moribund, and the Moorish American Temple, while continuing, had lost much of its earlier appeal. While each in its time had significant numbers of followers, neither Garvey nor Drew Ali was able to capture the imagination of "Negroes" in America as did one small black man from Detroit, with his emblematic cap of stars and crescents. That man was Elijah Poole, later assuming the name Elijah Muhammad, first prophet of the first indigenous American movement claiming an affiliation with Islam to gain the attention of the country, namely the Nation of Islam, or NOI. (It should be noted that the designation "black Muslims," popular because of C. Eric Lincoln's sociological study of that title, has never been one by which the

Nation of Islam has called itself.[5]) Malcolm X and Louis Farrakhan, both recipients of continuing publicity, were products of the NOI movement.

In part because of director Spike Lee's popular film about Malcolm X, the story of the rise of the NOI is one with which most people are quite familiar. It bears repeating, however, as a fascinating example of a truly indigenous socioreligious, even political, movement that played a unique role in meeting the needs of significant numbers of African Americans. The very inclusion of the word *nation* in its title set forth the ideal of a political as well as an ethical and religious entity, grounded at least nominally in a faith whose roots are far from the racist society of America. That it advocated a doctrine of human origin far from the ideals of an egalitarian Islam mattered little and, in fact, was scarcely realized by those who found in it a means of recapturing personal identity through a standard of performance that was strict, clean, and economically viable.

The precise beginnings of the movement remain hazy, despite the exacting scholarship that has tried to peel back the layers of mythology surrounding the appearance to African Americans in Detroit of a stranger named Wallace D. Fard. Among Fard's most ardent followers was Elijah Poole, son of a poor itinerant Baptist preacher. Poole was ripe for the kind of encouraging message that Fard preached. According to Poole's own account, Fard made his first appearance in Detroit on July 4, 1930, identifying himself as having come from the holy Muslim city of Mecca. He proclaimed a message that was specifically directed to the blacks of America, who were identified as members of the lost, and now found, ancient tribe of Shabazz, people of African descent who were said to have discovered the Nile Valley of Egypt and the holy city of Mecca. Poole believed that Fard's mission was to redeem and restore this lost tribe. Through one of Fard's early lectures, Poole came to understand that Fard was the personification of the promised *mahdi*, the guided one whose return is expected to initiate the final period before the Day of Resurrection and Judgment. Poole understood this identity actually to bestow upon Fard a form of divinity, an idea that, of course, is anathema to orthodox Islam. Later, in an apparently syncretistic blending of Islam and Christianity, he said that Fard was the one for whom the world has been waiting for two thousand years. Fard himself encouraged the interpretation that he was indeed a Christ figure, to displace the white Christ that Christians tried to give to blacks.

The real identity of W. D. Fard has been the subject of much ongoing debate. It was finally acknowledged that he was Caucasian, although later it was said that he actually embodied both black and white so that he could move with ease among both groups. Followers found the obscured identity a source of mystery and appeal rather than suspicion.

Fard first preached while traveling around peddling silks and artifacts. Initially meeting in private homes, his followers were soon sufficiently organized that they rented a meeting hall, which they called a temple. At this point, the Lost-Found Nation of Islam in the Wilderness of North America came officially into being, to be shortened simply to the Nation of Islam. Fard's ministry lasted only a little more than three years, during which he was able to develop an organization with educational resources for men, women, and children, as well as the still existing private security force known as the Fruit of Islam. His was, however, a ministry marked with some serious and unfortunate incidents. Fard was accused of inciting violence with his racist teachings, and he was arrested several times. He was finally expelled from Detroit on May 4, 1933. Soon afterward, he disappeared as mysteriously as he had first come, seen no more after 1934.

Elijah Poole found Fard's message compelling. As he himself began to pass the message on, he was accorded the status of minister and given the Muslim name of Elijah Muhammad. He quickly assumed a position of leadership in the movement and was eventually named chief minister of Islam. In 1932 he moved to Chicago, where he established what was known as Temple Number Two, the main headquarters for the NOI after the disappearance of W. D. Fard. A tough taskmaster, Elijah Muhammad ran the Nation with authority. He established a hierarchy with himself at the head. Under him were ministers, supreme captains, captains, and lieutenants. Those who wished to join the NOI had to submit a letter of application to the chief minister, who soon adopted the role of messenger of Allah. When accepted for membership, a new convert dropped his or her "slave," or last, name and adopted simply an X to signify an unknown African ancestry. Like Moorish Americans, NOI members referred to themselves not just as blacks or Negroes but also as Asiatics.

Many of the teachings of the NOI as developed by Elijah Muhammad are irreconcilable with the tradition of Islam. Mainstream Muslims today actively dissociate themselves from the current Nation under the leadership of Louis Farrakhan for a number of reasons, not the least being the extent to which he continues to preach what to them can only be understood as heresy or blasphemy. As we have seen, the *shahada* attests in its two articles that only God is divine and that Muhammad is God's Prophet, and the Qur'an affirms that Muhammad is the seal and the last in a long line of prophets. Elijah Muhammad's belief that Fard claimed for himself some kind of divine status belies the first part of the *shahada* and thus constitutes an act of *shirk*, or association with God, the greatest sin one can commit in orthodox Muslim understanding. NOI insistence that Elijah was the last messenger of W. D. Fard, which contradicts the second article, is abhorrent to most Muslims. Elijah Muhammad's son Warith Deen, leader of those who broke from the NOI after 1975, has said his father knew that some of his teachings were not in accord with true Islam. They were essential at the time he gave them, however, in order for blacks to pull themselves up from the circumstances of genuine degradation in which many found themselves and move to a station of pride and self-respect, thrift and discipline, and economic stability.

Muslims are proud of the acknowledgment fostered since the days of Prophet Muhammad that all people and all races are equal before God. The NOI teaching that whites are descended from the devil obviously contradicts this essential Muslim egalitarianism. An elaborate NOI mythology supports the identification of whites as evil and blacks as the chosen people of Allah. Briefly put, this account holds that a scientist named Yacub, descendant of the Shabazz tribe, after being exiled from Mecca, devised a plot to enslave the other members of the tribe. By clever genetics and cross-breeding he is said gradually to have developed the white race by matching recessive genes with recessive. The lightest in color of the races thus produced is the most inferior and, correspondingly, the most evil. Elijah Muhammad identified the process of coming to a knowledge of these realities and of the splendor of original black civilization, and thus to the place where whites can be overthrown, as a kind of resurrection for African Americans. This affirmation of the strength and goodness of blackness and the weakness and moral degeneration of whiteness was a powerful message for blacks who had been weaned in the culture of white supremacy. A member of Masjid Muhammad in Hartford tells about the prejudice and persecution that her father, who had been raised a Baptist in the South, experienced, including seeing his family's house burned down by whites. When he came north and heard the message of Elijah Muhammad, he especially listened to the part about the white man being the devil. "There is a connection between the devil and fire," she says with a smile.[6]

Elijah Muhammad preached that blacks are not American citizens because they are not Americans by race, and he was imprisoned during World War II for telling his followers that they should not participate in a war that was not their concern. The Nation, therefore, represented itself as a black entity within the United States, its members citizens of Mecca and its flag the emblem of Mecca. It considered the fall of America as a white

Elijah Muhammad, chief minister of the Nation of Islam until 1975. AGENCE FRANCE PRESSE/ARCHIVE PHOTOS

society to be imminent. The key for Elijah Muhammad was not integration into American society but separation and the establishment of a political and social unit in which whites would have no role. If a separate state were not achievable—and Elijah Muhammad was under no illusions about the difficulty of such an attainment—the goal remained justice and equal opportunity for blacks. Like Noble Drew Ali, he therefore advocated the establishment of black-owned businesses and other means of self-provision. To foster economic independence and security, essential for the goal of political independence, Elijah Muhammad encouraged members to think black, invest black, buy black. Economics and ethics were combined into a structure in which NOI members were required to be personally abstemious and professionally industrious.

In addition to prayer five times a day—one of the most obvious borrowings from traditional Islam—he enjoined members not to eat more than one meal a day and to avoid pork, alcohol, gambling, undue emphasis on athletics, laziness, and excessive sleeping. In order to maintain the purity of the black race, intermarriage was strictly forbidden. Following the Islamic duty of *zakat*, or almsgiving, he also asked members to give a regular part of their income to the Nation, whatever it was possible for them to afford. Education was extremely important to Elijah Muhammad, who himself never went past the fourth grade, and he fully supported the establishment of Muslim schools. Already in the 1930s the University of Islam, really a set of parochial schools, had begun in association with the Muslim temples to educate children through high school. This institution operated under the name of the Sister Clara Muhammad School, after Elijah's wife, with a highly organized curriculum and strict discipline for students.

Malcolm X

Among those most persuaded of the imminent fall of America's white leadership was Malcolm Little. Malcolm tells in his autobiography an intricate and compelling story of his family (whose home was burned by the Ku Klux Klan when Malcolm was six), his friends, his temptations as he grew through early manhood, and especially his bitter anger with the white society that had so demoralized and devalued blacks.[7] "Do you mean to tell me that in a powerful country like this, a so-called Christian country, that a handful of men from the South can prevent the North, the West, the Central States and the East from giving Negroes the rights the Constitution says they already have?" demanded Malcolm years later in an address at Boston University. "No! I don't believe that and neither do you. No white man really wants the black Man to have his rights, or he'd have them."[8]

Having spent much of his young adulthood in the inner cities of Boston, Hartford, and New York indulging in various forms of vice and crime, including bootlegging, pimping, and selling drugs, Malcolm was serving a seven-year sentence in the maximum-security Massachusetts Norfolk Prison when he first became aware of the Nation of Islam and its teaching through his brother Reginald. He was absolutely ripe for the message of black liberation preached by Elijah Muhammad, and in 1947, at the age of twenty-two, he became an ardent member of the NOI.

Malcolm X's role in the propagation of Nation of Islam ideology in the years succeeding his release from prison in 1952 is a well-known and much-discussed part of recent American history. A highly intelligent man, Malcolm submitted himself wholeheartedly to the discipline as well as the advocacy of the movement. He was to become the national representative of the Honorable Elijah Muhammad for the next twelve years, speaking nationally and internationally about the circumstances of blacks in American society and about the opportunity presented by the NOI to alter those circumstances. In 1959 he was interviewed by Mike Wallace for a controversial television documentary on the Nation titled *The Hate That Hate Produced*. Major newsmagazines and journals vied for coverage of Malcolm and his inflammatory messages about white bigotry.

Malcolm's autobiography and other records attest to his friendship with Elijah's son Wallace, later to be known as Imam Warith Deen, a deeply spiritual and well-trained Muslim who even in the early years had questions about some of his father's doctrines and interpretations. Many have speculated that this relationship was significant to Malcolm's eventual change from the hatred-of-whites mentality of his earlier years, consonant with NOI ideology, to an appreciation and advocacy of orthodox Islam's racial tolerance and inclusiveness. Recent investigations into Malcolm's early days as a member of the NOI reveal that he seems to have been influenced by some of the Ahmadi missionaries active in the middle of the twentieth century. Several top figures of the 1950s jazz world were Ahmadi or had Ahmadi connections, including John Coltrane, as shown in his "A Love Supreme."

Meanwhile, the FBI was stepping up its systematic efforts, begun in the 1950s and 1960s, to monitor the Nation, changing from simple surveillance to active intelligence. "The Holy Qur'an warns the Muslims that the devils see you," said Louis Farrakhan in 1974. "The United States Government has paid enemies and informers in every temple, among every society of Muslims. Whenever you meet, the devil meets with us. Whenever you pick up the phone to talk, the devil is listening."[9] The FBI has been accused of trying to destroy the Nation not only through the gathering of information "leaked" by informants but by actually creating disputes between the members of the NOI and other movements for black liberation, such as the Black Panthers. The tactics did not work, partly because they reinforced the ideology that whites really are devils.

Malcolm's presence as a spokesman for the Nation of Islam influenced numbers of African Americans, including some public figures. In February 1965, immediately after his heavyweight fight against Sonny Liston, boxer

Malcolm X, later to become El Hajj Malik el-Shabazz.
ARCHIVE PHOTOS

Cassius Clay, whom Malcolm had befriended, became one of the first of a significant number of athletes to become a Muslim, known thereafter as Muhammad Ali. Adopting his Muslim name, Ali always insisted, was one of the most important occurrences of his life. Because he did it at a time when the Nation of Islam was unpopular in the United States, however, the boxing commission was furious. Though he had been a hero, Ali quickly became the object of intense suspicion.

A number of events led to Malcolm's deep disappointment and eventual disenchantment with Elijah Muhammad, whom he professed to have loved and respected deeply for more than twelve years. "I have sat at our Messenger's feet, hearing the truth from his own mouth! I have pledged on my knees to Allah to tell the white man about his crimes and the black man

the true teachings of our Honorable Elijah Muhammad," he had said earlier. "I don't care if it costs my life."[10] In the early 1960s it appeared that
with Elijah's declining health the leadership of the NOI would go directly
to Malcolm. Jealousy on the part of other members, however, led to dis-
crediting rumors. Malcolm began to receive less frequent coverage in Nation
organs, such as its newspaper *Muhammad Speaks* (which Malcolm himself
founded in 1961), and he was discouraged from being such a public spokesman. This coincided with rumors concerning illicit relations on the part of
Elijah Muhammad with two of his former secretaries, rumors that Malcolm
felt he could confirm. Probably influenced by Wallace, Malcolm also began
to question more seriously some of the doctrines and beliefs of the Nation.
His disillusionment with Elijah, the jealousy of his fellow Nation members,
and his questioning of basic NOI doctrines, along with his increasingly vocal
opposition to American policy in the Vietnam War, were a combination that
ultimately would prove deadly to Malcolm. Responding to charges that he
was a dangerous extremist, Malcolm affirmed that only a radical stance could
address the extremely bad conditions in which blacks found themselves in
racist America.

Malcolm's widely quoted comment that John F. Kennedy's assassination
was a case of chickens coming home to roost, the natural outcome of the violence prevalent in America, was interpreted as his somehow sanctioning the
president's death. Elijah silenced Malcolm for three months. The rift grew
deeper. In January 1964 Malcolm was removed as a minister of New York's
Temple Number Seven, and at the same time Wallace was excommunicated
for his association with Malcolm. The scene was set for a dramatic change.

Three months later, Malcolm X set out for Mecca to participate in the
pilgrimage that is required of all Muslims at least once in a lifetime. It was,
indeed, to be the experience of a lifetime for Malcolm. His autobiography
describes his deep sense of shame as he realized that while he called himself a
minister of Islam, he did not know the ritual for prayer or some of the basic
requirements of living an Islamic life. The realization of the inadequacy of
his training, as well as the quite overwhelming recognition that people of
all races can and do participate together without rancor or prejudice in the
great ceremonial pilgrimage, shocked and humbled Malcolm. His ensuing
speaking tour through Africa after the *hajj*, in which he outlined his ideas for
an international black liberation movement, included visits to a number of
African Muslim heads of state. Conversations with these leaders opened his
eyes further to the incongruity of separatist Nation of Islam doctrines with
the inclusiveness of worldwide Islam.

The die was cast for Malcolm's break with the Nation. On March 8, 1964, he left his once-beloved association and organized a new group called the Muslim Mosque, Inc., with its political wing the Organization of Afro-American Unity (OAAU). In recognition of his pilgrimage and his new identity as an orthodox Muslim, he changed his name to El Hajj Malik el-Shabazz. He was attacked severely from within the Nation, and even his brother Philbert X was persuaded to denounce Malcolm publicly as a false prophet.

On February 21, 1965, the former Malcolm Little was shot and killed while addressing his newly formed OAAU in New York City, leaving his wife of seven years, Betty Shabazz, a widow. When Malcolm was shot, it was Betty who shielded her daughter with her own body. The actual assailant was never determined, though many might have wished for his death, and the world lost one of the most compelling political and religious leaders of the twentieth century.

By the 1960s, turbulent days for black Americans, many who saw themselves as political activists had affiliated with some kind of Islam. This was particularly true of those who worked in the arts, such as writers, poets, musicians, and others who in their public presentations were symbolizing their break with white society and their encouragement of other African Americans to view Islam as a vehicle for personal achievement as well as communal advancement. Some black intellectuals such as LeRoi Jones (Amiri Baraka) were analyzing the social and political issues current in the black community and advocating Islam as a solution to societal ills. Meanwhile the NOI was continuing to grow, and by the middle of the 1970s it claimed a million members. Some seventy-five temples were in operation in the United States and outside the country.

For many African Americans, adopting Islam served to set them apart from white society, Muslim or not. Since that time, and particularly after the death of Elijah Muhammad, others have moved consciously to look for the unity of all American Muslims, regardless of color or cultural background. One of those who pioneered the effort to bring African American and immigrant Islam closer together is Elijah Muhammad's son Wallace.

Wallace Muhammad (Warith Deen Mohammed)

Early in 1975, the Nation of Islam was stunned to hear of the death of its longtime leader, the Honorable Elijah Muhammad, of congestive heart failure. For some ardent followers of Elijah, this was a staggering event, sorely testing their faith, as they had believed that their leader would never suc-cumb to the throes of mortality. At the annual Savior's Day rally the day after the death, the public announcement was made that Wallace was to succeed his father as Supreme Minister of the NOI. Many were shocked because of the checkered history of Wallace's relationship with his father, and because of his lack of public exposure. Those on the inside, however, knew that Elijah wanted leadership to stay within the family. For the time being, most of the more visible leaders of the Nation, including Louis Farrakhan (whose support was reluctant, since he had expected to be the leader), gave their allegiance to Wallace. With his succession were to come momentous changes within the movement itself in the following years as the political millenarianism of the earlier Nation gave way to a visible move toward orthodox Islam.

Wallace, born in 1933, was the seventh of Elijah and Clara Muhammad's eight children. From an early age interested in the academic and spiritual disciplines of Islam, Wallace immersed himself in the study of Arabic and the Qur'an. He made his own first pilgrimage to Mecca in 1967, three years after Malcolm's momentous journey. Immediately upon assuming leader-ship of the NOI Wallace began to rethink publicly the ideology that had characterized the Nation in its earlier days. While always careful to credit his father with wise and skilled leadership, he soon clarified several things. First, Fard was not to be thought of as divine. Second, Elijah was not the pure and unblemished messenger of Allah that so many of his followers believed him to be, but only a very gifted man.

Central to Wallace Muhammad's early preaching was the rebuttal of the doctrine of black superiority, a keystone of Fard's and Elijah Muhammad's teachings. Only a few months after his father's death, Wallace announced that whites were to be considered fully human and even encouraged to become members of the Nation of Islam. He also posthumously brought Malcolm X back within the fold. Wallace evidenced his obvious interest in Islam as a spiritual force rather than a political tool by de-emphasizing the nationalism that in different ways had characterized the preaching of both his father and Malcolm. With the end of the demand for a separate state came his call for acknowledgment of citizenship within the United States of America and respect for the U.S. Constitution.

Among the many organizational changes Wallace effected was the aboli-tion of the men's Islamic security force, the notorious Fruit of Islam. This ban was probably a strategic action, as the FOI was the only unit within the Nation that could offer organized opposition to the direction in which he was taking the movement. Wallace also moved to separate business from the practice of religion. He basically began to take apart the huge but unwieldy and unsound business empire his father had tried so hard to build, leasing some small businesses to non-Muslims and liquidating large long-term debts by selling off those components that were not profitable.

Much of the community's evolution under Wallace Muhammad's leadership reveals itself in the succession of name changes he introduced. Moving the locus of identity from Asiatic to Islam in its more global connotation, he also emphasized the link with black Africa. In recognition of the Prophet Muhammad's original choice of a black Ethiopian named Bilal to give the first call to prayer, Wallace referred to his members as Bilalians. He changed the name of the NOI journal *Muhammad Speaks* to *Bilalian News*, and its content became much less political and more inclusive. "Bilalian" continues to be a general identification for black American Muslims. Initially, he saw the former Nation members as continuing to have their own group identity, which he called "the World Community of Al-Islam in the West" (WCIW).

Other external changes signaled the community's adoption of a new identity. What had been called temples were now referred to by their Arabic name *masjid* (literally, "the place of prostration"), the decor was Arabic symbols instead of the former slogans that denounced America and Christianity, Islamic prayers were broadcast, and seats were replaced with carpets so that all could sit on the floor as in a traditional mosque. Savior's Day, one of the most important observances of the Nation, became Ethnic Survival Week, to celebrate the achievements of black Americans. While the importance of cleanliness and honest, upright behavior continued from the old NOI days, Wallace relaxed the strict dress code. The subordinate role assigned to women under Elijah Muhammad gave way to equality of participation and function for men and women, with equal educational opportunities.

In 1978 Wallace began restructuring and decentralizing, resigning his own direct leadership in favor of an elected council of six people serving as imams. Two years later he announced that he had officially changed his name to Warith Deen Mohammed, which in Arabic means "the inheritor of the religion of (Prophet) Muhammad." At the same time, to emphasize the significance of a specifically American Islam, he changed the name of the organization from the World Community of Islam in the West to the American Muslim Mission. The journal received yet another title, changing from *Bilalian News* to the *American Muslim Journal*. In the mid-1980s, to signal the movement's identification with worldwide orthodox Islam, the periodical

Warith Deen Mohammed, imam of the Muslim American Society. © TED GRAY

was called simply *Muslim Journal*, a title it retains today. Published out of Chicago, it contains articles primarily but not exclusively about African American Muslims, highlighting their community achievements and recognition. It also includes basic Arabic lessons, as well as listings of literary and technological resources available for the study of Islam and Arabic.

In 1985 Warith Deen felt that the decentralization he had begun some years earlier was complete, and he declared that his followers were no longer to be characterized by any distinguishing name. We are simply Muslims, he affirmed, members of the worldwide body of Sunni Islam. Even after that, however, apparently by request of those in the community he represented, he decided to refer to them as the Muslim American Society.

Warith Deen emerged from this long process as a significant, recognized, and respected leader of American Islam, one whose vision highly influenced American blacks, both Muslim and non-Muslim. He has been called the contemporary *mujaddid*, the renewer of the religion of Islam for his age. In 1990 Imam Warith Deen was the first Muslim to be asked to open the U.S. Senate with prayer, and later he participated in President Bill Clinton's inaugural celebration. About his own status, he said: "I hope what I leave behind is enough evidence of my sincerity as a Muslim for people to say, well, maybe he had ups and downs, maybe he didn't do a lot of things we thought he should do, but one thing we have no doubts about: he was a sincere believer in his religion."[11]

Warith Deen Mohammed was a revered leader and an articulate voice in American Islam, as well as an advocate of strong interfaith relations. He pioneered a special program with the Roman Catholic Focolare Movement headed by the Blessed Lady Chiara Lubich. Together they hosted a series of public events in the United States. Immediately after 9/11 Warith Deen appeared on public television, where he declared that his community no longer has to look to Muslims overseas for true Islam because we have true Islam in America.

Warith Deen Mohammed died on September 8, 2008. His passing was a deep shock to his community and a loss to American Islam, of which he was the single most prominent leader of the early twenty-first century.

Louis Farrakhan

The former Nation of Islam was resuscitated under the leadership of the fiery Louis Farrakhan, generally following the ideology of Elijah Muhammad. Despite his earlier assurances of allegiance to Wallace, Farrakhan soon felt that Elijah's son was leading the group in a direction that would neglect the immediate task of addressing the still unfortunate circumstances of American blacks. In 1978 he publicly stated that he no longer felt welcome within the World Community of Al-Islam in the West and was cutting off all ties with Wallace. "When I could not agree with him any longer," he said, "I separated myself from him. Not to take up stones to throw them at him but because I honestly could not abide his criticism of his father, who had laid the basis for our development Islamically in America."[12] His plan, Farrakhan said, was to rebuild the old Nation of Islam, and to some extent he succeeded.

Some of Farrakhan's followers were former Nation members who disapproved of the changes proposed by Wallace, while others were new converts from within the African American community. The current NOI is basically a black-power movement dedicated to the old separatist ideal of establishing an independent nation. It continues to proclaim the injustices visited on the black community by racist white American society. Farrakhan has insisted that integration simply cannot solve the problems of blacks who have not achieved at least middle-class status. The *Final Call* newspaper resumed publication in 1979, featuring Farrakhan's speeches and activities, the involvements of other current NOI members, and a regular replay of the writings and talks of Elijah Muhammad. Farrakhan spearheads efforts by NOI members to work for the betterment of the black community. While still a small organization, the Nation continues to engage the attention of the American public because of its community efforts to clean up drug-infested areas and otherwise work to improve the lives of inner-city blacks. In 1997 Farrakhan's call for a "million man march" in Washington, D.C., brought together African Americans from across the nation.

Who is this figure who has continued to capture the imagination of significant, if small, numbers of African Americans with his message of black supremacy and separatism, to elicit other Muslims' constant insistence that the Nation is not part of their fold, and to intrigue and sometimes frighten those who listen to his rhetoric and experience his charisma? Born Louis Eugene Wolcott in 1933, the same year in which Wallace Muhammad was born, he pursued a musical career as a violinist and calypso singer. He gave this vocation up in 1955, however, after hearing the preaching of Elijah Muhammad and vowing his commitment to the NOI. He professed to have been strongly influenced by Malcolm X, whom he heard and knew in Boston, but said that it was Elijah who really brought him around. When Malcolm was killed, the former Louis Wolcott became Minister Louis Farrakhan of the New York Temple and acted as the national representative for the Honorable Elijah Muhammad.

For the most part, tensions between Imam Warith Deen Mohammed and his followers and Farrakhan's NOI were controlled, perhaps because there was little interaction. Certainly, mutual resentments were never absent, and Warith Deen indicated that his followers should not acknowledge Farrakhan at all. Farrakhan periodically erupted into national prominence by making inflammatory statements, as during Jesse Jackson's 1984 candidacy for president of the United States, when he was quoted as referring to Zionism as a "gutter religion" and hailing Adolf Hitler as a "great man." Despite his attempts to distinguish between Zionism and Judaism, the charge of anti-Semitism has stuck. Subsequent statements by some of Farrakhan's followers have served to substantiate the charge. While Warith Deen continually affirmed the egalitarian nature of true Islam, Farrakhan has identified what he sees as strong color prejudice among some immigrant Muslims, supporting his efforts to affirm the importance of black consciousness.

In the late 1980s Louis Farrakhan began to redefine the mission of the NOI. Still preaching the basic doctrines that had long characterized the

Nation, he began also to stress elements of the Islamic faith such as prayer and fasting, seemingly wishing to align the NOI more closely with traditional Islam. Friday prayers are strongly encouraged, particularly in Mosque Maryam, which serves as the national headquarters, on the south side of Chicago. Farrakhan has always attempted to affirm his allegiance to Elijah Muhammad and his teachings, but more recently he seems to have reinterpreted these teachings a bit. He always affirmed his own succession from Elijah, implicitly denying that of Warith Deen.

In the apparent effort to "Islamicize" his movement, Farrakhan began to emphasize the importance of closer ties with other Muslim communities in the Middle East and Africa. Thus he became a frequent and highly visible international visitor. For a number of years Islamic countries overseas contributed significant funding to the NOI movement, which they saw as helping to propagate the religion of Islam in America. Sunni Muslims waited to see whether Farrakhan was serious about his desire to bring the NOI more fully in line with orthodox Islam, but they remained skeptical. In 1990, at the Palmer House in Chicago, he moved his listeners with an inspiring profession of the two elements of the *shahada*, faith in one God and belief in Muhammad ibn Abdullah as his Prophet. Sunni Muslims, however, have been deeply disappointed that the NOI leader nonetheless has continued to maintain many of the original tenets of Elijah Muhammad.

NOI members are generally quite strict in their dress code (women do not wear makeup and must cover their hair), in their observance of dietary laws, and in their disavowal of tobacco, narcotics, and such habits as overeating and oversleeping. Normally they do not, however, pray five times a day. Unlike orthodox Muslims, they believe in a resurrection of the mind in which people are freed, rather than in the classic doctrine of the resurrection of the body on the Day of Judgment. Members tithe to the organization— and that income, along with sales of *Final Call*, provides the major source of funding.

Louis Farrakhan's Nation of Islam, while obviously controversial, has unquestionably provided important social and community services. The U.S. government supports its drug and AIDS programs and security efforts in crime- and drug-infested federal housing units. Members of the reconstituted Fruit of Islam serve as patrols in a number of large urban areas, wearing their recognizable uniforms of pressed shirts, ties, and dark suits. The Nation has had notable success working with gangs and drug dealers, especially young blacks and Hispanics, in an effort that has few parallels. While most Muslims in America, black and immigrant, continue to say that the Nation is not to be considered part of the community of Islam, some are less willing to be so dismissive, urging that the changes gradually introduced in the Nation may perhaps indicate steady, if slow, movement in the right direction.

Louis Farrakhan, at this writing, is suffering serious illness and has indicated that he is not able to remain as head of the NOI. Two important leaders of the African American community lived and worked at the same time, each influencing large numbers of adherents and each espousing a clearly different interpretation of what Islam can mean for American blacks. Never friends but never enemies either, Warith Deen Mohammed and Louis Farrakhan will remain—like Malcolm X—figures of stature. It is yet to be seen how the leadership of the community will evolve.

African American Sunni Movements

Followers of Warith Deen Mohammed and Louis Farrakhan, of course, are not the only African Americans to associate themselves with Islam. A number of others serve as examples of Islam's appeal to blacks, especially in the urban American context. Some of these identify themselves specifically as Sunni and attempt to follow the teachings of orthodox Islam with diligence, often in opposition to Nation of Islam teachings.

The Hanafi Madhhab movement, for example, was first begun fairly early in the century by a Pakistani immigrant. His follower Khalifa Hammas Abdul Khaalis tried unsuccessfully to infiltrate the NOI and change its direction. Failing that objective, he established the Hanafi Madhhab Center in Washington, D.C., in the late 1950s. Its members express their public commitment to America, a stand that has sometimes made the movement unpopular with other black groups and especially with the Nation. In an ugly incident in 1973, unknown assailants killed seven Hanafis, four children among them. Three years later Hanafis themselves, in protest against the showing of a film titled *Mohammad, Messenger of God*, which they felt to be blasphemous, raided office buildings in Washington, D.C., and took hostages. A man was killed, and ambassadors from several Muslim countries were called in to resolve the matter. The Hanafis have since stayed well out of the public eye. One of the most prominent Hanafi members has been basketball star Kareem Abdul-Jabbar.

Another group self-identified as Sunni is the Darul Islam movement[13] (also rendered as the Dar ul-Islam), begun in Brooklyn in the early 1960s. The first converts were men who had been associated with the black power movement and who, despite their pledge to follow the Prophet Muhammad and the *shari'a*, in the beginning adopted an agenda of racial separatism. From its earliest days, the group suffered from internal conflicts and several times disbanded and then reassembled. A new association was formed in the late 1960s, meeting in a small flat in Brooklyn that served as a house of prayer, instruction, and even communal living for those who chose it. The movement solidified, grew, and began to establish branches in many major U.S. cities. Various ministries were set up, including one for self-defense training, required of all young men. By the time of Elijah Muhammad's death in 1975, the Dar claimed more than thirty mosque-based Sunni Muslim communities. At that point, before Warith Deen began to move former NOI members toward orthodox Islam, the Dar was the largest black Sunni Muslim organization in the country, with mosques as far west as Colorado and in the West Indies, Ontario, and Alaska. While each chapter had its own imam, the leader was Imam Yahya Abdul-Kareem of the Brooklyn mosque. The various branches were joined in a federation modeled on the Treaty of Medina fashioned by the Prophet Muhammad.

The Darul Islam movement at its height took its Islam seriously. Members were asked upon entry to take a pledge that amounted to a lifetime commitment. They were challenged to follow a rigorous course of religious teaching, including classical training in Arabic, the Qur'an, and Sunna. As the Dar developed, it moved away from its earlier agenda of separatism, although the theme of racism and the belief that Islam could be the liberating force was always present. Unwilling to advocate some of the theories that have made the Nation so unpalatable to orthodox Islam, the Dar has actually held more strictly to the tenets and practices of Islam than many other Muslims might feel necessary. Members have been encouraged to dress in Muslim fashion and to avoid contact with non-Muslims. At times, strong enmities have arisen between the strict observers of the Dar movement and other Muslims, especially immigrants, who seemed to Dar members to be buying into the American system. In the 1970s some members again broke off to establish a separate and ultraconservative group, identifying themselves as the Fuqra.

Gradually, Dar members were also introduced to elements of the Sufi tradition of Islam, as Imam Yahya understood these from his study with a Pakistani Sufi *shaykh* of the Qadiriyya order. By 1980 Imam Yahya, under the influence of his Sufi master, announced the end of the Dar as a separate movement—much as Warith Deen did with his followers—and its assimilation into Sufi Islam. He gave up his own leadership role, and the Ya-Sin mosque in Brooklyn ceased functioning and was sold.

One Atlanta Darul Islam member who opposed the absorption into Sufism and led the attempts to reaffiliate Dar members was former chairman of the Student Nonviolent Coordinating Committee (SNCC) H. Rap Brown. In his new identity as Imam Jamil Abdullah al-Amin, Brown helped form and lead another much smaller federation now called the National Community. The Community, along with the Islamic Society of North America, the Islamic Circle of North America, and Warith Deen Mohammed's Muslim American Society, once constituted the National Shura Council in America. In 2002 Imam Jamil al-Amin was found guilty of murder and is now serving a life sentence without parole in Georgia. His movement continues to have branches in various parts of America as well as in the Caribbean.

Among the Sunni African American Muslim groups who reacted against NOI teachings, two others deserve brief mention. Shaykh Khalid Ahmad Tawfiq began the Mosque of Islamic Brotherhood (MIB) in 1970 in Harlem. Tawfiq, a former member of the Moorish Science Temple, became a follower of Malcolm X. He never accepted the racist doctrines of the Nation, and under Malcolm's sponsorship left to study at al-Azhar in Cairo, bastion of Islamic orthodoxy. On his return to Harlem, he began the MIB in an attempt to adapt what he understood to be true Islam to the specific needs of African Americans. He tried to blend the teachings of Marcus Garvey's UNIA with those of Hasan al-Banna and the Egyptian Muslim Brotherhood. Tawfiq died in 1988, and the MIB has continued as a relatively small movement in Harlem.

Another group that arose during the same period is the Islamic Party, begun by jazz musician D. C. Muzzafruddin in 1971. Also influenced by Malcolm, like Tawfiq he traveled in the Middle East to learn more about Islam. In addition to the Muslim Brotherhood, he was influenced by the teachings of Pakistani leader Maulana Mawdudi. He began the Islamic Party in Washington, D.C., to spread a better understanding of Islam and to counter what Muzzafruddin saw as the apathy of immigrant Muslims in not attend ing appropriately to the task of spreading the faith. Branches were later established in other major American cities such as Chicago, New York, and Houston. During the 1970s the movement gained considerable strength, and numbers of students at Howard University joined the da'wa effort. Many saw the party as a substitute for the flagging civil rights movement. In 1975 the Islamic Party received a significant gift from Libya's Colonel Qadaffi. The group's decision in the late 1970s to move to Georgia to live in a rural context proved its undoing. It suffered a series of splits, offices in other major cities were forced to close, and a surviving faction moved to Trinidad and finally to the Dominican Republic. Muzzafruddin returned to America, where he died in 1983, but the movement was effectively finished. A few of his followers, attracted by the Iranian revolution, became affiliated with Shi'ism.

A highly visible Sunni Muslim personality in the public arena today is Imam Siraj Wahaj, congregational leader of Masjid al-Taqwa in Brooklyn, New York. Siraj Wahaj has served as vice president of ISNA and president of the Majlis al-Shura (consultative council) of New York. He travels around the world speaking to Muslim and other groups about a range of issues from an Islamic perspective. Originally a Baptist, the Imam has been a Muslim since the late 1960s. He is an enthusiastic speaker who knows how to ignite a crowd, never hesitating to identify what he sees to be the current ills of American society and the solutions provided by Islam as both a social system and a set of religious beliefs. He is very popular with young people, and is regularly invited to address conferences such as Muslim Youth of North America (MYNA). Among the Imam's many local endeavors is an active program spearheading an antidrug campaign in New York City, which has resulted in the closure of a number of drug houses. In 1991 Imam Siraj Wahaj was the first Muslim invited to give the invocation prayer at the opening session of Congress in Washington, D.C.

African American Sectarian Movements

Meanwhile, a number of other African American groups have spun off from the ideology of the Nation of Islam, manifesting themselves as quasi-Islamic as they borrow some elements from orthodox Islam and disregard others. The extent to which these sectarian groups are accepted by Muslims as part of the fabric of Islam is often difficult to gauge, although they are increasingly accused by Sunni Muslims, African American and those from the immigrant community, of being beyond the boundaries of what is Islamically acceptable. Looking to Asia and/or Africa as the source of identity continues to be a common theme for black sectarian movements. Two examples can serve to illustrate the nature of some of these groups.

The Ansaru Allah community is a black sect founded almost thirty years ago by Isa Muhammad, who was familiar with the teachings of both the Moorish Science Temple and the Nation of Islam. Like those groups, the Ansar consistently emphasized the importance of American blacks breaking free of the inferior status to which whites consigned them. Isa Muhammad, however, rejected the claims of both Drew Ali and Elijah Muhammad to prophethood and proclaimed his own message to supersede theirs and others. Isa Muhammad's origins seem deliberately to have been obscured, though he said he was born in 1945 in the Sudan. He claimed to have written more than 365 books and pamphlets by the power of Allah speaking through him, and indeed many of these are available. After 1990 all of his written works appeared under the name As Sayyid Isa al Haadi al-Mahdi.

Originally called the Ansar Pure Sufi in the late 1960s, with the Star of David and an Egyptian ankh part of its symbolism, the group changed its name to Nubian Islamic Hebrews. The *mahdist* Islamic crescent was added to its symbols, and its members were requested to wear long African robes. Soon the group began to publish a newspaper and several journals. In 1973 Isa traveled to Egypt and the Sudan, where he says he was visited by the figure of Khidr, said to be a spiritual guide of Muslim mystics. From that point, his teachings began to sound much more specifically Islamic, and he portrayed himself as responsible for propagation of the Qur'anic message in the West. His affirmation of the importance of being black carried the corresponding condemnation of the "pale-skinned" race in a series of attacks on whites that rivaled even early NOI ideology. The "Nubian Islamic Hebrews" terminology was dropped, and the community was officially named the Ansaru Allah, from Sura 61:14 of the Qur'an, which refers to the "helpers [*ansar*] of Allah." In 1981 Isa seemed to proclaim himself the promised messiah of Islam. By the early 1990s, he began to sound more orthodox in his preaching and teaching, modifying earlier attacks on whites. Much of the more recent literature shows him proclaiming that the members of Ansaru Allah follow the teachings of the Qur'an more closely than any other Muslims, especially those of Saudi Arabia. By the 1990s Ansaru Allah communities were located in many cities of the United States, as well as in a number of countries in Africa, the Caribbean, and even Europe.

Isa Muhammad officially retired as Imam of the Ansaru Allah community in 1988, and is now serving a prison sentence in Georgia. The group has continued to exist and to redefine itself. At times it has seemed to be strictly Muslim, and at others to reflect strong influences of Christianity and Judaism. The Ansar thus serves as a fascinating example of the mixture of Islam, black nationalism, and many of the traditions that make up the fabric of American religion.

Another spin-off from the Nation of Islam is a group called Allah's Nation of the Five Percenters.[14] The movement, founded in Harlem in 1964 by former NOI member Clarence "Pudding" 13X, has spread across urban America and is now found in major cities from New York to Los Angeles.

Its direct appeal affirms even more immediately than the NOI doctrine the value of being black, and it especially attracts African American youth. Clarence came to believe and teach not only that God is black but, by extension, that all blacks are themselves God. After being reprimanded by the Nation, Clarence 13X left with some of his associates to begin preaching to black street youth.

Always a smooth and articulate speaker, Clarence first developed what has become the popular fast rap message of the Five Percenters. Each youth who learns the ideology is charged to pass it on to someone even younger. For more than two decades the movement was headquartered at the "Allah School in Mecca" in Harlem. In June of 1969 Clarence met the fate of Malcolm and others, shot by unidentified gunmen. Some blamed the NOI for avenging his departure, although Farrakhan, who was then head of Harlem's Temple Number Seven, strongly denied it. Like Malcolm's, Clarence 13X's murderer was never caught.

Five Percenter ideology is a complex combination of vaguely Islamic symbolism, black supremacy theory, and popular culture. To NOI teachings about the original black man, Clarence added a classification of people according to percentages. Only five percent of all people understand that the Living God is the black man. They are the ones who are the righteous teachers of freedom, justice, and equality to all others. Five Percenter ideology borrows from Sufism the science of interpreting the meaning of letters of the Arabic alphabet. The Five Percenters, also called the Nation of Gods and Earths, acknowledge the status of males as gods by teaching that the proper name for the black man is Allah, which stands for the physical members of arm, leg, leg, arm, and head. Black men often adopt names that reflect their divine status, such as "Allah Supreme" or "God Allah Mind." Such references appear in the music of the Notorious B.I.G. and Mos Def, showing Five Percenter ideology's influence on the hip-hop movement.

The medium of rap music is an effective tool for propagating a message based on fast talk and slick reinterpretations, and several popular rap recording artists have consciously identified with and propagated Five Percenter ideology. The rap never goes stale because it keeps incorporating the latest in slang expressions and developing new and fresh interpretations to fit the conditions of each new set of possible recruits. For the further development of Islamic rap in America see chapter 7.

Islam in the African American community has changed greatly since the early days of such pioneering figures as Noble Drew Ali and Elijah Muhammad. Strong leaders like Warith Deen Mohammed have worked hard to bring together African American and immigrant Islam. African Americans have come far in their quest for full social and economic participation in America. While racism is still alive and reasonably well, the fact is that African Americans, Muslims and others, are now entrenched in the American middle class. They have also made great strides in American professional life. The world of academia, which until fairly recently had no Muslim university faculty at all, now sees African American Muslim scholars such as Sherman Jackson, Aminah McCloud, Edward Curtis, and many others working creatively in new fields of academic investigation.

Immigrants, African Americans, and converts from other groups all combine to illustrate the many ways in which it is possible to be Muslim in America. Just as many characteristics distinguish them from one another, so too they share many concerns. In the following chapters we will look at some of the issues members of all of these communities face as they try to define who is Muslim and who is not, to assess what roles are appropriate and necessary in a Western context, and to determine what as Americans they share as they attempt to forge an Islamic *umma* in the West.

CHAPTER FIVE

The Public Practice of Islam

Think about it: Living in the West is the real test of a believer. You're living Islam in place where there are no restrictions against your worship. No one will prevent you from praying here, no one will make you shave your beard or remove your *hijab*. . . . America today is a place where anything, including Islam, is allowed.[1]

This freedom to practice the faith in public—to build and attend mosques, to train indigenous Islamic leadership, to contribute to the spread of knowledge about Islam, to form organizations that will reflect the issues and concerns of American Muslims—is now being accepted by American society as a right and an expectation for this growing religious neighbor. Following is a brief look at how the public face of Islam is being expressed.

Mosques (*Masjids*)

A Muslim architect who came from Pakistan to the United States as a student in 1960 describes his attempts to find a mosque in the Pittsburgh area. His host family, eager to make him feel at home, took him to the closest facsimile they could find. "As we turned onto a minor street on the University of Pittsburgh campus," Gulzar Haider writes, "[my host] pointed to a vertical neon sign that said in no uncertain terms 'Syria Mosque.' . . . Horseshoe arches, horizontal bands of different colored bricks, decorative terra-cotta—all were devices to invoke a Moorish memory. Excitedly, I took a youthful step towards the lobby, when my host turned around and said, 'This is not the kind of mosque in which you bend up and down facing Mecca. This is a meeting hall-theater built by Shriners. . . . They are the guys who dress up in satin baggies, embroidered vests, and fez caps.'"[2]

As a result of this and other fruitless attempts to find an American mosque that both looked and functioned like one, this architect has devoted his career to designing Islamic mosques for the Western context. In 1979 he was invited to draw up plans for the mosque located at the national headquarters of the Islamic Society of North America (ISNA) in Plainfield, Indiana. The movement to create an Islamic architecture for the American environment is both fascinating and challenging. It is, in effect, the latest chapter in a long struggle among American Muslims to find or create worship spaces appropriate for the particular needs of their communities and faith.

Many Muslims who came to America earlier in this century had little overt interest in participating in Islamic functions or even in identifying themselves specifically as members of the Islamic tradition. In many cases, however, they found their attitudes changing. Their frequent frustration in not finding a social group of other Americans with whom they could feel comfortable and accepted, or the satisfaction of sharing experiences that reflected their commonality with other Muslims, encouraged them to participate more openly in religiously based activities. They gravitated toward common worship, Qur'an study groups, and other gatherings that reinforced their affiliation with the religion of Islam. As second-generation Muslims reached the age to marry and have children, they often became more aware of the importance of providing a social, cultural, and religious context for their children. Most of the new Muslim communities, however, had no easy access to trained leadership to instruct them in the elements of the faith or to lead the prayer. Those who had even a little education in the Qur'an or Islamic law were looked to for guidance. Sometimes people with no training at all had to gather the faithful together on Friday and perform the function of imam, or prayer leader.

Before long, a number of immigrant Muslim communities across the nation began to think about more structured ways to observe their religion and ensure its continuity. They were concerned about the difficulty of finding an appropriate place in which to worship and observe the Friday prayers. Sometimes they held services in one another's homes. But as the community began to grow, this arrangement became increasingly less feasible. Some congregations leased abandoned buildings or other spaces, while others occasionally shared space in local churches. Often these facilities were dreary and at best unsuited for sitting and praying on the floor, without pews or chairs, as is the Muslim custom. Slowly, more and more Muslims began to think and dream about establishing their own mosques. To possess such a building would, of course, make it much easier to gather together and perform the actual worship. The building would also enable the community to have pride in its identification with Islam and its ability to provide its own facility. And finally, it would serve as a means of legitimating Islam as part of the American religious scene, providing visible structures and institutions that could "stand up and be counted" alongside the many churches and synagogues across America.

We have already noted the pioneering efforts in building mosques in the early decades of the twentieth century. The mosque movement began to gain real momentum by the middle of the century. The opening of the Islamic Center of Washington in Washington, D.C., completed in 1957, was an important signal to Muslims and non-Muslims alike that Islam was being recognized by Islamic countries abroad as a significant presence in the American context. The center was built as a cooperative venture between U.S. Muslims and Islamic governments overseas. The first building in America to have been professionally designed as a mosque, it has since attracted visitors and dignitaries from across the Muslim world. From its minaret, archways, and columns to its spacious and carpeted worship hall, the mosque of the center was constructed according to the highest standards of Islamic architecture. Designed particularly to serve the diplomatic community of Washington, it has also been the locus of missionary and educational activities.

Since the construction of the Washington, D.C., mosque, numerous structures have been architecturally conceived and built for the specific purpose of serving as mosque or Islamic center, and many other buildings have been converted for mosque use. That there are now some 35 mosques and Islamic centers in the greater Washington, D.C., area illustrates the enormous growth of the mosque movement in America over the last half century. According to recent surveys, well over 2,000 institutions identify themselves as mosques or Islamic centers in the United States. Almost 80 percent of these have been established since 1980. Massachusetts (297), California (248), and New York (147) boast the largest number of *masjids* (*masjid* is the literal translation of the word meaning "place of prostration") in the country. New Jersey, Texas, and Michigan also have significant numbers of mosques, and virtually no state is unable to point to some structure functioning in this capacity. In terms of ethnic identification, Indo-Pakistanis claim the most mosques, with Arabs next, although as racial-ethnic identities have begun to give way to more integrated congregations, such distinctions have become less meaningful.

There is growing sentiment today among some American Muslims to avoid use of the word *mosque* in favor of the Arabic term *masjid*. The story is circulating that during the reign of Fernando and Isabella in Spain, when Christianity was growing at the expense of Islam, one of them supposedly

The Islamic Center in Washington, D.C. Courtesy Islamic Center, Washington, D.C.

said that they were going to swat the Muslims in the *masjid* where they congregate like mosquitoes. Thus, it is said, arose the term *mosque*. While the story is most likely apocryphal, it is true that *masjid* is preferred over *mosque* by many Muslims.

While many of the structures designed as mosques follow a classical style of Islamic architecture, it appears that a new American style is gradually emerging, related to the particular locations of these edifices. We saw in chapter 3 Hasan Fathi's attempt to blend traditional Islamic architecture with the style of the New Mexico desert. The Massachusetts Institute of Technology's project to document the growth of mosques in the United States and Canada has a traveling photography exhibit of this American phenomenon. Muslim architects have actually designed only a few of these buildings, and well-meaning efforts in some cases have resulted in structures actually not well conceived to meet the various needs of their congregations. Those who wish to design and build their own mosques can find assistance through such companies as Kinoo, Inc. "The Principals, as Muslims, have direct concern and knowledge of contemporary and traditional norms important to the program, development, design, and construction of mosques and Islamic centers," Kinoo assures potential clients.[3] Muslims themselves are increasingly "owning" the task of designing the mosque or community center in their self-conscious efforts to "create Muslim space" within the American continent.

Many different styles, then, characterize American mosques. Some are converted storefronts, offices, or houses, made to look at least somewhat Islamic by the removal of chairs and other furniture and the addition of Qur'anic verses on the wall and some kind of marker to indicate the direction of prayer. Others are well-financed, full-fledged mosques, constructed according to architecture appropriate to the Middle East or other parts of the Muslim world. Some emphasize ethnic identity and serve as centers in which members work together for survival in a sometimes hostile American context. Others are more heterogeneous in character, not only serving as centers for prayer and social activities but also maintaining an active outreach to the surrounding community with various kinds of social services. Many work in the schools and other public contexts for education about Islamic beliefs and practices, as well as for better interfaith understanding. After 9/11 the Council on American-Islamic Relations (CAIR) encouraged all American mosques to join in an "open house project" in which they were to invite non-Muslim neighbors to see where and how Muslims worship and enjoy hospitality and information sharing. A significant number of mosques around the country did issue such invitations. Efforts by the National Council of Churches to persuade Christian congregations to reciprocate were generally unsuccessful.

Some major Islamic centers have been likened to Christian "mega-churches," large racially and ethnically diverse institutions with a variety of educational and social services. These large mosques and Islamic centers often provide education at a range of levels for children and adults, with well-equipped classrooms and libraries. They feature social and sporting facilities, and occasionally even a restaurant, a funeral home, or offices to let for Islamic-oriented businesses. Muslims are encouraged by a variety of means to contribute to the construction of these large Islamic centers, assured that their contributions are tax deductible and vital to providing an Islamic environment for worship and education.

Several of these mega-mosques are particularly noticeable on the American landscape, such as the Islamic Center of Greater Cincinnati (ICGC). The ICGC is a neighbor to the large Ohio Islamic center in Toledo, both eye-openers for those not expecting to see such visible evidence of the presence of Islam in the state. The ICGC is an interesting example of the way in which such centers are entering the American scene. It was born in the early 1960s when a small group of Muslims first gathered for prayer in Cincinnati.

As the community grew, it began to press more steadily for a facility that could provide not only a worship context but a place for the education of the community. Constant efforts at planning and fund-raising finally paid off, with the assistance of some support from the Middle East, and the resulting center abounds with a range of facilities. At its heart is a lovely mosque with the capacity to accommodate more than a thousand worshipers. The larger facility includes a community center, gymnasium, school, recreational center, and house for the resident imam. Plans are under way for the construction of senior citizens housing near the center to allow elderly members the chance to participate in center activities.

Despite the impressive nature of these large institutions, the vast majority of buildings currently being used as mosques neither were built for that purpose nor have facilities adequate for the various demands of their congregations. Most are converted houses, offices, former churches, or other buildings originally constructed for different purposes. In every instance, efforts are put forth to make the structure appear as "Islamic" as possible, including clearing space and adding carpets in the largest room to serve as the prayer hall, ensuring that washing facilities are available for ablutions, marking the prayer direction in some visible way, decorating the walls with Arabic calligraphy, turning rooms into classrooms, adding a sign in the front of the building to indicate its present use, and perhaps putting a crescent in some visible place. Often most, if not all, of the labor required to maintain these facilities comes from the volunteer services of members of the congregation.

There is a small but growing movement in the United States to provide public space for Muslim prayer. In January 1996, Denver's new international airport became the first in America to feature a mosque. The space designated for Muslim worship is on the sixth-floor mezzanine looking out on the main terminal, adjacent to a combined Christian and Jewish chapel. At first, discussion was held about a common worship space for all three religions, but the Muslims chose for both practical (no chairs or pews occupy a Muslim prayer hall) and religious (many Muslims would not avail themselves of a worship space that had Christian or Jewish symbols) reasons to keep the mosque separate, with its own entrance. Private donations financed half of the whole worship complex, and the other half came from the airlines servicing the airport. The international airport in Columbus, Ohio, has an interfaith meditation room that includes a separate prayer area for Muslims. John F. Kennedy International Airport in New York has an interfaith chapel that is largely utilized by Muslims and, along with a number of other public buildings in the city, features the Muslim crescent and star on one of its

Masjid Al Faatir Islamic Center in Chicago, Illinois, can accommodate up to three thousand worshipers.   © TED GRAY

outdoor flagpoles. Such efforts intend not only to provide services for American Muslims and those traveling from abroad but also to raise the visibility of Islam in America—one more tool in the effort to foster the faith and its better understanding.

Imams

Technically, nothing in Islam corresponds to the ordained clergy of Christianity and Judaism. Nonetheless, the forms of religious leadership throughout the history of Islam have been many and varied, with high degrees of specialization. As Islam in the United States has grown and developed, so has the need for people to serve in leadership capacities. Normally, the person who assumes the function of leading the prayer in a mosque or Islamic gathering is known as the imam (to be distinguished from the technical term referring to the hidden leader of the Shi'ites). It is not unusual to find today that those within and outside the American Muslim community see imams as functioning in ways that reflect, if not parallel, the clergy of other faiths.

Islamic worship area of the interfaith chapel at Denver International Airport.
COURTESY DENVER INTERNATIONAL AIRPORT

Some mosque communities active since the earlier part of the century have found that with the arrival of new and more conservative coreligionists, certain of their mosques' practices are being challenged. It is not unusual for a newly arrived imam who received his training in a place like Cairo or Saudi Arabia to introduce changes to make the mosque more traditional. In the late twentieth century oil-producing Muslim countries, eager to support the growth of Islam in areas in which it is a minority faith, often financed and sent these imams to America. They were classically educated, and were usually the first trained leaders in established mosque communities. However, they tended to insist on more strict interpretations of mosque usage and practice than was customary for some American Muslims. As one imam put it, "If you are talking about performing a wedding in the mosque, there is nothing in Islam which will say to you, 'no.' The Prophet used to do that in the mosque. But if you are talking about having the wedding in the form of music and dancing in the mosque, we will not allow it. Anyone who wants to do that, he can go and rent a hall outside, but it will not be accepted in the mosque."[4] Imams who come to the United States for the purpose of serving and educating mosque communities here may find themselves challenged by the customs of already established communities. Often they have difficulty with English, which can curtail their effective leadership and diminish their ability to communicate with American-born Muslim children.

If some imams assume their responsibilities with full Islamic training, others may be pressed into service when they are not well prepared because of the needs of the community for leadership. Particularly in less affluent communities, imams serve their congregations with only a partial knowledge of Arabic, the Qur'an, Islamic law, and Sunna. Sometimes they work in the capacity of imam without remuneration from their poor congregations and find themselves having to carry out those responsibilities while maintaining full-time employment elsewhere. In fact, only relatively few *masjids* in America actually have the services of a full-time trained imam. If a mosque community is located near a university, students from Muslim countries or resident chaplains may serve as temporary imams or assist in teaching Arabic and the Qur'an. The need for better training facilities for imams in the United States is widely recognized, although at present the opportunities to receive such training, particularly when communities are under severe financial constraints, are extremely limited.

Muslims who are most active in large mosques and Islamic centers, and who are their strongest financial supporters, are often professionals who are trained in the sciences (especially medicine) and who have not had extensive religious instruction. While grateful for the support that has come from the international Islamic community in sending trained religious leadership to American mosques, Muslims in the United States are deeply aware of the crucial necessity of developing an Islamically well-educated but distinctively indigenous American religious leadership. The issue of attracting and appropriately training an indigenous leadership for mosques and Islamic centers is of utmost importance. Clearly, one of the ways in which American Muslims can begin to extricate themselves from the influences of overseas Islam, to the extent to which this is considered desirable or necessary, is by developing their own education and training for imams.

Those imams who do have classical Islamic training often find that the expectations of their constituents differ from those in traditional Islamic societies. As *masjids* assume functions and activities that make them seem more like American churches and synagogues than mosques, so imams are asked to carry out a range of responsibilities more characteristic of pastors and rabbis than has ever been the case for Muslim prayer leaders. The very word *imam* refers, among other things, to "the one who stands in front of the congregation and leads the prayer." In traditional Muslim societies, other professionals perform weddings and funerals, give legal advice, provide education in matters of faith and practice, and the like.

In America imams are called upon to do all of these things and more. In addition to knowledge of the Qur'an, *hadith*, and Islamic law and theology, they must have good managerial and financial skills, provide pastoral care and counseling for congregants with particular needs, visit the sick and elderly, organize the community in cleaning up neighborhoods from drugs and other illicit activities, train members to teach in after-school and weekend mosque-school sessions, adjudicate when disputes over procedure arise among members, combat anti-Islamic prejudice and promote a better understanding of Islam, participate in interfaith community activities, and do many other things not part of the traditional role of imam. These expectations are often difficult to meet, not only because the imam may not be trained to do them but also because in so many cases he is working with the *masjid* in only a part-time capacity at best. In some cases new models are under experimentation, such as having a "team" of leaders to rotate through the responsibilities and take turns in actually leading the prayer. Since 9/11 imams have regularly been called on to explain and defend Islam as a religion of peace and moderation rather than one of violence and extremism in a wide range of public forums.

One of the leaders in helping Muslim imams understand their roles and responsibilities in America for many years has been Muzammil Siddiqi, director of the Islamic Society of Orange County, California. A member of the Fiqh (Islamic law) Council of North America, he has served as director of the Islamic Center of Washington, D.C., and as president of the Islamic Society of North America. Siddiqi is a Muslim intellectual who is also deeply concerned with helping Muslims live authentically in America. A visible presence on the international Muslim scene, Siddiqi has served as a member of the Supreme Islamic Council of Egypt and the Supreme Council of Mosques in Mecca, Saudi Arabia. Muzammil Siddiqi models a deep concern for interreligious dialogue and exchange. A frequent participant in presentations with Christian and Jewish colleagues, he has been extremely active in helping to foster better Muslim-Christian-Jewish relations, especially since 9/11.

In March 2008 a conference on mosque leadership was held in Washington, D.C., at which a number of Muslim religious leaders reflected on the theme "The American Mosque in the 21st Century: Identity, Education, and Empowerment." The conference was part of the ongoing project Muslims in the American Public Square, headed by Zahid Bukhari of Georgetown

University and Sulayman Nyang of Howard University. Among the topics under consideration were issues of identity, Muslim communal presence, governance, worship, social cohesion, sacred space, mosques as centers of learning, and inter-mosque relationships. Recognizing that American Islam is at a point where specific criteria are needed to assess who is ready and able to serve the position of imam, they agreed on a set of minimal standards. While a master's degree in Islam is desirable, these leaders agreed that what is really needed are the following: (a) an *ijaza* or license testifying to at least one year of study overseas at an internationally recognized Islamic institute, (b) experience in American language and culture, and (c) a working knowledge of Arabic. As these standards are proposed to apply to imams of mosques, so too they should be relevant to the qualifications of trained chaplains.

Chaplains

A recent and growing phenomenon on the American scene is the presence of Muslims serving in a chaplaincy capacity in educational institutions, the military, hospitals, and the prison system. Sometimes these people have imam status and sometimes not. Chapter 7 describes the activities of Muslim chaplains in American colleges and universities.

The 1990s saw the first several Muslim chaplains in the U.S. armed forces. The number of Muslim men and women currently serving in all branches of the U.S. military is estimated to be some twenty thousand, some of whom embraced Islam during the Gulf War and the invasions of Iraq and Afghanistan. Although only a fairly small number are actually identified as Muslim in military records, the several branches of the military are beginning to recognize the importance of providing assistance for Muslim men and women. In addition to attending to their spiritual needs, chaplains help create appropriate contexts in which Muslims can observe their faith through practice, diet, and dress, and they work to ensure the granting of appropriate rights.

In 1993 Captain Abdul-Rasheed Muhammad became the first commissioned Islamic chaplain in the U.S. Army, with the title of imam. Officially listed as chaplain to both Muslims and non-Muslims, he carried the responsibility for creating ways in which people of all religious faiths could practice their religion, although his primary work was with Muslims. Serving both male and female Muslims, he argued for the right of men to wear beards, for appropriate Islamic dress such as *hijabs* and *kufis*, for allowing women to wear modified uniforms during physical training for purposes of modesty, for special areas in which prayers can be said, and for the right to perform Muslim wedding ceremonies and burial services. "I think the Army bringing in an Islamic chaplain is a symbol of the increased sensitivity toward Islam," said Muhammad. "The armed forces have taken important steps to accommodate Muslim beliefs."[5] The second Muslim to be commissioned as a member of the Military Chaplains Corps was Lieutenant (Junior Grade) Monje Malak Abd al-Muta Ali Noel, Jr., of the U.S. Navy, appointed three years after Muhammad. Chaplain Noel received a master of divinity degree from the Lutheran School of Theology in Chicago, conferred jointly with the American Islamic College.

Thanks to the work of people like Muhammad and Noel, and aided by the continuing efforts of the Office of Armed Forces and Veteran Affairs of the American Muslim Council, Muslims in the armed services are allowed to observe the Friday prayer, to go to Mecca to perform *hajj*, and in general to practice their faith appropriately. During Ramadan 1998 the Pentagon hosted the first *iftar* meal for all Muslims on active duty in the armed services or employed by the Department of Defense. Women's dress remains an issue in the military, however, and in 1996 a female Muslim soldier was discharged, albeit honorably, after she refused to stop wearing the head scarf. Muslim women in the military are still not allowed to wear *hijab* under their military headgear. Currently there are only twelve Muslim chaplains in the military, of whom none is female. A fully qualified female U.S. Army major has been waiting for years for an appointment as chaplain, which does not seem to be forthcoming.

With regard to trained chaplains in the prison system, it is clear that far more are needed to meet the needs of a rapidly growing Muslim (primarily African American) inmate population. Department of Health and Human Services statistics reveal that prisons are in a state of crisis. The largest and most quickly growing ethnic group of American Muslims is African American, and within those the most explosive growth is among black inmates. According to one estimate the number of Muslim converts in prison exceeds 250,000. The current "war on terror" being conducted by the U.S. government is extremely disturbing to many of these inmates, with the result that they are susceptible to recruitment by extremist groups such as Al Qaeda that are present within the American penal system. In one famous case Chaplain James Lee, an army captain, was accused of passing secrets to Al Qaeda from prisoners held at Guantánamo. Eight months later the charges were dropped.

Some government experts fear that correctional facilities may represent a new U.S. front in the war on terrorism, referring to prisoners and former inmates who have ties to Islamic extremists.[6] The Department of Justice in 2006 put out this warning: "The potential for radicalization of prison inmates in the United States poses a threat of unknown magnitude to the national security of the U.S. Prisons have long been places where extremist ideology and calls to violence could find a willing ear."[7] Some have referred to the form of Islam unique to prison as "Jailhouse Islam," warning that it constitutes a significant threat to prison security. Chaplains teaching a moderate interpretation of Islam and providing more opportunities for prayer services could be effective tools in countering this potential threat. Islamic programming is underfunded, and there is a serious shortage of Muslim chaplains. Religious programs are desperately needed to provide both spiritual guidance and education and to advocate for other inmate services. Without a Muslim chaplain to educate new converts about correct Islamic doctrine, argues anthropologist Anna Bowers,[8] inmates become self-appointed religious leaders and the chances of exposure to more extremist views of Islam are bound to rise. Bowers recommends that prison staff be educated about Islam, that more Muslim chaplains be recruited, that funding be provided for outreach and reentry programs for inmates, and that research be done on the possible connection between involvement in a Muslim community upon release and the decreased likelihood of recidivism.

Currently there are ten Muslim chaplains working for the federal Bureau of Prisons, with many more affiliated with numerous state correctional institutions. A few states, like California and New York, have numerous positions because of the size of the inmate population (California alone had thirty full- and part-time chaplains in 2005). More lay Muslims are now coming to share in the responsibility for working with inmates. In many cases, Catholic and Protestant chaplains find themselves called on to minister also to Muslims, and they are trying hard to educate themselves about Islam as well as to find ways to provide religious materials for Muslim inmates. A Protestant chaplain working in a prison in New York State, for example, in 2007 completed a project in which he brought together Muslim and Christian inmates to talk about how they understood their own faith and that of the other.

Many local mosques and Islamic centers, including Sufi communities, are working actively with prisoners in their areas to provide support and instruction, members in some cases serving in the capacity of imams and chaplains. In a few cases, Muslim women work in female correctional institutions, providing instruction and counseling to female Muslim inmates

First Muslim Navy chaplain, Monje Malak Abd al-Muta Ali Noel Jr.
GEOFF LUMETTA/*THE WASHINGTON REPORT ON MIDDLE EAST AFFAIRS*

and helping them find Islamic solutions to the chronic problems of abuse, drug addiction, prostitution, and poverty that may have contributed to their incarceration. The Muslim Chaplains Association serves as the certifying body for professional chaplains. Its vision statement affirms its intention to be the leading membership organization for professional Muslim chaplains, integrating multicultural and multi-ethnic perspectives. The association provides spiritual counseling, working in partnership with similar organizations to train and support professional religious leadership.

Spreading the Faith (*Da'wa*)

Muslims in America feel a particular responsibility for the exercise of *da'wa*, which as we have seen means, literally, "calling" (to God, to faith, to Islam). It has been likened to the missionary efforts of Christianity and some other religions, although it has distinctive meanings within the Islamic context. For some, *da'wa* means the active business of the propagation of Islam with the end of making conversions, and a number of immigrant groups work regularly in the United States to disseminate the faith. For others, *da'wa* involves the effort to bring those who have fallen away from Islam back to active involvement in the faith. That may mean encouraging Muslims who are not observant or who participate only in the major holidays to pray regularly, attend the mosque, and pay *zakat*. And for still others, *da'wa* means the responsibility simply to live quiet lives of Muslim piety and charity, with the hope that by example they can encourage wayward coreligionists as well as others to believe that Islam is the right and appropriate response to God.

Many different arenas can support any of these interpretations of *da'wa*, including mosques and Islamic centers themselves, prisons, interfaith activities, schools, and universities. As Muslims become more self-conscious about the establishment and promotion of Islam in America, increasing numbers of books and journal articles are appearing on the subject of *da'wa*. Muslims often cite Qur'an 2:256, "There is no compulsion in religion," in support of their unwillingness to press for the conversion of others. Many of the immigrants who would have been less proactive about Islam in their home country, however, find themselves seriously involved in the identification and propagation of the faith in the West. "We have the primary task of Islamizing America. We have to carefully select our priorities, set achievable targets, and concentrate. . . . We have Allah's message, and a 250 million person-large target group."[9] Especially since 9/11 *da'wa* has become part of the effort to make Islam better understood, to lobby for political and other kinds of rights for Muslims, and to offer the Islamic lifestyle as a viable alternative to the perceived perils of American secular life.

Many of those who are classified as actively pursuing *da'wa* are influenced by the writings of such twentieth-century Muslim leaders as Abu'l-A'la al-Mawdudi of Pakistan and Sayyid Qutb of Egypt. They argue that the more Muslims there are in America, the more opportunities they will have to express their voice in public life, and the better chance Muslims in general will have to combat American prejudice against Islam. As with the spread of Islam over much of the world, Muslims involved in active propagation in America stress its rationality, the simplicity of its beliefs and requirements, its ethical content and emphasis on responsible living in this world, and its ideals of racial harmony and human brotherhood.

The propagation of Islam in America has ranked high on the agenda of a number of other Muslim countries. The Tableeghi Jamaat (Tablighi Jama'at) of the Indian subcontinent regularly sends itinerant missionaries to the United States and Canada to preach and practice *da'wa* through meetings and lectures, using local mosques as the base for their activities. The Jamaat is a movement of spiritual renewal that began in India in the early part of the century, attempting to imitate the practice of the Prophet's community in Medina. It began its missionary work in the United States in 1952 and since then has preached spiritual revival and social isolation, directed both to wayward Muslims and to those whom it hopes to convert. Urging Muslims in America to avoid any unnecessary contact with people who do not share its beliefs, the Jamaat preaches resistance to Western culture whenever possible and strongly opposes Muslim involvement in any kind of political activity save the propagation of the faith. A small number of mosques are directly affiliated with the Tableeghi Jamaat, although its influence extends considerably further. Tableeghi members are sophisticated in the use of new media techniques.

That some revivalist Muslim groups abroad have targeted American Muslims as the recipients of financial assistance has greatly aided the *da'wa* effort. The Salafiyya movement, associated with conservative Saudi ideology and strongly supportive of the establishment of *shari'a* law, claims to be non-political, though as conservative Sunnis its members take an active stance in attempting to denounce Shi'i movements in this country and abroad. American Shi'ites themselves, as has been noted, receive a great deal of attention through such institutions as the Kho'i Foundation, formerly under the leadership of Imam Kho'i from Najaf in Iraq. Such efforts, of course, illustrate not only the range of foreign-supported *da'wa* activities in America but also the traditional historical and geographical tensions and divisions in Islam now being played out in the West.

One of the richest fields for the propagation of *da'wa*, particularly but not exclusively among African Americans, is the prison system. In some senses, Malcolm Little's experience of finding Islam while he was incarcerated, and the way it truly changed his life, has been repeated in less dramatic ways in the lives of many hundreds of people over the last half century. Certainly, Malcolm's story is well known and influential among young blacks who hope to find in Islam a way to make serious changes in their lives. Their struggle to practice Islam while in prison has a number of interesting dimensions. On the one hand, the fight to achieve the freedom to express their faith appropriately, paralleling the struggle of members of the armed forces in terms of dress, space, diet, and opportunity, has been hard fought and is still not fully achieved. On the other hand, prison guards and other personnel, aware that Muslims who observe the discipline of the faith and stand by its moral code are less likely to "cause trouble" than other inmates, have often tried to support and encourage rather than obstruct their practice of Islam.

While exact figures are hard to determine, it is estimated that some 350,000 prisoners in U.S. correctional institutions are Muslims, most of them having converted to Islam in prison. A higher proportion of ethnic minorities is represented in the American prison system than in the population as a whole, including Hispanics and Native Americans as well as blacks. Estimates suggest that four-fifths of inmates who convert to any religion while incarcerated choose Islam. The particular appeal to African American inmates seems to be its egalitarianism, sense of brotherhood, and emphasis on self-discipline and devotion.

When a prisoner accepts Islam, he or she recites the *shahada*, or profession of faith, before witnesses in whatever facility of the prison is set aside for Islamic practice. In some cases, the appeal of a new identity is so strong that inmates wish to "take their *shahada*" well before they have a clear idea of what they are really professing. Part of the instructional effort in the prisons is to make sure that inmates receive an adequate introduction to Islam before they decide whether they wish to convert. Once the *shahada* is made, a number of things combine to ensure a new identity. Generally, one adopts an Islamic name and begins to wear whatever form of dress is allowed in a given facility. Acceptance into the community of those prisoners who are already Muslim is immediate, and the participation in communal prayers and other Islamic activities helps solidify the new convert's sense of identity and belonging. In some larger facilities, rows of Muslims can be seen praying together in exercise yards or in special rooms segregated from the rest of the prison complex. Many inmates spend hours every day reading the Qur'an as well as performing the obligatory and special prayers.

Personal modesty and cleanliness become of primary importance, as does one's general appearance, with all efforts made to demonstrate that one has entered the community of Islam. Many choose to give up smoking and use particular toiletries, such as aromatic oils, to enhance the image of Muslims as different from other inmates. Rigorous programs of study and prayer are designed to divert attention from any sexual temptations. Such disciplines are particularly important in maximum-security facilities to help maintain a sense of pride, worth, and belonging. Unfortunately a high proportion of inmates, whatever their religion or ethnicity, enter prison with some kind of substance addiction. Anti-addiction groups working with Muslim inmates have had encouraging success in rehabilitating addicts through emphasis on piety, repentance, and seeking God's forgiveness.

The growing numbers of trained imams and Muslim leaders active in the prisons, working with Christian and Jewish clergy to ensure equal opportunities for observance, encourage such study. The Islamic Society of North America (ISNA) sponsors an annual national conference on the subject of Islam in American prisons, bringing together people who have been involved in *da'wa* and assistance to the incarcerated. Presentations at the conference help workers introduce the message of Islam, lobby for improved opportunities to practice the faith, and develop techniques for rehabilitation, post-prison support, and finding jobs upon release.

Some inmates feel that the Islamic community at large is not doing enough to help address the plight of Muslims in prison. Nonetheless, significant efforts are being made, particularly among young Muslim converts in prison. The Junior Association of Muslim Men (JAMM), for example, was established at Sing Sing prison in 1994 under the leadership of Imam Warith Deen Mohammed. The first program of its kind, JAMM is designed to create a sense of responsibility in young Muslims, training them in the elements of Islam and providing tools for their reentry into society. Inmates under the age of thirty-five are targeted, along with others possibly interested in adopting Islam. The message is that Islam provides the structure through which they can transform their lives, and they can become leaders in society upon their release. JAMM, which forms a significant bridge between prison and community life, hopes to extend its activities to other penal institutions.

The struggle for the recognition of Islam as a religion that deserves constitutional protection has not been easy. For several decades, virtually the only Muslims in prison belonged to the Nation of Islam, considered by the state to be a dangerous racist cult. Since the 1960s the attempt simply to contain and manage Muslims in the prisons has gradually changed to recognition of religious liberty and a Muslim's right as an American citizen to practice the faith. Issues have been resolved primarily as a result of Muslim prison inmates' bringing these issues to court. Slowly, the courts have come to acknowledge that Islam is a faith that deserves the same constitutional safeguards as Christianity and Judaism. Muslims have fought for, and in many cases won, the right to have *halal* food, to wear beards, to gather for Friday prayer, and to observe the fast of Ramadan with *iftar* meals at the end of the day.

Many times courts have had to try cases in which Muslim prisoners have charged authorities with First Amendment violations of discrimination and even religious persecution, and in general the decisions have supported these charges. In a few penal institutions the creation of what has been called "Islamic space" allows Muslim prisoners to feel that their religion actually allows them to exist separately defined from their fellow inmates and in some senses from the institution in which they are incarcerated. In addition to having access to facilities for performing *salat* and being allowed to observe other basic elements of Islam such as food and dress, some are now studying the Qur'an and Arabic as well as the elements of Islamic finance in preparation for eventual financial autonomy. Many continue to argue that Muslim converts in the prison system still do not receive religious rights equal to those accorded Christians and Jews. That there has been great progress over the last several decades, however, is certainly acknowledged.

Studies indicate that the rate of recidivism, the return to crime and imprisonment, is lower among Muslims than other groups, although certainly the adoption of Islam is not a guarantee that incarceration is a thing of the past for an individual. Muslims have also demonstrated relatively greater success in rehabilitation from drug and alcohol addiction.

While programs designed for the support of newly released Muslim converts are not abundant, the American Muslim community shows growing awareness of the needs of former inmates and is developing initiatives to continue their education in Islam and to help integrate them into the community.

Islamic Organizations

Behind many of the efforts to facilitate life for Muslims living in America are the numerous organizations developed for the guidance and support of the community. The earliest movements toward such organization began in the middle of the twentieth century with the attempt to bring together for a national conference the small but growing number of mosques begun in various parts of the country. In 1952 in Cedar Rapids, Iowa, some four hundred Muslims representing the United States and Canada gathered with the intent to form a national organization. The idea for such a union came to one Abdullah Ingram, a Muslim serving in the American army during World War II. He was frustrated that the armed services did not recognize his identity as a Muslim, and no such notice could be made on his dog tag. After returning home, he began to work for the recognition of Muslims in America. After a second and third meeting, the Federation of Islamic Organizations was formed, with Ingram as its president and fifty-two mosques as members, mainly Lebanese and Syrian.

Later, under the expanded name Federation of Islamic Associations in the United States and Canada and assisted by funding from Saudi Arabia, the organization moved its headquarters to Detroit. The FIA played a key role in providing an umbrella of unity for American mosques in the middle of the century and was the first attempt to provide for conversation and collaboration among Muslims in the United States. After a series of national meetings, however, it gave way as the major American Islamic organization to other groups, among which the most influential was the Muslim Student Association (MSA).

The MSA was formed to strengthen national and international ties among Muslims of all national origins and ethnicities. Following the ideology of the Muslim Brotherhood of Egypt and the Jama'at-i-Islami of the Indian subcontinent, the group was created to provide a structure through which the Muslim student associations that had begun to appear on a number of American campuses could relate to one another. It soon developed into an agency with enormous influence in helping to redefine Islamic identity in America as something beyond national, ethnic, and linguistic allegiances. The first national conference, held at the University of Illinois in 1963, was attended by a variety of Muslims. These students brought with them numerous ideologies, all of them subsumed under the banner of Islam. Most of the students in America planned to return to their home countries as educated, informed, and influential participants in the process of furthering international Islam. An elaborate organizational structure was soon developed, with local chapters of the MSA established across the country, connected both nationally and regionally. Each year an annual convention was held, activities multiplied, and the influence of the association extended. Finally, in 1975 a national headquarters was set up in Plainfield, Indiana, with a general secretary and a significant support staff.

Under the general structure of the MSA, a number of subsidiary organizations have been established. The North American Islamic Trust (NAIT) handles financial matters, including investments, loans, mutual funds, book services, and the like. The Islamic Teaching Center (ITC) deals with matters related to the education of American Muslims through the development of publications and promotional literature, materials for da'wa, and other means of spreading information about the faith and practice of Islam. A series of groups emerged under the aegis of the MSA, focusing on the professional expertise of those who graduated and stayed on to become employed in the United States. Among them were the Islamic Medical Association (IMA), which held annual conferences to discuss different aspects of medicine and health; the Association of Muslim Social Scientists (AMSS), dedicated to connecting social science research and Islamic tradition; the Association of Muslim Businessmen and Professionals (AMBP), whose purpose was to provide links for Muslims in business and commerce; and the Association of Muslim Scientists and Engineers (AMSE). As the MSA grew and time passed, it was obviously no longer simply a vehicle for uniting student groups and working on college campuses; it had become the strongest Islamic structure in North America.

By 1981, after much consultation, a plan was put forward to establish an organization that would reflect the range of activities and interests of American Muslims that the MSA, originally designed to meet the needs of students, actually carried out. That organization has been known ever since as the Islamic Society of North America (ISNA). ISNA, in effect, has become the overseeing body for a great number of emerging Islamic organizations. These include local organizations devoted to community work in specific locations, campus student groups (still referred to as MSA, one of the largest and best connected of the Islamic groups), organizations designed to foster the activities of Muslim professionals and to the service of the Muslim community in America and abroad (such as the Muslim Community Association, and the very popular Muslim Youth of North America (MYNA). The overall organization is complex and expansive. Constituent groups function with their own boards and committees but are responsible overall to ISNA and its executive council, called the Majlis al-Shura. ISNA sponsors national weekend conferences each year, which draw large numbers of Muslims from the United States to hear speakers and to debate issues of ethical, social, and religious interest. Those who attend share common prayer and worship, meet and mix with Muslims from their home countries as well as other parts of the world, and experience a strong and reassuring sense of the strength and power of the Muslim community in America. Many youth participate in these national meetings and have an opportunity to talk with one another and with Muslim leaders about how to grow up with Islamic values intact. MSA itself also holds annual conferences for students across America.

ISNA activities range widely and attend to virtually every aspect of Islam in twenty-first-century America. Instruction and sometimes financial assistance are provided to local groups that wish to organize around particular issues of Islamic interest, and ISNA's national services include a great repertoire of instructional materials, workshops, library facilities, housing assistance, a marriage bureau operating a computerized database for matching partners, certificates for marriage and for taking the *shahada*, a *zakat* fund, *da'wa* literature, an Islamic book service and audiovisual center, the AMANA Mutual Trust Fund, and the ISNA women's committee. Among the journals published by ISNA are *Islamic Horizons*, the *American Journal of Islamic Studies*, and *Al-Ittihad*. ISNA is now headed by a Canadian woman convert to Islam, the first time a woman has held a comparable position in a national Muslim organization.

While ISNA is designed to be an organization of all American Muslims, some African Americans still perceive it as devoted primarily to the needs of members of the immigrant community. Imam Warith Deen Mohammed's followers in the Muslim American Society tend not to go to annual ISNA conferences but to hold their own national meetings to address topics of particular interest to African American Muslims. In some cases, blacks even feel that they are unwelcome and unappreciated by those involved in ISNA, although the identification of most African Americans with Sunni Islam is contributing to solving that problem.

Another national organization of Muslims, which has been present on the American scene for more than two decades but claims considerably fewer affiliates than ISNA, is the Islamic Circle of North America. Comprising primarily Indian subcontinent followers of al-Mawdudi, ICNA is known for its strict adherence to the spirit and the law of Islam, exemplified in its national meetings at which separate sessions are arranged for women. Most of ICNA's members are from the East Coast and Canada. While there are occasional tensions between ICNA and ISNA, increased efforts are being made to build bridges between the organizations. Representatives of each group generally attend the meetings and conferences of the other, and efforts are made to see that their respective conventions, workshops, and seminars are not scheduled in conflict with each other. ICNA focuses less on pressing social and political concerns than ISNA and more on the spiritual regeneration of American Muslims and the direction of youth to righteous living. Its primary publication is the monthly journal *The Message*.

An organization formed in 1993 specifically for the pursuit of *da'wa* in the United States is the Islamic Assembly of North America (IANA). Its stated goal is to gather all energies and potential resources, human and financial, to revive Islam and meet the needs of Muslims.

National Muslim women's organizations are growing rapidly in America. KARAMAH: Muslim Women Lawyers for Human Rights devotes itself to helping Muslim women understand and work for their legal rights. The North American Council for Muslim Women, headquartered in northern Virginia, and the Toronto-based Canadian Council of Muslim Women work to promote the welfare of American Muslim women. They host annual conferences on issues such as violence against women, law and policies applicable to women, youth concerns, and the like. Women work in nongovernment organizations (NGOs) and civic organizations, in the political arena and anti-defamation movements, and in religious activist groups. Some have grown up under the influence of national Muslim organizations such as MYNA (Muslim Youth of North America) and are now taking their place in the leadership of the American Muslim community. Women's organizations are vocal and enthusiastic participants in the efforts to bring about better understanding of rights, responsibilities, and opportunities within the Islamic context.

In addition, women are becoming connected on an international scale through such groups as IMAN, the International Muslimah Artists Network, created by and for Muslim women artists, and the World Council of Muslim Women Foundation, a nonprofit organization whose goals are the teaching of women's rights, global peace, and interfaith education from a worldwide perspective.

A great many organizations function at the national level to bring together special groups and to promote particular causes related to Muslim life in America. The North American Association of Muslim Professionals and Scholars (NAAMPS) is designed to attract Muslim intellectuals and scholars from different ethnic and cultural groups who are interested in discussing the challenge of Muslim community life in America. Some organizations are geared to particular ethnic and professional identities, such as the Association of Pakistani Physicians in North America (APPNA), offering its members opportunities to develop their organizational skills within an Islamic ethos. APPNA works to sponsor grassroots activities, such as free clinics for local communities, to emphasize that Islam teaches love and care for neighbors.

Sometimes aided by and sometimes independent of these national organizations, Muslims are forming groups at all local and regional levels. Islamic councils in many areas of the United States serve as organizing units for centers and mosques. In many cases, a membership fee for local congregations provides a budget for annual meetings and services such as financial assistance, family counseling, and support of international Muslim causes. Also developing at the local and regional levels are numbers of *shura* councils (consultative bodies). The Islamic Shura Council of New York, for example, evolved from a small study group of Muslim city leaders. Members of the council now meet monthly to work for the promotion of Islam, better prison conditions for Muslim inmates, drug control, and other forms of community service. Warith Deen Mohammed recently reactivated the Illinois Shuraa of Imams, calling it simply the Illinois Shuraa, to support the imams' ministry in the state. It supervises the work of a number of subcommittees headed by male and female Muslim leaders and works for the establishment of schools and mosques throughout the state.

Increasing numbers of organizations at both national and local levels concentrate specifically on the political arena. The American Muslim Council (AMC) in Washington, D.C., is a nonprofit, sociopolitical organization established in 1990 that works to promote ethical values among Muslims and to educate voters about the electoral process. It is interested in developing increased political power for Muslims. The AMC regularly puts on registration drives in coordination with local Muslim groups. Since 9/11 the AMC has been invited to host an annual 'eid al-fitr (breaking of the fast of Ramadan) celebration at the White House. The AMC is campaigning for official recognition of the two Islamic 'eids as national holidays, and is responsible for the issuing of the Muslim 'eid stamp by the U.S. Postal Service in 2002. The Muslim Public Affairs Council (MPAC) is a bipartisan organization that also concentrates on voter education, helping Muslims to understand how to make political decisions within the context of Islam. The MPAC is present at both political party conventions.

For a long time Muslims in this country had very little involvement with either local or national politics. Those from immigrant families often wanted to keep to themselves as much as possible, fearing that involvement in American political life might break the bonds of protection they were trying to forge around themselves and their children. African Americans have long been disillusioned with American politics anyway. Then in the year 2000, Muslims for the first time tried to vote as a national bloc, thinking that they now had enough numbers to influence the direction of national policies. The idea was good, though for several reasons the effort was not successful. The decision was made by a group of Muslims of immigrant heritage. African Americans were not included in the consultation, which resulted in some unfortunate ill feelings. The decision was to vote Republican, which did not sit well with a number of staunchly Democratic Muslim voters. And in the end the process backfired anyway, as the newly elected president, George W. Bush, who had promised to protect Muslim rights, ended up doing the opposite in the succeeding war on terror.

What the decision to try to organize politically did do, however, was to begin a serious engagement of American Muslims in national politics. Since then both men and women have been strongly encouraged to get out and vote, and even to run for political office. During voter registration time young people often stand outside mosques with sign-up sheets for those coming to the service. In 2007 Minnesota Democrat Keith Maurice Ellison became the first Muslim U.S. senator. He gained considerable notoriety for taking the oath of office by placing his hand on a Koran (Qur'an) previously owned by Thomas Jefferson. A few Muslim women have also run for public office. In 2002 an African American Muslim woman was elected to the Missouri House of Representatives, and other women focusing on local issues are trying to enter their states' legislatures. In 2004, in a highly publicized campaign, a female Democrat from California ran for the U.S. Congress, but unfortunately she lost.

Muslims have learned another lesson from 2000, which is the necessity of working on the local level to get elected. They understand that they have to be part of the political process from the ground up. The increasing participation of Muslims in American political life is seen as an affirmation of the essentially democratic nature of Islam, which they are trying hard to demonstrate to the general public.

In a range of different ways, then, Muslims are becoming a more visible part of the religious face of America. They are insisting that the facilities necessary for worship and religious instruction be there for public as well as private use, and that the requisite forms of trained Islamic leadership be available to the various institutions and people that need them. They are recognizing that it is to their advantage as individuals and communities to be as involved in the national political life as possible. It is clear that this movement for religious visibility is gaining momentum and that the coming decades will see more mosques, more imams, more chaplains, and more organizations dedicated to the practice and, indeed, the spread of Islam in the American arena.

CHAPTER SIX

Women and the Muslim American Family

As an American Muslim woman, I am free to decide what I want my own wedding to be like. . . . I'll make my own tradition—one that embodies *my own American Muslim ethnic culture*. You see, Islam allows for my full identity. And that's just one of the reasons why I am a Muslim.[1]

So says Asma Gull Hasan, an American Muslim of South Asian descent, speaking of her struggle with her family about whether or not to follow the traditions of their culture of origin when planning her wedding. Hasan and many other American Muslim women are attempting to show that they can follow the dictates of the Qur'an as well as be sensitive to familial expectations and at the same time experience the freedom to act and to define themselves in new ways. That freedom, for many women, extends from personal life circumstances to education to jobs to involvement in a great variety of organizations. Women and men across the country are increasingly turning their attention to the ways in which women contribute to the formulation of American Islam as they participate in the public as well as the private spheres of Muslim life.

Many of the arenas that traditionally have been open only to men are now considered legitimate for females as well. In the same way, those fields of operation that classically have been seen as women's domain, such as home and family, are in many cases understood in America to provide opportunities for shared participation and responsibility. In this chapter we will look at a range of concerns that both deal specifically with women's rights and roles and illustrate what seems to be a growing American movement toward cooperation and co-involvement as men and women raise families that reflect traditional Islamic values and are viable in the new American environment.

Roles and Responsibilities of Women

Educated American Muslim women are increasingly vocal in their insistence that Islam provides for equal rights and opportunities for women and men. While certainly not a new argument, this rhetoric is part of the post-9/11 Muslim defense when critics question the equality of women in Islam. In general, however, roles are seen as complementary rather than identical. In the case of more conservative Muslims, this balance may involve separation of the sexes in the public sphere. It is evident, for example, in the practice of men and women being separated in worship, meetings, and other public gatherings. While maintaining different space is certainly not mandatory, and many Muslims do not observe it, for others it signifies that women have as much right to define their own space as do men. Many women feel that such separation certainly does not curtail their vocal participation in public forums and discussions. "This is not forced segregation," commented a participant in a regional Muslim conference on women in New England. "Often we just feel more comfortable being able to relax with our friends, not worry if our knees happen to touch those of the person next to us, and enjoy a time of comradeship and even a little friendly gossip. Besides, if we object to what is being said we can do it as a block, or in small groups." Many other Muslim women and men, while supporting the idea of complementary roles, see little point in not having a free mixing of men and women in most public areas, although not in worship. To some extent, of course, their opinion is a reflection of class and culture. Upper-middle-class and upper-class urban immigrants generally take a more relaxed attitude toward gender mixing.

American Muslim women often invoke the "mothers of the faithful," as Muhammad's wives have been referred to, as models for their own behavior and professional involvement. Khadija, first wife of the Prophet and the owner of a successful camel caravan business, is cited as the earliest Muslim "businesswoman." 'A'isha, his beloved young wife, is said to have been the first female great religious and spiritual authority and the most important collector of traditions about the Prophet, and she was also the first female leader of a Muslim army. Attempts to relegate women to the private sphere, keep them from active professional and public involvement, and remove them from positions of religious authority are vigorously opposed as antithetical to the intentions of the Prophet and the way in which his early community functioned.

The Qur'an is cited as being fully egalitarian in its treatment of men and women, insisting that both have the same religious responsibilities in this life and affirming that both will be called to exactly the same accountability on the Day of Resurrection. Muslims generally insist that this equality represents a great improvement over the circumstances of women before Islam and that the Qur'an is a remarkably equitable document in comparison with the sacred scriptures of other religious traditions. They also acknowledge that there has been a great disparity in many cultures throughout the history of Islam between the opportunities for women outlined in the Qur'an and the ways in which women have actually been treated. America as a land of religious freedom is seen as the ground on which true Islam can again be realized.

Some non-Muslims, particularly Western feminists, point to a few verses in the Qur'an that they say indicate the inferior status of women. Muslims argue that it is necessary to understand such verses in the context in which they were revealed. Women inherit only half of what men inherit, for example, and the testimony of two women is equal to that of one man in a court of law. These injunctions are interpreted as viable because of the Muslim man's responsibility to take care of and provide for the woman. Some Muslims feel that *equity* is probably a better term than *equality* in comparing expectations for men and women and that the distinctions between men's and women's roles and the resulting differences in some of the responsibilities do not mean that one is better or more privileged than the other. More progressive voices can be heard saying that some of the passages suggesting what appears to be an inferior status for women must be interpreted in the light of new contexts and new roles for women. The one male prerogative that is generally not challenged is the right to serve as imam, or religious leader, of a worshiping Muslim congregation. The primary reason given for women's disqualification is menstruation, which renders them impure and thus unfit to lead the prayer. Women normally do not participate in religious activities, including fasting during the month of Ramadan, while menstruating, though they must fulfill any religious responsibilities for that month at a later time.

Increasingly, both women and men are insisting that women play a dynamic part in shaping American Islam. Even women with families are encouraged to find ways to participate and not use the excuse of responsibilities in the home to avoid their communal obligations. While there is little disagreement that Muslim women are allowed to have full professional lives (most American Muslims acknowledge and lament that women in some Muslim countries are still denied these opportunities), there is much discussion about what kinds of professions are appropriate and what family sacrifices, if any, should be made to allow a woman to maintain a full-time job.

Many women of immigrant origin note how much more difficult it is to work in the United States because here they do not have an extended family to help care for children. Reluctant to leave their children at a day-care center, women may choose to stay home with them while they are young to provide the family environment and support they feel is crucial for development during the early years. When asked if they would be more willing to use day care if it were run by Muslims "in an Islamic way," some say yes, while others still feel that being at home with young children is essential. Some professional women are willing to risk becoming dated in their fields of expertise, even jeopardizing their professional reentry, rather than leave their children to the care of those who are not family members. When elderly parents are in the home, often experiencing loneliness and isolation, added pressures are put on younger women to remain at home rather than go out to work.

There is little disagreement among American Muslims about the importance of adequate education for girls and women. As they often cite, the first word revealed by God to the Prophet Muhammad was "to read," the word also meaning "to recite." The modern expectation is that all Muslims, women as well as men, must be as well educated as possible. One argument in favor of education is that part of a woman's religious responsibility is to accept the challenge to expand her knowledge, and that God will ask her on the judgment day why she did not take advantage of all the opportunities available to learn. Another is that if women do not educate themselves, un-Islamic sexist and repressive customs will be allowed to continue. Implied is the assumption that what men will not do for women in terms of reform must come from their own initiative. Both women and men insist that the voices of women are necessary for *da'wa* and that women must be able to participate intelligently in the mutual consultation that is the ideal Islamic way of governing the community. Arguments about what subjects may be appropriate for women to study are still occurring in many parts of the world but do not seem to be a high priority among American Muslims.

Islamic Dress

One of the most controversial subjects in the American Islamic community is that of appropriate dress for religiously observant women. Clearly, this is a topic about which many women feel strongly, one way or the other, and about which they are interested in coming to their own determination, apart from the discourse of Western feminism or secular critique. Most

Muslims feel that it is appropriate for both men and women, as the Qur'an makes clear, to dress modestly. The issue is what constitutes modesty. (The Qur'an, despite what some Muslim women believe, does not clearly specify exactly how much of the body has to be covered.) The choice of how to dress is the woman's and cannot, or should not, be forced on her by males in her family.

Conservative clothing for women really began to reappear in various parts of the Arab world after 1967 and the devastating defeat of the Arabs (Muslims) at the hands of Israel. Political observers have noted that the defeat brought about much Muslim introspection as to what it means to live Islamically, to be assured of victory and success under God's guidance. Many women began to wear the *hijab* (head covering) after that time as a sign of their allegiance to Islam, and it soon became one of the manifestations of the so-called Islamic revival.

One of the main issues for American Muslims is whether all women must dress conservatively, or Islamically, to be considered good Muslims, and what, in fact, exactly constitutes such dress. The question has been particularly important since 9/11. Since that time more women in the United States have adopted some form of dress that signifies their affiliation with Islam. More-conservative women adopt clothing that covers everything except the hands and face and also wear a head covering. A very few choose to wear a full-face veil. Others may simply add a scarf completely covering the hair to their usual attire.

As issues of appropriate dress have become more prominent over the past several decades, especially but not exclusively for women, so they are reflected in the availability of many different kinds of Muslim clothing. Islamic dress can now readily be found in special stores and retail houses, and on many online sites. A range of products is available for women, from various kinds of *hijabs*, or headdresses, to embroidered dresses that reach the ankles and wrists, often with matching shoes. Sometimes these are for the business or daytime public sphere and are often featured in gray or tan tones. Other creations are designed for the world of full fashion. Most Islamic clothing businesses use the terminology of *jilbab* for an overgarment, *hijab* or *khimar* for the head scarf, and *niqab* for the full-face veil. Some companies feature women's clothing in a more India/Pakistan or Malaysian style, often called *shalwar khameez*, with loose trousers and tunics. One can purchase rings, earrings, pins, pendants, and other kinds of jewelry in gold or silver featuring Islamic inscriptions such as "*Allahu akbar*" ("God is greater"). For those who would like to dress more casually but still carry the message of their identity, custom-made Islamic and Arabic T-shirts are available for businesses, schools, and other organizations. The pictures of women in graceful garb portrayed in catalogs and magazine advertisements are often very alluring, and some Muslims worry that Islamic dress may sometimes be more a question of high fashion than of piety.

Many Muslim circles engage in a quite lively discussion about the role of Islamic dress in the success, or the lack of it, of women in the workplace. Some women insist that having adopted conservative clothing, they now feel free to enter fully into public life, secure in the knowledge that people will respect them as women of faith and piety. Some even argue that dressing Islamically makes it easier to move up in one's professional field. Many, however, cite the opposite experience. "When I was up for promotion," says a middle-aged Palestinian woman, "my boss called me in and said candidly that because of the public relations aspects of the new position it would be much better if I did not have to wear what he called 'that hat' all the time. I replied that the 'hat' was more important to me than the promotion, and I was not surprised when I didn't get it."

Some cite more blatant examples of prejudice, such as women who wear *hijabs* to work being called "ragheads" or "mops." Though such incidents may give pause to some professional Muslim women, they seem to energize others to be even more intentional about their dress.

Sometimes the discussion about dress centers on *when* rather than *whether* to adopt the *hijab*. Most young people who decide to dress Islamically do so in high school or college, although among a few Shi'ite groups girls as young as six or seven wear long dresses and head coverings. While some women believe that they will appear more attractive as marriage partners if they wear Islamic dress, others fear that men will think that they are too pious. Many Muslim women in America, of course, completely reject the notion that they should have to wear long sleeves and a scarf. Acknowledging that dressing as revealingly as some Western women do is inappropriate, they argue that modesty is a matter of judgment and that the mark of a good Muslim should be her behavior and not her appearance. An Egyptian woman who has lived in America for decades expresses the feeling of a number of American Muslims about wearing the veil: "At home," she says, "no woman in my family has worn a veil or head covering since the early part of the twentieth century. I find it very painful to come to this country and feel so much pressure to adopt a form of dress that feels just like that which it took so much courage for Muslim feminists to get rid of so many years ago."[2]

Women's Religious Practices

The role of women in the mosques is another issue that has received much attention from American Muslims. Until fairly recently most Muslim women in America did not attend the mosque. Some still do not, either because they are not interested in doing so or because they question the appropriateness of women in that space. In the immigrant community, the roles that women play institutionally to a large extent are still circumscribed by the cultural expectations of the countries from which they or their families originally came, and they may have little public religious activity.

Other women have been deeply involved in the activities related to organizing and establishing mosques for most of the history of American Islam, and both men and women are listed as founders of some of the early institutions. They often have played strong organizing roles and, not surprisingly, have been involved in the social side of mosque activities such as dinners, bake sales, and other occasions to bring people together. Today women are playing stronger and more visible roles in mosques than ever before. Some 15 percent of mosque attendees at Friday services are now women. Occasionally, though not often, a woman serves as president of the congregation. Approximately half of immigrant mosques allow women to serve on governing boards, as do most African American mosques. Since many American Muslims live away from the context of an extended family, the mosque often fulfills that social role. Mosques and Islamic centers are increasingly the locus of activity for the entire family, such as holiday observances and celebrations.

Muslims deal with issues of appropriate dress and location during the prayer service itself in a variety of different ways, according to the constituency and orientation of the mosque and the direction of its leadership. Women generally dress conservatively when participating in mosque activities, being particularly careful to cover their hair as well as their arms and legs. Many of the newly constructed mosques have separate entrances for women. Where women sit during the prayer is related to tradition, the inclination of the imam or other mosque leaders, and the mosque facility itself. Buildings converted to *masjids* may not have a place where women can be located separately during the prayers. A number of different models are currently used in American mosques, although the general rule is that men and women do not sit together in mixed groupings for worship. No matter what the configuration, the rationale is that the very physical nature of the prayer prostrations, with one's forehead sometimes touching the floor and one's rear parts elevated, necessitates the separation of men and women to avoid distraction from attention to God.

In more "liberal" *masjids*, men may be located on one side of the prayer hall and women on the other, equidistant from the front and perhaps separated by a low partition. Another possibility, based on what is understood to have been the practice in the Prophet's Medinan community, is for men to worship at the front of the prayer hall and women in the back. In a number of mosques, particularly those that are purpose-built, women move through their private entrance directly to facilities for performing ablutions and then to a second-floor balcony, where they gather with their children. Generally there is a railing of some sort over or through which they are able to look down on the imam and men assembled below. In more conservative mosques, women may be located in a completely separate room with no visual access to the main prayer hall. Here the actual prayer service is often broadcast on closed-circuit TV or over a loudspeaker so that the women can watch or listen and participate as they choose. It is estimated that two-thirds of the women who attend mosque services pray in some space separate from men.

Over the last few years there have been several efforts by Muslim women to defy traditional standards that they believe were determined by men and are disadvantageous to women. In 2003, for example, a young journalist named Asra Nomani gained publicity by going into a mosque in West Virginia using the men's rather than the women's entrance. She sat down in the men's section, and when asked to leave she refused. Her story generated a great deal of media coverage, which was short-lived. She went on to write a book, *Standing Alone at Mecca*, about her experience on the pilgrimage as a single woman.[3] The book contains her own "Islamic Bill of Rights for Women in Mosques," which she intended to help make mosques more accessible to women. Several mosques in California and elsewhere have also put forth efforts toward the greater inclusion of women.

The year after Nomani's attempts to change tradition, in New York City Amina Wadud, an African American scholar-activist famous for her groundbreaking work on the Qur'an,[4] became the first woman to lead a mixed-gender congregation and give the sermon at a Friday prayer service. Several mosques refused her request to host the service, and she finally held it at the Synod House of the Cathedral of St. John the Divine. The event, which has been accused of being a stunt to publicize Nomani's book, led to a lively international controversy, with correspondents around the world weighing in on whether or not what Wadud did was Islamically acceptable. While neither of these events led to much lasting change, a very few women have continued to break with tradition by engaging in such typically male activities as giving the *khutba* (Friday sermon) or performing a wedding ceremony. What is most appropriate for worship in America is under continuing discussion, and certainly refinements will continue.

In some cases women are making public their frustration at the perpetuation of what they see as inappropriate customs related to women's access. In 2008 a woman described the annoyance she felt when she and her non-Muslim mother and her children tried to enter a mosque in Colorado. They were told that there were no women in that *masjid* and that she would not be allowed to pray there. "As a Muslima," she said, "I felt humiliated and angry, and I was embarrassed for the Ummah. . . . Nothing like reinforcing negative stereotypes, is there?"[5] The author begins the online article in which she vents her frustration about this event by citing the well-known *hadith* from Imam Malik, "Do not stop the maid servants from going to the mosques of Allah!"

Meanwhile Muslim women are finding a variety of ways in which to participate in religious activities and to educate themselves in the Islamic arts and sciences. While they cannot serve as imams, some are serving different constituencies such as universities, prisons, hospitals, and the military as chaplains (see chapter 7). A number of women are attracted by the dancing and chanting involved in Sufi *dhikrs* (exercises for the remembrance of God), finding possibilities for personal engagement that go beyond the opportunities that are available in the mosque. Sufism has been a path that white American women have followed on the way to conversion to Islam. Many women fast during the month of Ramadan, and more are involved in the daily preparation of elaborate meals to acknowledge the breaking of the fast at the end of each day and the *'eid al-fitr* or holiday by which the community celebrates the conclusion of the month of abstaining. The daily *iftars*, where the fast is broken either privately in the home or sometimes in community in the mosque, since 9/11 have offered important opportunities for Muslims to share their customs and their faith with non-Muslim friends and acquaintances. More women are going on the *hajj* or pilgrimage than ever before, and some make the journey more than the required one time. Again, a return from *hajj* provides an excellent opportunity for Muslim women to talk with other women in their communities about what it means to engage in this "journey of a lifetime."

Shi'ite women have their own special religious duties and rituals, particularly during the month of Muharram. Prayers, lamentations, and fasting in that month and especially on the day of 'Ashura are considered highly meritorious. Recounting the sad tale of the martyrdom of their revered Husayn, grandson of the Prophet Muhammad, has traditionally been the role of certain Shi'ite women who are trained in the art of storytelling. As each stage of the drama unfolds the women, gathered together for these occasions, moan and weep for the loss of their beloved hero. This is the women's version of the reenactment of the drama of the battle of Karbala that is often carried out in Shi'ite mosques for all members of the community. Children watch in fascination as the battle lines are drawn and the audience participates with shouts and groans. Whether at the mosque or listening with their mothers to the storytelling, young Shi'ite children learn early how in some respects Shi'ite Islam differs from Sunni Islam.

Women in the United States are increasingly aware of the importance of their own religious education. In part this affirms their full participation in the community of Islam, including those realms that have traditionally been the arena of men's activities. It also provides women with the appropriate tools for doing the task of educational *da'wa*, sharing their knowledge about Islam with Muslim sisters and brothers and also helping non-Muslims to understand what Islam is all about. Using resources provided by mosques and national organizations such as ISNA and ICNA, as well as the many books and articles written about Islam and the amazing amounts of information found on the Internet, individually or in groups, women are advancing themselves significantly in the traditional Islamic sciences such as study of the Qur'an and traditions, *tafsir* or exegesis of the holy text, *tajwid* or recitation of the Qur'an, and knowledge of the main systems of Islamic law.

Women's study groups (*dars*, plural *durus*) are becoming very popular, sometimes referred to as *halaqas* or circles. First begun by African American Sunni women in the 1990s as Qur'an study sessions, they are now part of the practice of many women from immigrant families. Women gather at one another's homes, or occasionally at the mosque, to learn together under the leadership of someone (usually another woman) trained in the Islamic sciences. Sometimes these groups are composed of women of common ethnic identification, and sometimes they are mixed and serve the purpose of fostering an interethnic sense of community. Women enjoy the fellowship and share the freedom to talk freely with one another that they might not have were men present. "I feel empowered," said one frequent attendee at a circle in the Washington, D.C., area. "It is as if we are taking Islam into our own hands."

Marriage and Divorce

Marriage is of great importance in Islam, so much so that traditional societies have not had a place for the unmarried man or woman. That importance continues in the West, although circumstances dictate changes from traditional patterns.

By Islamic legal stipulation, Muslim men are free to marry Jews and Christians, on the understanding that the male head of the household determines the religion in which the children will be brought up. Muslim women, on the other hand, are not permitted by law or custom to marry anyone but another Muslim. The potential lack of marriage partners makes the situation difficult for young women in America, who sometimes break with these prescriptions and customs. In some circumstances families of eligible young Muslim women have had to look to their home countries to find suitable husbands.

The conviction of many families that they do not want their daughters to date or socialize with available men stems not only from a desire to protect them (from the possibility of premarital sex) but also from fear that dating will inevitably lead to greater instances of intermarriage. Often parents put pressure on their children to marry not only other Muslims but also to select their husbands strictly from within their particular ethnic or cultural group, a situation that further complicates the marriage issue. Some Anglo Americans who have converted to Islam, for example, are frustrated in their attempts to marry immigrant Muslim women because the families of the women will not permit it. "What can I do?" asked one young white convert. "I want to marry a Muslim, but I'm not Palestinian or Indonesian or Turkish. How do I find a wife?" On the whole, African American, Latino/Latina, and other ethnic minority Muslims tend to marry within their own groups.

Marriages between Muslim men and Christian women, while legally permitted, often encounter serious problems despite the best intentions of the two parties and sometimes even when they have the support of their families. One of the most difficult realities is that marriage in the American context generally means a union of two individuals, with the families somewhat incidentally and rather uncertainly joined only for family occasions. For Muslims, however, marriage is still seen as the union of families, with parents or other relatives traditionally making all of the arrangements. While these so-called arranged marriages are now less common in urban areas of Islamic countries, many immigrant families bring with them expectations that hamper the contracting of marriage in the United States between Muslims and non-Muslims.

Premarital counseling is beginning to play a role in American Islam. A few years ago, for example, the imam of the All Dulles Area Muslim Society in Sterling, Virginia, began to require such counseling of everyone who wanted to get married at his mosque. A few similar programs are getting started, focusing on issues such as interfaith marriage, knowing one's partner before the wedding, and what constitutes a wali—a person who is supposed to help a woman pick the right husband. New York activist Daisy Khan counsels couples along with her husband, an imam, especially those who want to enter into interfaith relationships. Khan prefers to connect Muslim couples, but recognizes that in American society a woman may need to marry outside the faith or remain single.[6] Issues relating to marriage are on the agenda of the Muslim Alliance in North America, a national group consisting mainly of African Americans whose first national conference, in 2008, featured marriage as one of its main topics.

Many young Muslim men are convinced that they want a marriage of equality in which both partners share responsibility for home and family and both contribute financially to the family budget. Then they begin to feel pressure from other Muslims in the mosque or in their community who may not agree with these contemporary American liberal standards. Or these men may return home for an extended visit, wherever home originally was, and without realizing what is happening they may slip back into the old ways of doing things. Such occurrences happen often enough to warrant some serious forethought, and they suggest again the importance of premarital conversation and advice.

Traditional relationships between men and women within the family structure are under a great deal of scrutiny in America. One of the most highly debated verses in the Qur'an is Sura 4:34, often cited to affirm male authority: "Men have authority over women, because God made the one of them to excel the other, and because they spend of their property [for the support of women]. So good women are obedient. . . . As for those on whose part you fear insubordination, admonish them and banish them to beds apart, and beat them."

As the verse is traditionally interpreted, Muslim men are to be financially responsible for women. Thus, either her husband or some other male relative must see to a woman's material needs. At least in theory, this verse ensures that a woman will always be taken care of, and Muslims are eager to point out that the American reality of so many single women, and single mothers, living below the poverty line with no men to support them would be inconceivable in the Islamic system. The rub is, this financial responsibility means that final decision making lies with the man. Many Muslim women who think about the matter seriously, even in the American context, consider that this is a small price to pay for security. A young Egyptian was asked by an American friend, "Doesn't it really annoy you to think that your future husband will have the last word?" "Yes," said the Muslim girl, "it is frustrating. But I honestly think that if you don't make a big deal out of it, finally it is the only system that works." But many contemporary Muslims, especially those raised or educated in the American context, are challenging the question of final authority. "Muslims are simply having to figure out new kinds of interpretations that respect the integrity of the Qur'anic text but allow for the kind of give-and-take that Western women generally insist on," says columnist Michele Boorstein. "And the fact is that in most Muslim marriages today, whatever lip service is given to male authority, the woman knows exactly how to exert power, as she has always known."[7]

Although "beating" seems to be allowable in the last part of this Qur'anic passage, no reputable Muslim interpreters would suggest that it should involve anything more than the lightest of taps as a reminder to the wife of her conjugal responsibilities. Never can this legitimately be cited as justification for wife beating, although Muslim men, like Christian and other men, have on occasion resorted to such measures. Domestic violence has been very little discussed in the American Muslim community until recently. Now there is more public recognition that domestic violence in Muslim families is on the rise, although Muslims profess that they are less culpable than non-Muslims. Articles in Muslim journals encourage their readers to face the reality of increasing violence, understand the stress factors that contribute to it, and work for its elimination. "Only a strong Islamic character, that condemns anger and emphasizes tolerance and compassion," writes one journalist pleading for Muslim attention to this potential problem, "can reduce the tendency toward violence."[8]

Americans who are not Muslim have always had difficulty with the justification for what they understand to be the Islamic sanction of polygamy or, more technically, polygyny (the taking of more than one wife). Muslims explain that, indeed, the Qur'an does specify that under certain conditions a man may marry up to four wives. It stipulates, however, that the husband must treat each of his wives as equal to all the others. Many modern commentators on the Qur'an have interpreted that requirement to mean that God really does not want a man to marry more than once or he would not have levied such a difficult stipulation on multiple marriages. Others point out that at the time when the Qur'an was being revealed, women were losing their husbands in battle. The injunction to take up to four wives, they argue, was out of charity to these husbandless women. Some American Muslim women, as is true of their educated counterparts in other countries, understand that it is their prerogative to stipulate in the marriage contract that the husband may not take a second wife.

Multiple marriages are generally not an issue in America for the simple reason that they are prohibited by law, although they are also not unknown. Nonetheless, the matter is not irrelevant in this Western context, and some women still express fear that they may find themselves one of several wives. "Dear [Islamic counselor]," writes one worried wife in an advice column. "My husband has confided in me that he would like to take a second wife . . . that he would like for us to help a widowed woman and her sons by his getting married to her." The writer confesses that she feels guilty because she is sorry for the other woman but does not want to share her husband. What, she asks, should she do? The counselor responds that because polygamy is illegal in the United States, the husband cannot take a second wife, and the husband's concern for the widow's welfare must be balanced by concern for the mental welfare of his own wife.[9] Muslims sometimes counter Western ridicule of polygyny with the accusation that more Americans have multiple wives than Muslims. The difference, they say, is that Americans take their wives in serial order, through divorce and remarriage.

Islamic journals publish articles on the elements of a good Islamic marriage, what potential partners should be looking for, and the importance for both parties of a well-thought-out and reasonable marriage contract. Marriage is a legal arrangement in Islam, not a sacrament as in the Christian sense, and is secured with a written contract. Female advocates and others are prompting young women to be wise in their insistence on such a contract as an essential component of a truly Islamic marriage, urging them to see that a carefully crafted contract can be an effective deterrent to future problems in the marriage. The importance of *mahr* or dowry as essential to a valid Islamic marriage contract is also stressed. Challenging the traditional understanding of *mahr* as a kind of bride-price, they insist rather that it is the element of the contract that makes clear the conditions by which a woman is willing to engage in marriage. Many young Muslim women, while accepting the importance of this contractual element, are using it as a way not only of providing security for themselves but of ensuring a fair and equitable basis for marriage by insisting that the amount not be more than the male can easily afford.

In traditional Muslim cultures marriage is negotiated by families, though this practice is undergoing significant change and rethinking in many Islamic societies today. Some immigrant groups in the United States still adhere to arranged marriages, although with subtle differences from traditional expectations. Such customs vary with the length of time that immigrants have been in the West. Younger women generally refuse to accept such an arrangement, insisting that they are capable of making their own choice or that God will lead them to an appropriate union. In a few recent cases, however, youth are expressing their concern that they see marriages in the United States as too unstable, and are wondering if going back to arranged marriages might, in fact, not have some merit.

Matrimonial services are provided by many of the major Islamic organizations. The annual national conventions of the Islamic Society of North America, the Islamic Circle of North America, the Muslim Student Association, and various professional associations are sometimes often referred to as "meat markets," where young Muslims can get to know each other in structured situations. At some professional meetings, for example, girls' parents can showcase their daughters while parents of the potential grooms weigh the choices. Dozens of Web sites offer matchmaking services to Muslim women and men, providing chat rooms where singles can get to know each other. Muslim women, young and not so young, may spend months chatting with men online, exchanging comments and information and determining whether or not they might want to change their electronic relationship to a more personal one. In addition to exploring opportunities on the Internet, many Muslims look to the matrimonial sections of popular monthly and quarterly journals.

Young men and women, or sometimes their parents acting on their behalf, can post their own credentials and their hopes for qualities that they would like to see exhibited in their mates. "Young man of Pakistani heritage, full-time professional, seeking educated young woman, aged 20–25, light-skinned, Islamically observant and enjoys homemaking." Once a contact is made, the two parties (or their families) may decide that they would like to carry on a courtship. For those who want to honor traditional cultural practices, Islamically appropriate ways for potential mates to meet and get acquainted can be set up, including the use of chaperones. Other young people may simply arrange to get together and decide whether or not to see each other again.

There is a consensus among Muslim religious leaders that Western-style dating is forbidden, some even saying that voice contact through telephone conversations is sexually arousing for the man. Matrimonial Web sites are therefore gaining acceptance even among more conservative Muslims. Electronic communication gives single adults some degree of control over their relationships at the same time that they are operating within accepted cultural and religious boundaries, and it also can allow for the participation of their parents should the relationship flourish.

American Muslims are also paying more attention to the matter of divorce. They are quick to note that while Muslims are often accused of "easy divorce," statistics among Muslims worldwide show a much lower rate of separation than among Western Christians. Nonetheless, the fact that many men in the history of Islam have rid themselves of unwanted wives by uttering what is called the triple *talaq*, or divorce, has without question been an affliction for many women. While considered a reprehensible practice, it has been possible for a husband simply to say three times in a row, "I divorce you, I divorce you, I divorce you." According to Islamic law, practices are not just required or forbidden but fall into grades of acceptability and non-acceptability. This triple divorce, while historically common, is legally barely acceptable in most modern states. American Muslims know that the Prophet Muhammad deemed divorce in any case to be the worst of solutions, one that is to be avoided at almost any cost.

The question is often asked whether the husband must initiate the divorce or if a wife, who for whatever reason cannot stand living with her husband anymore, can initiate divorce proceedings. While the system may seem to favor the man, who can divorce at will although certainly not with license, a woman does have recourse in the termination of a marriage if there is good reason. The problem for many women, especially those who are not educated, is that they simply do not know their rights. In many Muslim countries, helping women understand their legal prerogatives has been identified as an important task. Another deeply problematic matter for the divorced women in many cultures has been the fate of the children when divorce occurs. The four major schools of Islamic law, while differing on the age of the child, eventually give custody of both sons and daughters to the father. Like everything else, however, these stipulations are subject to the modifications of American civil law and are often interpreted differently in the Western context.

Children and Youth

As is true of Muslim cultures across the world, having children is a matter of great importance to Muslims living in America. While certain realities such as the employment of the wife may place constraints on the number of children a couple will decide to have, to be childless or even to have only one child is often considered a deep disappointment to the larger family. Children are very much a part of the family from birth and accompany their parents outside as well as inside the home as often as possible. At most social occasions, in the women's section of the mosque, or even in group meetings and conferences, children are present and occupy themselves by playing around their mothers. Muslims use babysitters only when they absolutely have to, believing that the more their children are with them the better they will understand, and feel a part of, family and community events. The occasional disruptions caused by children's squabbling, crying, or making demands on their parents are generally seen as normal and perfectly acceptable. On the whole, Muslim children are well behaved and learn at an early age how to amuse themselves in public and social gatherings that may keep them up past their usual bedtime.

How to raise children in American society and culture is an ongoing concern to all Muslim parents. Deeply worried about the influences of American television, for example, many families have strict rules for the number and kind of shows their children may watch, and they try to find acceptable alternatives. Muslim organizations and businesses are helping parents in both the entertainment and the instruction of their children in the home context by producing a rapidly growing number of games, videos, and other Islamic products that allow for the family to interact together in an Islamically oriented atmosphere. Mothers looking for ways to both educate and entertain their children can choose from a wide selection of Islamically sponsored products. Fine Media Group (FMG) introduces movie hits of the year for children and family entertainment. For those who want to engage in family activities, a variety of games and puzzles is available, all with Islamic themes. Families can construct three-dimensional models of the Ka'ba in Mecca (fully assembled models are more than a foot high and two feet wide), quiz each other about Islamic history or facts of the faith, or play Islamic card games. Mission: Survival is an educational adventure game designed to preserve Islamic identity, cope with societal challenges, and reinforce Islamic values. And for little girls unable to resist the Barbie doll phenomenon, NoorArt says, "Move over, Barbie! Razanne is here." Razanne, according to the ad, means a woman who is beautifully modest and shy in the best Islamic manner, "a doll that is 'just like Mom'—one who could serve as a role model for young Muslims." Razanne is twelve inches tall and wears a solid color *jilbaab* (robe) and a white *hijab*. The scarf is removable so that the child can practice the correct way of putting it on. The doll comes in three skin tones—white, tan, and dark brown—to appeal to different racial-ethnic groups. She also can be purchased dressed as a Muslim Girl Scout, a teacher, or one of several other professionals. An African American Razanne is ready to demonstrate the positions of prayer.

Many Muslim parents discuss with one another ways to reinforce Islamic identity in their young children and teenagers. Interaction with non-Muslim children and youth is both inevitable and, in the view of most Muslims, a good thing. But it can lead to difficulties if the young people of the community do not possess the tools to help them understand their differences and see them as a matter of personal pride and significance. As children reach the teenage years, issues of identity become more complicated for young Muslims. Sometimes they may feel some pressure to live double lives. Comfortable with their Muslim identity at home, and at least reasonably willing to conform to the expectations of their elders while with relatives, they may find it tempting to drop that identity in the more public aspects of their lives, especially as they socialize with friends who are not Muslim. Some girls may even leave home wearing Islamic head covering with the intention of removing it when out of sight. Others, of course, find that they want to adopt the *hijab* when they see their friends wearing it. This is especially true of college girls who have become active in local MSA chapters since 9/11. Muslim journals are eager to report the testimonies of young women who insist that they find the *hijab* a source of pride and distinction when they do wear it to school.

Sometimes the different expectations of private and public come into direct conflict, as, for example, when Muslim young people want to date and attend social functions sponsored by their schools or private parties given by non-Muslim friends. Muslim parents whose children still live at home struggle with how to respond to these issues, and again the answers range widely. Some simply refuse to allow either boys or girls to socialize outside the home or mosque community, with varying results. Others, more willing to accommodate the American social system, hope that the Islamic values they have instilled in their children will shield them against inevitable temptations. They espouse a more moderate view of social interaction for boys and girls, yet still do not allow their daughters to date or in general to participate in out-of-school activities. Some young people, however, rebel against this restriction, feeling that it is prejudicial in favor of boys. "Most of the Muslim girls I know are like me and not allowed to date or even to go to social activities at the school like dances or parties," complains a Pakistani teenager. "Our parents don't seem to notice when the boys go out, but the door gets locked even when a group of girls wants to go to the mall together or something." That girls in Islamic society have always been highly protected is a legacy that has both positive and negative repercussions for young American Muslims.

Some families take a more "integrationist" view, questioning why they should have come to this country at all if they are simply going to hide from it. They argue that Muslims have to learn how to live *in* America and to deal with it as it is, rather than trying to find ways to circumvent it. Children should be given solid training in Islamic morality in the home and the mosque insofar as is possible, they say, and then they should be trusted to use their good judgment when interacting with friends in the public school. Some even insist that girls should be allowed to date after a certain age, although this remains a highly controversial topic among most American Muslims.

Alternative means of socialization are being developed both locally and nationally, providing opportunities for youth to meet and get acquainted that do not involve the dating process per se. Mosques and Islamic centers feature activities for mixed groups of chaperoned youth, bringing them together through service opportunities or social encounters. Organizations such as Muslim Youth of North America (MYNA), sponsored by the Islamic Society of North America (ISNA) invite youth to conferences, summer camps, and other activities in which they interact with members of the opposite gender, but not in all activities and with carefully selected adult chaperones. Each summer young people from across America gather to meet one another, hear speakers of prominence, and talk about issues of common concern. These meetings provide an opportunity for young Muslims to socialize "in an Islamic environment." Many of the activities planned for Muslim youth are designed to provide opportunities for them to meet eligible marriage partners. Often the youth stress the things they have in common, affirming the importance of being Muslim together in America and rejecting their families' attempts to focus on ethnic identities that separate rather than join them. MYNA emphasizes the benefits of recreation, and youth are instructed in the appropriate activities for girls and boys, young men and women. The organization also sponsors seminars and retreats throughout the year, as well as winter conferences during Thanksgiving and Christmas breaks.

Numerous other opportunities fill the time of young Muslim Americans. An increasing number of public high schools are organizing Islamic clubs for their students, providing friendship and support in a common context. The Islamic Assembly of North America provides summer interns with travel, lodging, and expenses to give them the opportunity to work with the IANA staff and learn professional and organizational skills. Muslim Boy and Girl Scout troops organizing across America are particularly attractive to young African Americans, especially those from the inner city. Young Muslims (YM), an organization of the Islamic Circle of North America based in Jamaica, New York, provides a network for youth across North America who are active in the propagation of Islam among their peers. In a slick brochure featuring a canoe and paddles, the organizers of YM urge prospective participants to "get in the boat and grab the oars as you make the journey through the currents of life. . . . One must gather the oars of Al-Qur'an & Sunnah to maneuver past the dangers and reach the harbor of Jannah [heaven]." Organizations such as the Muslim Arab Youth Association (MAYA), affiliated with ISNA, have sponsored regional meetings and annually bring together Muslim youth to talk about Islamic law and its implications for their lives, issues of marriage and social life, Islamic culture, and many other topics related to participation in the community of Islam.

Behind all these efforts is the hope that Muslim youth can see Islam in positive, enlightened ways rather than as something shameful or as something that keeps them from enjoying their teen years as they see other young people apparently enjoying theirs.

Many Muslim families who choose to make mosque participation part of their family activity are experiencing the same problems in keeping young people interested in learning about their religion as Christians and Jews are facing in America. "I just can't see why what some old guys said centuries ago is still so important for us," argued one thirteen-year-old to his parents. "They didn't live in America! They didn't face the kinds of issues we are facing! I don't mind the social activities in the mosque, but going to the classes and listening to the sermons is just unreal." Here we see the jarring collision of old and new, of youth and the elder generation, of former cultural associations and the challenges of Western society. Muslims struggle to keep their families religiously intact and their youth involved, as they look to the mosque both for communal affiliation and for sophisticated forms of religious education. In that effort they have much in common with people in other religious traditions in America. Some inevitably choose to move away from mosque life and adopt more secularized forms of Islamic identity.

Care of the Elderly

Muslims are keenly aware of the concerns facing their families in terms of care of the elderly. Living in a different situation from the extended family in which they were raised, many Muslims of immigrant origin do not have the support of large numbers of relatives nearby. If husband and wife are both working, an elderly parent may find himself or herself alone for long periods of time, and may be exceedingly lonely. This isolation, of course, is exacerbated when elderly immigrants speak little English and thus do not find much comfort in watching television or listening to the radio. Many of America's older immigrants have come originally from situations in which they were actively employed, but in their new life they do not work outside the home and feel isolated and often quite useless. If they cannot drive, they may feel trapped in the home.

Worse, families arriving in refugee status with little skill in English often do not understand and thus are not able to access the American health care system. The elderly, who are often the ones most clearly in need of medication and health care, are completely cut off from assistance until the younger members of the family master the system and are able to get access to health care for their elders. Churches and other institutions working to rehabilitate Muslim refugees recognize the vital necessity of helping as many members of the families as possible to gain basic language skills.

Mosques and Islamic centers are beginning to understand the importance of providing special services for the elderly. Some organize activities to bring together members of the older generation to socialize and feel welcome in an Islamically defined space. This effort may involve providing special transportation. It is often the elderly, particularly those more recently arrived in America, who feel the sharpest pain at the anti-Muslim prejudice they experience through the media. Participation in the mosque offers them at least a temporary refuge from loneliness and social isolation. Imams increasingly have to assume roles similar to those of Christian pastors, sometimes making "house calls" to the parents of people who are active in their mosque congregations. Individuals and programs also focus on advising elderly people about such matters as health care, finances, and nutrition.

Elderly parents, certainly those who still follow the norms of the cultures in which they were raised, expect to live with their adult children, most normally with the son and his family. And whenever possible, Muslim families try to meet that expectation. There are, however, obvious problems. Often families with limited incomes have very little extra space in their homes. The traditional role of the mother-in-law as "boss" of her son and especially of her daughter-in-law meets with scant approval in most American-oriented families. In many cases, however, grandparents in the home provide a wonderful source of support and identification for the children. Many adults busy outside the home rely on elderly parents not only to provide babysitting services but also to give foundational instruction in what it means to be Muslim. On the other hand, the elderly are sometimes so baffled by aspects of American culture that they appear to be disapproving of the dress, activities, and worldviews of the younger generation. The pressure not to "Americanize" that teenagers may feel from their grandparents can lead to tensions between the generations and even greater feelings of loneliness on the part of the elderly.

African Americans, especially those in urban areas, have long struggled with the problem of broken homes and disappearing fathers. Becoming Muslim may not mean that the problem is left behind. Grandmothers are called on to take care of children while the mothers are at work. They may understand American culture better than their counterparts in immigrant generations, but that does not necessarily ease the pressures of trying to raise children to be good Muslims, good citizens, and good family members. African American Muslim organizations that are trying to support family structures and help keep the males home and responsible for their duties to their wives, children, and parents are recognizing the crucial importance of appropriate care for the elderly.

The initial response of most Muslims to the growing American custom of moving elderly relatives into retirement homes or even nursing homes is denial, shock, and anger. It is not the Islamic way, they insist, to isolate older people and deprive them of the fellowship of the family. "I would never dream of putting an elderly relative in a nursing home," says a first-generation immigrant. "I do not believe, whether you are Muslim or not, you should put your parents in a nursing home—unless, God forbid, they are seriously ill and need the care of a professional person."[10] Still, as families face the realities of having two working adults away from the home for a long period each day or of their inability to meet the health care needs of the aging, as well as the simple fact that people are living much longer than previously, Muslim groups are trying to find Islamic solutions. A few of the larger centers are constructing special housing for older Muslims near the mosque so that residents can experience greater community support.

The July 26, 2008, issue of the magazine *Islamic Horizons* was devoted to a study of aging Muslims in America. Here the problems faced by families with aging parents are addressed directly: "In some Muslim families elder parents are admitted to nursing or senior citizen homes, and children don't have the time to visit. There are other instances where no next of kin showed up when a Muslim senior citizen died in a hospital."[11]

The literature coming from national organizations and publications reminds Muslim individuals, families, and communities that just as children must have constant care, so too older people need as much love and attention as can possibly be given. "Just as helpless infants need parents, older people need their children to give constant loving care," says one health care expert. "An infant cannot explain its needs in words. Elders also experience many moments when they find it difficult to express their needs. It is up to the care-giver to search out the real needs of those he serves. Elders need love and compassion, therefore, it is important that the community adopt older citizens who do not have willing children."[12]

New Horizons for Women

While bearing the inevitable responsibility of taking care of their children, their parents, and others in their families, as well as reaching out to new forms of religious practice and community participation, Muslim women in the United States are becoming visible on other fronts as well.

Organizationally they have come into their own. The Islamic Society of North America now has Ingrid Mattson as its president. Mattson, a professor at Hartford Seminary in Connecticut, is the first woman ever to hold elected national office in a major Muslim organization. Only a few years ago the national Muslim Student Association elected its first woman leader. National and local organizations created and run by and for women are burgeoning, many of them maintaining Internet connections with corresponding organizations abroad. Some of the organizations are professional, providing connections among working women, but many others are intended as service providers, helping women with everything from counseling to health care to knowledge of Islamic law. "Women working together have always gotten things done, while the men just sit and talk," commented a visitor from

Ghana recently. Whether it can be said of American Muslim men that they only sit and talk is questionable, but certainly the former is being proven every day.

It takes only a few taps of the computer keys to discover the world of new American art being created by Muslim women across the country. They work in a huge range of media, from painting to silverworking to tapestry to pottery, creating and marketing their products, which usually combine a theme from a Muslim culture with some of the realities of living in America. Women are novelists, playwrights, poets, and creators of a variety of different kinds of film and video scripts.

In 2002 *Azizah*, the first journal specifically for Muslim women, was initiated. Designed to present the issues, accomplishments, and interests of Muslim women in North America, the journal contains pictures and articles on topics ranging from beauty to health to helping refugees to get settled in the United States. Each issue features on its cover a woman in Islamic dress, the many different styles showing how many ways there are for women to dress according to their faith (and still, of course, be very stylish!). *Azizah* has been criticized for consistently following this pattern, but as editor and founder Tayyibah Taylor retorts, what other journal in America is going to have a Muslim woman on its cover?

Women are writing for other women, for Muslims in general, and for American consumption. They are courageously addressing issues of health, family violence, education, politics, and a great number of other topics that they think need finally to be brought to public attention. Even teenage girls are getting involved in writing. *The American Muslim Teenager's Handbook*, written by Dilara, Imran, and Yasmine Hafiz, won CAIR's 2007 "Outstanding Youth" Award.[13] It provides a paperback guide to the essential beliefs and practices of Islam, including questions and comments from Muslim teens across the United States. The book includes information about prayer and pilgrimage, suggestions as to how to read the Qur'an, and discussions about controversial issues such as dating, dancing, drinking, and drugs (which it labels "the 4 'D's").

These, then, are some of the issues and concerns that Muslim women in America face as they consider their rights and roles, work for the establishment and maintenance of sound family structures, struggle to raise and support their children and provide for the needs of those who are reaching the end of their more productive days, and maintain active lives beyond the family structure. While many women remain uneducated, unemployed (although working long hours in unpaid occupations), and uninformed about their Islamic rights, others are speaking and writing articulately about their roles as participants in what they see as a new American *umma*, giving fresh and exciting interpretations to material from the Qur'an and the traditions that are classically understood to isolate women from the public realm. Encouraged to claim their rightful roles in the public functioning of the community, they are actively advocating for women's participation in politics and government as well as in the more traditional realms of education and home care.

Muslim women in America are subject to influences from a great many directions. Some are persuaded that the conservative traditions in which they have been raised still offer the most appropriate understanding of how they should behave and what roles they should play. Others hear and are deeply influenced by the exciting new interpretations coming from various areas of the Muslim world or have themselves made those contributions in different contexts before coming to America. They are increasingly raising their voices in conversations about what is most appropriate and effective for American Muslim women. While initially many Muslim women found feminist discourse elitist, racist, and irrelevant to their concerns, many more attempts are now being made by Muslim and non-Muslim women to engage in conversations that are mutually enriching and beneficial.

Women continue to push at the margins of what is considered Islamically acceptable, in their actions and in their interpretations. The first "feminist" translation of the Qur'an, for example, has been done by Laleh Bakhtiar, associate editor of Kazi Publications in Chicago. Trained in philosophy, psychology, and religious studies, Bakhtiar has used some of the methods of traditional Sufi psychology as therapy in working especially with Muslim teenage girls. She sees great hope in the young adult generation, especially those who have been able to survive a parenting system often inappropriate to current American culture. Her Qur'an translation is designed for women of all ages, as well as for men, in an effort to make the Holy Word as relevant as possible for contemporary American Islam.

Considerably more controversial among members of the Muslim community, especially conservatives, is the work of Canadian writer and journalist Irshad Manji, which has received a great deal of publicity in the last few years. Initiating what she calls "Operation Jihad," Manji hopes to encourage reflection and reform on the part of her fellow Muslims in the United States and Canada. Manji is a self-professed lesbian who works as producer-reporter for Queer Television in Toronto. Her most explosive book is titled *The Trouble with Islam: A Muslim's Call for Reform in Her Faith*.[14] Manji insists that she is a practicing Muslim, and that her concern is to identify areas where tradition, prejudice, and narrow-minded thinking have served to make Islam irrelevant for many people. Manji has produced a documentary about young Muslim women, and she plans to create an institute for independent thinking in Islam as a result of the book. One of her proposals that many Muslims find most galling is the possibility that the Qur'an may not be completely "God-authored." We must be more flexible in interpreting scripture, she argues, and more willing to be open to tolerance and pluralism. Women must be empowered to take advantage of new economic initiatives and should be more active participants in media organizations. Manji is articulate and well informed, but her message is unlikely to appeal to more than a small portion of today's American Muslims.

The extent to which any or all of these different voices will affect the role of women in the Western *umma* is just starting to be seen.

CHAPTER SEVEN

Living a Muslim Life in American Society

Muslims face many questions as they try to live their lives as responsible citizens of their country, of their families, and in many cases, of their religious tradition. How do they provide appropriate education for their children? What economic strictures do they observe? How are matters of nutrition and health, Islamic music, burial of the dead dealt with? What special products are currently being designed for Muslims, how do they deal with the observance of holidays, both American and Islamic, what new forms of music and communication are now available? In this chapter we discuss daily concerns among American Muslims, whatever the extent to which they consider themselves practitioners of their faith.

Education

One of the most important issues for American Muslims is the education of members of the community, including Islamic parochial education for children, mosque instruction, and forms of continuing adult education. These concerns have been a primary consideration for more than four decades. The acquisition of knowledge has always been a fundamental issue in Islam, and American Muslims refer frequently to the Prophet's affirmation that every Muslim must attain as much knowledge as possible, even if he or she must go as far as China to get it. Such encouragement strengthens the educational resolve of Muslims of all ages, from young people to elderly immigrants who may need simply to improve their English. In the previous chapter we looked at some of the ways women are educating themselves in the Islamic sciences. Current conversations among Muslims in the United States also focus on better training for youth in history, technology, the sciences, and many other subjects that will allow them to find personal and professional success. Learning about elements of Islamic faith and law that are relevant to life in this society is given high priority for all age groups, and the study of Arabic is strongly encouraged whenever possible.

Many Muslim families are concerned about their children's experiences in the public schools. "In the good old days," writes one critic of public school education, "certainly it was easier to trust the public school system was going to do the job. Life has gotten increasingly complex, and [parents'] responsibilities now include involvement in the educational environment and curriculum of our children."[1] Parents worry about the quality of education provided to their children, particularly in some of the larger metropolitan areas. As we have seen, they are troubled about the influences to which their children are exposed, from societal ills such as drugs and crime to the pressures on young people to become more "Americanized." Some see the problems of American schools as reflecting an abdication on the part of Christian (and Jewish) America of its basic religious values. Many parents also worry that their children, especially the girls, may be exposed to un-Islamic requirements in public schools, such as wearing short clothing during gym classes, or having coeducational physical education, or being given sexual information that parents do not think is appropriate for them to hear.

Believing that an Islamic system of education would serve the community better in terms of both academic content and values training, many Muslims are turning their energies toward the establishment of private Islamic educational institutions. K–8 or K–12 Islamic schools, they believe, can provide alternative education for character development, protect children from stereotyping and taunting, offer Islamic alternatives to such social ills as premarital sex, drugs, and violence, and allow children to avoid public school curricula that misrepresent the teachings of Islam.

The number of private Islamic schools in America is slowly growing, but still totals fewer than 250. Some schools are well financed and equipped, with excellent teachers and resources. Of necessity, their fees are sometimes quite high. Even some children who are not Muslim are enrolling in these schools as their parents seek for them a first-rate parochial education. Many other Muslim schools, however, suffer from lack of funding, with teachers often underpaid and administrators not adequately trained for the work. Because many schools are still very new, it is not yet possible to assess the quality of the education that they offer. Most programs do not extend beyond eighth grade, although there are now a few good Islamic high schools. Advertisements for teachers and administrators, who do not necessarily need to be Muslim themselves, fill Islamic journals. The aim of Islamic schools is to provide education in an environment based on the Qur'an and Sunna. Although most states currently do not require accreditation for private educational institutions, major Islamic school organizations argue that accreditation of Islamic schools will signify high performance. Muslims are encouraged to make the funding of Islamic education a mainstay of their charitable giving.

Alternatively, a few Muslim families choose to educate their sons and daughters at home. A large and growing body of materials is available for those who wish to begin training youth at home or in private institutions. "Don't let valuable time slip away," urges an ad in a prominent Islamic journal. "Take the first step toward getting the assistance you need." Various Muslim organizations provide correspondence courses, suggestions for new literature and curricula, handbooks for educators, and other useful tools and information. The annual conventions of these organizations occasionally offer special sessions on homeschooling, which is becoming increasingly popular as electronic services provide access to significant educational materials. While some parents worry that their children will not be adequately socialized to enter mainstream American society if they learn only at home, others argue that the benefits of being in a completely Islamic environment, along with many opportunities to find instruction and interaction outside the home in museums, field trips, and other activities, outweigh such concerns. All parents hope that proper Islamic training at home and in the mosque or Islamic center will sufficiently "arm" their children to make wise decisions. Organizations such as the Muslim Home School Educators Network have been established in Massachusetts and Texas to share Internet-based information on curriculum, instructional resources, and legal issues for Muslim homeschooling families.

Among the first Islamic educational institutions in America were the Clara Muhammad primary schools known as the University of Islam. Begun by the wife of Elijah Muhammad, head of the Nation of Islam until his death in 1975, these schools, which were originally designed for African American children, now have students from all ethnic backgrounds. After the death of Elijah, his son Warith Deen sought a revamping of the curriculum, eliminating the racist content. He renamed them the Sister Clara Muhammad schools after his mother. They continue to provide education for grade-school children.

Youth at an Islamic school in Queens, New York. © Jolie Stahl

A few families who are sufficiently concerned about American education, and who have appropriate contacts and financial resources, send their
children abroad for their education. No matter what form of education is
chosen—public, private, home, or abroad—educators enjoin Muslim parents also to provide the resources and environment in the home that will help
the child learn not only more effectively but also "more Islamically."

Some parents choose to supplement their children's public school education with special training sessions after school and on weekends in their
homes, where copies of the Qur'an and *hadith* are readily available and
other symbols of Muslim culture and ethos create suitable surroundings for
Islamic education. Other groups work for the improvement of American
public education. Increasing efforts are being made to help non-Muslim public school teachers present the religion of Islam with better understanding
and more accuracy. The Council on Islamic Education (CIE), now part of a
new broader organization called the Institute on Religion and Civic Values
(IRCV), works with K–12 textbook publishers to produce more comprehen-
sive and balanced textbooks with respect to world religions, conducts in-ser-
vice workshops for teachers at national social studies conferences, and pro-
duces teaching units that shed light on various aspects of Muslim civilization.

TEACHER'S GUIDE

Answer Key

Comparison of Islam, Judaism and Christianity

Item	Judaism	Christianity	Islam
Belief in how many deities?	One (monotheism)	One (monotheism)	One (monotheism)
Name of Supreme Being	Jehovah (Yahweh)	God	Allah
Central Prophet/Figure	Moses	Jesus Christ	Muhammad
Holy City	Jerusalem	Jerusalem	Makkah, Madinah and Jerusalem
Ordained Religious Leader	rabbi	priest or minister	none, but imam leads worship
Sacred Writings	Hebrew Bible (Old Testament)	Bible (Old and New Testaments)	Qur'an
Name for Believers	Jews	Christians	Muslims
Worship and Use of Idols or Images	images and statues forbidden	statues allowed but not worshipped	images and statues forbidden
Symbol of Faith	Star of David	cross	none
House of Worship	synagogue	cathedral or church	masjid
Special Events	Passover, Yom Kippur	Christmas, Easter	Eid al-Fitr, Eid al-Adha
Beliefs concerning "the good life."	complete obedience to Mosaic law	love God and fellow humans	adherence to "Five Pillars" of faith
Beliefs concerning life after death.	Day of Judgment	Day of Judgment	Day of Judgment

Activity sheet from an instructional book on Islam from the Council on Islamic Education. COURTESY COUNCIL ON ISLAMIC EDUCATION

Among the resources available from CIE is a handbook for educators titled *Teaching About Islam and Muslims in the Public School Classroom*. It includes information on beliefs and practices, a section on issues about which Muslim students in the public school classroom may be particularly sensitive, activity sheets for students learning about Islam, and up-to-date information on books, videotapes, and other educational materials. CIE brings together representatives of the many cultural groupings of American Muslims (immigrant, African American, Latino/Latina, Native American) to talk about the ways in which American history textbooks represent different cultures. Members work with a number of publishers to encourage broader and more representative coverage, as well as the correction of errors and misperceptions about Islam and Muslim peoples. Muslims and others in the educational community join them in the effort to eliminate stereotyping and prejudicial presentations in the materials used in the public schools.

Meanwhile, some Muslims are joining forces with conservative Christian groups and others who are lobbying for prayer in the public schools. "The pro-school prayer coalition is changing," says a commentator on education for Muslim children. "Today, it includes Muslims, black urban leaders, and Christian clergy. Even liberal politicians are joining hands with religious conservatives. The increase in heinous crimes among youth and promiscuous sex has sounded the alarm and led to the broadening of the prayer lobby's base. It's important for young people to have a moment to reflect."[2]

The Islamic educational program in America also provides training for youth and adults in the weekend schools of mosques and Islamic centers. Again, journals and organizations make a great deal of material and assistance available. Instruction ranges from the Qur'an, Sunna, and Islamic history to issues of appropriate dress and behavior for Muslims in different circumstances. Realistic about the possible reasons their youth may have for not wanting to attend after-school or weekend instruction in the mosque, adults are working out strategies to make such activities more fun. Some of the larger Islamic centers, for example, offer athletic facilities such as basketball and volleyball courts to balance the classroom instruction. The study of Arabic is particularly encouraged, and mosques may hold contests for youth and adults in recitation and knowledge of the Qur'an.

One of the themes receiving particular attention is the importance of educating Muslims in Islamic ethics and equipping them to lead morally responsible lives. Reflecting concern for the perceived moral disintegration of American society, this stress on an Islamically defined morality serves both to provide a serious alternative for American Muslims and to witness to the great importance Muslims give to establishing a moral and ethical society. The Islamic Society of North America (ISNA) has a twelve-volume *Encyclopedia on Moral Excellence*, available on CD-ROM and translated into a number of languages. Organizations such as the Muslim Student Association periodically hold forums on topics related to the pursuit of moral excellence, a key ingredient in living a responsible life in contemporary America. Current articles and books are stressing the integration of moral responsibility with academic training. "From the Islamic perspective," writes one educator, "the purpose of education in general is the upbringing of righteous Muslims. This righteousness instills in the Muslim child a set of fundamental values which in turn make him observe his obligations as well as the correct norms of conduct in society naturally."[3]

The Islamic community is giving increasing attention to Islamic education at the college and university level, although to date only a few specifically Muslim institutions of higher learning have been developed. Among them is the American Islamic College, established in Chicago in 1983. The AIC, accredited by the Illinois Board of Higher Education, offers a range of undergraduate courses in the social and physical sciences, computer science, economics, history, and other areas, as well as a number of courses in Arabic and Islamic studies and a wide range of online instruction.

In 1996 the first Muslim school of graduate study in America was established as the Graduate School of Islamic and Social Sciences in Leesburg, Virginia, providing students an opportunity to study with an Islamic faculty in the traditions of Islam. Its goal was to train leaders dedicated to the establishment of Muslim culture and civilization in North America. GSISS formerly offered two areas of study, a master of arts program in Islamic studies and a master's program for the training of Muslim imams and chaplains. The school is now known as Cordoba University, and no longer offers a chaplaincy program, although as of 2007 it offers a certificate program in Muslim-Christian dialogue jointly with the Washington Theological Consortium. Hartford Seminary in Connecticut, a Christian institution, offers the only accredited Muslim chaplain training program combining master's-level training with field instruction. The Imam Ali Seminary in Medina, New York, a Shiʻi school that was dedicated to providing training for teachers to assist in the personal and community growth of Muslims living in America, is no longer in business.

Muslim students enrolled at other American colleges and universities are becoming increasingly vocal in their efforts to gain recognition for themselves and their community. These efforts, supported by national groups such as the MSA, are bringing results. Syracuse University was among the first to recognize ʻeid al-fitr at the end of Ramadan as an official school holiday, with the entire university closing for the day. Mount Holyoke College set a model for interfaith relations when it established a program whereby Muslim and Jewish students may elect once a week to share a common meal prepared in a kitchen that is both halal (permissible) and kosher. Harvard University attracted publicity a few years ago when it invited a Muslim to speak at graduation. These pioneering efforts are being followed by initiatives at a number of other colleges recognizing their growing Muslim student bodies. At many universities meat prepared in Islamically permissible ways is available to students by request.

Very new in American colleges and universities is the presence of full-time Muslim chaplains in offices of student affairs, although a number of institutions

The American Islamic College in Chicago, Illinois.
COURTESY AMERICAN ISLAMIC COLLEGE, CHICAGO, ILLINOIS

have had part-time assistance for some time. As of summer 2008, seven schools have full-time Muslim chaplains: Georgetown, Duke, Yale, Princeton, New York University, Brown, and the University of Pennsylvania. Emory has an associate chaplain, and both Smith and Mount Holyoke in Massachusetts and Trinity and Wesleyan in Connecticut have joint full-time positions. Competition among these East Coast schools is obviously a contributing factor to this spurt of attention to the needs of Muslim students; at present there do not appear to be any similar developments on the West Coast.

Meanwhile, Islamic periodicals and newspapers highlight the achievements of Muslim students everywhere, and many contain special sections devoted specifically to education, providing tips to prospective students on everything from filling out financial aid applications to requesting an appropriate roommate. Muslim students themselves are starting to write articles in school newspapers and in national Muslim journals warning of the difficulties of living Islamically in college and emphasizing the importance of keeping company with other young Muslims. "I would like to say that the secret to keeping your Iman [faith] and strengthening your Deen [religion] when you are in college lies in brotherhood and sisterhood. Muslims on campus don't have the Taqwa [piety] to live as an individual in their kafir [unbeliever] society," wrote a student at Rutgers University in the late 1990s. "Strength is in our numbers because Shaitan [Satan] finds difficulty in deceiving whole flocks as opposed to lone sheep."[4] Many young Muslim women who are eager to socialize when they come to college are shocked by what they find to be the pressure to drink and to engage in occasional sex. Often they find refuge by joining other Muslims for social gatherings, sometimes under the rubric of the MSA. Such association for some leads to their first venture into wearing Islamic dress, or at least a head scarf.

It has become clear over the last few years that young people need models of Islamic teaching and behavior to attract them to a new appreciation of their faith. As one young woman put it, "We need a new set of gurus. The old ones are either dead or out of date." That purpose is being served to some extent by the opportunity to study at institutes founded especially for learning "in the Islamic way." Several such institutes now exist, particularly in the West, where students can spend a few weeks or much longer in an environment of Islamic learning and culture. One of the most popular has been the Zaytuna Institute in California. Sheikh Hamza Yusuf, who teaches at Zaytuna, converted to Islam in 1977 and has devoted himself to the study of the Islamic sciences in many places in the Middle East and Africa. His goal is the preservation of traditional teaching methods in Islam. In recent years Sheikh Hamza has spoken out against terror and extremism, while promoting cooperation and education. Zaytuna Institute is temporarily closed while Sheikh Hamza studies the feasibility of reopening it as an Islamic seminary.

Several other opportunities exist for young Muslims to learn in Islamically designed contexts. An institution called Al-Maghrib sets up "tribes" in various cities, of which there are currently thirteen. It specializes in weekend education. The American Learning Institute for Muslims (ALIM) is designed for college students, bringing students of different spiritual orientations for the academic study of Islam. Some organizations, such as Rihla (spiritual journey), teach in the genre of Sufism. Rihla holds sessions at Dar al-Islam in Abiquiu, New Mexico.[5]

Since 9/11 Islamic education in all of its forms in America has been intensely scrutinized out of fear that Muslim institutions may be producing young radicals. Much of the alarm is raised in online articles claiming, for example, that Islamic schools may be sleeper cells or that they are teaching hatred of America (often based on what they fear are American parallels to the *madrasas* or religious schools of Pakistan and Afghanistan). Various approaches are being taken to address this issue. The Noor-Ul-Iman School in Monmouth Junction, New Jersey, for example, formed a media and public affairs committee that includes teachers and students in order to interact with the local media. The committee recruits teachers who speak with an American accent and are well versed in world affairs. The challenge for Muslims as they face the task of educating their youth and other members of the community is thus threefold: they must continue to improve the quality of education for their Muslim students; they must be very careful to ensure that the fears expressed by some Americans about Muslim institutions teaching extremism are not true; and they must intensify efforts to educate the American public about the elements of their religion that really do reflect the message of the Qur'an and the teachings of Prophet Muhammad.

Young Muslims who want to pursue Islam as a field of academic study can now do so under the tutelage of Muslim faculty at most colleges and universities in America. This relatively new phenomenon is partly a result of efforts of academic institutions to diversify their faculty and to acknowledge the advantage of having an academically well-qualified faculty member who is also a Muslim teaching in the various fields of Islamic studies.

Economics

Among the many difficult issues facing Muslims who want to live according to the strictures of Islamic law is that of proper financial stewardship. This problem has a number of dimensions, of which perhaps the most complex is the Qur'anic prohibition on the accumulation of interest (*riba*). "Is the money a Muslim earns from working at a bank *haram* [unlawful]?" writes a concerned reader to a national journal's *fatawa* (legal opinions) discussion forum. "Work at any bank that deals with *ribaa* [usury/interest] is *haram*," comes the answer, "because it is from the act of helping one another in sin and transgression."[6] Interpreted strictly, the term can be understood to refer to usury, or interest in excess of the legal rate.

Some Muslims, however, argue for a more flexible interpretation of the law that would allow for the accumulation of some reasonable interest on money invested. The detailed arguments require a subtle understanding of Islamic law and interpretation. The ramifications, however, are important for those Muslims who try conscientiously to adhere to the law. One of the obvious ways in which the prohibition on interest affects Muslims has to do with taking out mortgages on houses, mosques, and other Islamic institutions. In some instances, communities in America simply collect all the money needed to build an Islamic institution, thereby avoiding the necessity of having a mortgage and dealing with the matter of interest. The growth of Islamic banks across the world, and now also in America, helps provide some solutions.

Another financial issue attracting increased attention is whether capital gains on investments are Islamically acceptable. Some argue that capital gains should never be allowed, while others claim that they should be prohibited only when they would destabilize the smooth functioning of the economic order. Many banks in America now work with "bank deposits" and "Islamic deposits," in which money is entrusted to the bank for safekeeping and later returned without interest, upon request or the satisfaction of certain conditions. Such deposits may be accessed through checking accounts or may be put in term-limit accounts such as certificates of deposit.

As American Muslims articulate their economic concerns more specifically, more opportunities present themselves through advertisements for counseling and assistance in Islamic investing. The North American Islamic Trust, for example, provides counseling for investors about the ways in which they can achieve long-term growth at the same time that they avoid both the accumulation of interest and the possibility that their money will be invested in businesses that trade in alcohol, tobacco, pornography, or gambling.

Such debates remain to be settled by those with extensive knowledge of economics as well as Islamic law. In the meantime, Muslims in the United States raise practical questions about finances, and increasing attention is being given in the popular literature to helping them think through Islamically acceptable responses. "Have you fallen into the debt trap yet?" reads the opening line of an article in the journal *Al Jumuah*, warning its readers of the importance of avoiding outstanding loans and the inevitable payment of interest on those loans. Specific examples illustrate the concrete ways in which the sayings of the Prophet and the injunctions of the law can inform everyday financial decisions. For families living close to the economic margin, difficult questions often arise, particularly if for reasons of religious conviction a husband feels that it is Islamically unacceptable for his wife to participate in the workplace and contribute to the family income. Letters to religious advisors in Muslim journals often ponder how to be responsible both to Islamic expectations and to the exigencies of providing for the economic stability of one's family in the American context.

One response increasingly advocated is to manage one's money through investment clubs. "Muslims seeking *halal* [permissible], safe and rewarding means of making their money grow have a choice in the shape of an 'investment club,'" suggests a Muslim economist.[7] These clubs function as low-risk structured partnership agreements in which members pool money and invest, meeting regularly to explore new opportunities. Management and brokering costs are lowered, and members have an opportunity to share in broad expertise working for maximized investment returns.

The issue of how finances affect mosque growth and maintenance exceeds questions of interest and mortgage. Traditionally, members of Islamic societies do not pledge to the support of a religious institution, as such support comes from the state. Muslims in other parts of the world attend the mosque according to their needs and interests but do not consider themselves "members." In the American context, the situation differs markedly. Mosques and Islamic centers generally function as self-supporting units, often dependent on the contributions of the local Muslim community and on fund-raising activities for maintenance and continuation of services. Muslims who are conscientious about paying the *zakat*, or Islamically required tax for the care of the needy, may feel doubly pressured at the expectation of also having to contribute to the mosque or Islamic center. At the same time, they increasingly realize that such institutional support is crucial in America and needs to be thought about in new ways. Many mosques find that they are forced further to adopt American customs of seeking financial support, engaging in fund-raising activities such as dinners, rummage sales, special events, and direct-mail appeals. The matter of financing becomes even more complicated when foreign governments—Iran or Saudi Arabia, for example—offer support to communities in this country. While the infusion of monies may be welcome, the expectations that recipients assume certain social and political positions may not be.

National Islamic organizations make concerted efforts to help Muslims in America think creatively about their financial options. They put forth strategies to assist in economic advancement, such as better entry into the American mainstream, insofar as possible attempting to buy from and sell to Muslims only, and even international Muslim economic solidarity. Some argue that the American *umma* must have its own treasury (*bait al-mal*) for the collection of *zakat* and other kinds of charitable donations on the local, state, and national levels. The hope is that such a central agency could not only deploy charitable giving most effectively but could also develop a surplus of its own resources to assist in financing Muslim projects.

One of the managing directors of the first full-service Muslim-owned investment bank in America, located on Wall Street, argues for the importance of establishing a chair in Islamic finance at a major university. Acknowledging that many schools teach courses about Islam, he says, "Now, it is vitally important to take the next logical step, which is to establish a Chair on Islamic Finance to not only create and fulfill a demand in our youth (our future), but also explain why high profile conventional financial institutions . . . have established Islamic financial 'Windows' for business."[8]

Considerable debate in national and local forums examines such issues as whether Muslims should try to benefit from affirmative-action hiring programs as long as they exist. Some leaders urge Muslims to look more closely at the history of Jews in America for examples of how to succeed financially in the face of prejudice and minority status. In the current U.S. environment, financial institutions are experiencing a lack of stability. It is not surprising that Islamic banks are also in trouble. In September 2008, for example, Sunrise Equities, a Chicago-based financial services firm that claimed to be compliant with the *shari'* failed. Many Muslims living in the area who used the services of the bank lost all their savings. Sunrise Equities, unfortunately, is under somewhat of a cloud with accusations that the bank has been less than candid with its clients about the state of their assets.

American Muslims will most certainly continue to address with great seriousness the many factors relating to economics and their impact upon Muslim life in America in the coming years.

Nutrition and Health

American Muslims have long been concerned lest they be unable to observe the dietary restrictions of Islam. These, including the prohibition on pork products and alcohol, they understand both to be based on the commands of God in the Qur'an and to reflect concerns for health and hygiene. African

American converts to the Nation of Islam from the middle of the century on were enjoined in the strongest terms to abandon completely all former customs of eating any parts of the pig. Books and pamphlets still available in Muslim bookstores warn of the disastrous effects of disregarding these rules, complete with graphic depictions of the one who succumbs to such temptation and then begins to acquire porcine characteristics. Extensive efforts over the last several decades have determined the ingredients used in breads, pastries, and other products found in grocery stores, fast-food establishments, and other places where Muslims might buy their food. This endeavor has caused Muslims to discontinue use of a number of products, such as those that may contain lard. The movement to focus public attention on the importance of proper diet in Islam is growing and includes warnings about the necessity of moderate and supervised consumption of any pharmaceutical products that might contain alcohol or narcotics.

In recent years, more attention has also been given to the proper ritual slaughter of animals prepared for consumption. Earlier, those Muslims who wanted to ensure that their meat was permissible were forced to buy it from Jewish kosher butchers. Now many more places sell Islamically slaughtered meat, generally known as *halal* (from the Arabic word meaning "allowed" or "lawful"). The proper Islamic slaughtering of an animal has both health and ritual dimensions. The animal's throat should be slit cleanly with a sharp instrument, cutting through the windpipe, gullet, and jugular vein. After the throat is cut, the blood must be drained before the head is fully removed. This method contrasts with the typical American way of slaughter, in which the animal is stunned with an electric shock before being killed and the blood is not fully drained. Meat from which blood is removed is much less prone to fermentation and the accumulation of bacteria. In addition, while the animal is being slaughtered, the name of God is to be recited, as is indicated in Sura 6:118 of the Qur'an: "Eat of that over which the name of God has been mentioned."

It is generally considered permissible to have a tape of Qur'an recitation running during the slaughter as an alternative to having someone speaking in person. The issue of *halal* meat includes the slaughter not only of beef and sheep but also of poultry. North Carolina, a large chicken-producing state, exports Islamically slaughtered birds to Muslim countries, especially in the Middle East. Groups such as the Islamic Food and Nutrition Council of America, located in Bedford Park, Illinois, are preparing information kits to assist Muslims employed in various parts of the American food industry.

An issue of particular interest to many Muslim Americans, and to which Islamic scholars give a number of answers, is whether Muslims should be allowed to eat food prepared by non-Muslims, specifically Christians and Jews. "This day all things good are made lawful unto you," says the Qur'an. "The food of the Prophet is lawful unto you and yours is lawful unto them" (Sura 5:5). Some conservative scholars argue that the answer is no because one cannot be sure that it has been prepared in the proper way. Others agree with the Egyptian reformer Rashid Rida, who early in this century argued that if the Qur'an allows a man to marry one of the People of the Book, surely it is not wrong to eat the food of Christians or Jews. Obviously, the increasing social interactions of Muslims and non-Muslims, through business and other contacts and in the various events that have been scheduled for better interfaith understanding since 9/11, make it difficult to maintain the strictest dietary observance.

Some Muslims refuse to attend any occasion at which alcohol is served, while others simply abstain from drinking it themselves and leave their neighbors to make their own decisions. Some wonder whether it is necessary to serve alcohol to guests. "In our family . . . we used to serve liquor to our American guests," reports a Muslim from upstate New York. "We would just put it on the table and leave it there for them to help themselves. But we stopped doing this as a result of comments made by my older daughter—that when we don't drink, why do we serve drinks?" The issue of whether a Muslim should work in a store or restaurant that sells alcohol has greatly concerned some Muslims, particularly when the job is essential for the support of their families, and the decisions have varied. Some question whether Muslims should be allowed to take any drugs that possibly contain traces of forbidden substances such as alcohol. Again, responses differ, with most affirming such use if it is necessary for the patient's life and no substitute is available. The general rule is that substances that impair one's mind or cloud one's discernment are to be avoided at all costs short of life endangerment.

Also receiving considerable attention in the American Muslim community is the matter of proper health care opportunities. In some cases, organizations are planning for free care for the needy, such as that provided by the University Muslim Medical Association (UMMA) Free Health Clinic in Los Angeles, run by Muslim physicians and medical students. Located in the heart of gang-troubled south central Los Angeles, the clinic focuses on issues of health care and social welfare. It runs on the charitable donations of money and supplies by hospitals, businesses, and other agencies and donations of time by medical and other staff. In other cases, efforts are being made to ensure that Muslims under medical care in public and private hospitals in America are treated in ways that accord with their beliefs.

Riverview Hospital in Detroit, Michigan, in collaboration with Islamic Health and Human Services, made an unprecedented decision to provide for Islamic practices as a regular part of its hospital services. "Al-Hamdilullah [praise be to God]!" cried the Muslim reporter describing the consequences of this decision. "This is not a dream. You are not in a Muslim country. You are in Detroit."[9] The *adhan*, or call to prayer, is whispered in the ear of a newborn baby, *halal* food is prepared in the hospital kitchen, Muslim patients and caregivers do *salat* in the meditation room, Qur'ans are available by request, and female hospital personnel are allowed to go about their work in full *hijab* if they so choose. Lists of patients contain the reference "Muslim" by their names when appropriate. Riverview is the first to offer total Islamic care to Muslim patients, but it is being joined by others. Slowly other health care facilities in the United States are acknowledging the multiethnic and multi-religious representation among their patients and are taking steps to adopt policies and make changes to meet the needs of their patients and clients. A growing number of trained Muslim chaplains are now available to serve at hospitals and health care centers.

Holidays

As Muslims become more aware of their presence in North America as a definable religious entity, they are also becoming more clear about the importance of distinguishing between their own holidays and festivals and those of Christian or secular America. It is often difficult for some Muslim children to understand why they are not allowed to participate in the holidays their classmates enjoy. For more-observant Muslims, the problem is exacerbated when many of their fellow Muslims enjoy all the holidays, taking what is fun and ignoring specifically religious implications. Other Muslim parents want to encourage their children to "own" their Muslim holidays and distance themselves from American observances that they feel are specific to Jews and Christians or are too secular to have a part in Islam.

Questions arise especially around Christmastime. Why not let our children have a Christmas tree and exchange gifts, some argue, especially since Muslims, along with Christians, honor the birth of Jesus? Others try to compromise or avoid any observance of the holiday at all. Still others decide that observing Christmas has some advantages. "We celebrate Christmas for two reasons," says one woman. "It is important to get involved with American society, and if you don't celebrate Christmas and if you don't celebrate

Thanksgiving, to me really you are telling those people you are not part of American society. . . . The second reason is that we do believe in Jesus. We don't believe that he was a god, but we do believe he was a prophet."[10] Muslim parents who are not happy when their children come home singing Christmas carols may be even more startled when they hear "Happy Hanukkah" songs.

Other holidays present fewer immediate problems. Easter is so clearly an acknowledgment of a Christian belief denied by Islam, namely the resurrection of Jesus, that there is little at issue, aside from wondering whether to allow children to color eggs or have bunny baskets. Muslims may see the Fourth of July as a time to affirm their participation in American civic life. Halloween for the most part is deemed rather harmless, although most parents do not want their children trick-or-treating and they recognize that the holiday observed is really the Christian All Saints' Day. Thanksgiving can easily be appreciated as a truly Islamic event insofar as it is a time to appreciate God's bounty with one's family and friends.

Nonetheless, occasions in the calendar in which the vast majority of Americans participate to some degree or other continue to raise questions. These may be compounded as Muslims develop friendships with non-Muslims and may be invited to such holiday celebrations. Young people especially may find it difficult to understand why they cannot participate in holidays celebrated by non-Muslim friends, such as birthdays or other occasions. The conservative response, calling on the rulings of Muslim legists over the centuries, is a firm *no*, some insisting that one should not even congratulate Christians, Jews, or others at the time of their holidays. Some Muslims, however, do send Christmas cards to their Christian friends. Many Muslims are trying modifications of strict Islamic regulations that can satisfy both their own consciences and their desire not to isolate themselves and their children unduly from the influences of a culture in which they are, in fact, citizens and participants. Secular Muslims, of course, are not involved with such detailed decision making and do not observe any holidays except insofar as they serve as social or family occasions.

Much thought has been given to rethinking how to observe the traditional Islamic holidays in the Western context. Although the *'eid al-fitr*, the breaking of the fast of Ramadan described in chapter 1, may be the most publicized and thus the most evident Islamic holiday to Americans who are not Muslims, in fact it is considered to be the minor, or lesser, *'eid*, or celebration. The major *'eid* is the *'eid al-adha*, the festival commemorating Abraham's response to God's instruction to offer his son as a sacrifice, whom

Muslims believe to have been Ishmael rather than Isaac. During the 'eid al-adha, which occurs at the end of the pilgrimage to Mecca, Muslims traditionally sacrifice animals, or purchase halal meat, to distribute to the needy of the community. Muslims in America observe the holiday at the same time that pilgrims are completing their hajj in Mecca. Many Muslims choose to celebrate the birthday of the Prophet, mulid al-nabi, often according to the particular customs of the country or society from which they originally came, insofar as that is possible in their new context. One of the most important yearly observances for American Shi'ites is that known as Muharram, during which they recollect and reenact the events that took place at the time of the killing of Prophet Muhammad's grandson Husayn at Karbala. The month itself is already sacred to all Muslims, as it was the time when Muhammad changed the direction in which Muslims were to face when performing the ritual prayer from Jerusalem to Mecca. "The Muharram majlis [lamentation assembly] provides each successive generation with the religious instruction necessary for the continuance of Shi'i identity. Throughout the year the verity of the emotional experience of Karbala that begins in childhood is repeatedly reaffirmed."[11] Shi'ites are being creative both in carrying out this observation and in translating it to the better understanding of their non-Muslim neighbors.

Public schools in America are becoming more aware of all these holidays and often encourage Muslim students to tell the other members of the class what their celebrations mean. School calendars in more progressive institutions record the major Islamic holidays as well as those of Christians and Jews.

Islamic "Products"

Muslims who want to eat, dress, and comport themselves in recognizably Islamic ways have access to a great range of commodities designed to assist, enhance, and promote their identity. In most urban areas of America today one can find numerous products in markets and stores designed particularly for Muslim consumption. Many of these products are also available by mail or e-mail order, evidenced in the growing number of advertisements online, in Islamic journals and newspapers, in other publications, and through other media. One of the most attractive aspects of the various local and national meetings of Muslim organizations is the bazaar area, where a variety of Islamic products can be purchased.

Web sites and home pages giving information on Islamic materials multiply daily, and one faces more information and products than can easily be imagined. Most obvious are the great numbers of books, videos, CDs, software packages, and instructional materials about Islam. Many of these educational materials are designed for entertainment at the same time that they instruct, such as videos with Islamic cartoons for children. Increasing numbers of games and puzzles attract families who seek to engage in wholesome group activity. Family members may wish to quiz one another about Islamic history or salient facts about the faith and practice of Islam with Islamic game cards. Some journals contain quizzes about Islam, with the answers provided on a separate page.

The Muslim who wants to ensure that her or his diet is appropriate to the strictures of the law can order from a number of food production companies that feature such treats as *shawarma* (a Middle Eastern mixture of rotisserie-grilled meat and spices), Vienna sausage, corned beef and pastrami, turkey ham, and even pizza toppings, all prepared according to strict *halal* standards. The Islamic Book Center in Richmond Hill, New York, offers *A Handbook of Halaal and Haraam Products* with more than six thousand

A *halal* store sells Islamically acceptable food products. © THE PHOTO WORKS

listings and articles on how to select one's diet wisely. Companies such as Midamar Corporation in Cedar Rapids, Iowa, assure customers that they have worked for many years with selected USDA-approved companies to ensure product quality and integrity. Even *halal* marshmallows are available in large and small sizes, prepared appropriately from beef gelatin. Along with foods, one can order exclusive skin-care products like eye-lift hydrating gel and mystic musk night cream, also designed to meet Islamic requirements by avoiding the use of animal fats or alcohol and guaranteed not to have been tested on animals. Weight-loss programs advertise products in line with Islamic dietary requirements. Men can even hope to have their hair restored using Islamically appropriate products for hair and scalp. A great variety of women's and men's clothing is available, as described in chapter 6.

Products are designed both to help Muslims affirm their identity and to make life easier and more convenient for them in a Western context. Special package tours to Saudi Arabia at the time of the *hajj* advertise "the best service and lowest prices for the pilgrimage," some geared for the traveler who would prefer economy and others combining stays in luxury hotels with the rigors of the pilgrimage. A number of travel agencies offer special service and low prices for arranging special *'umra* (the lesser pilgrimage not made during the time of *hajj*) trips. Information on pilgrimage opportunities is available on the Internet at *hajj* and *'umrah* Web sites. Muslims who want to know the exact times for prayer and breaking the daily fast during Ramadan may purchase a variety of specially designed watches and clocks. "Don't pray when you remember," advertises Casio, "pray when it is time to pray!" What is billed as its "Amazing AL-ASR Islamic Watch" points to Mecca from any location without using a compass, gives the time of prayer for more than two hundred cities around the world, and displays a thirty-day *hijra* calendar.

New Forms of Communication

It might well be argued that nothing has so dramatically changed American Islam as the increased use of various means of communication. The most potent is the Internet, on which Muslims can find information of every kind from religious to political to homemaking aids. Alexis Kort in a 2005 article, "Dar al-Cyber Islam," argues that the Internet may be for Islam what the printing press was for Christianity—a vehicle for shifting the structures and hierarchies of religious knowledge within Islam through the ways in which it shifts accessibility, participation, and authority.[12] Young people are the primary, though by no means the only, Internet customers. Their use of English as a means of communication has created a universal language of Islamic discourse separate from the claims either of classical Arabic or of other languages of immigrant cultures.

Muslims and those who want to learn more about Islam literally have both classical and contemporary religious information at their fingertips. There are numerous editions and translations of the Qur'an, including chanting with variant vocalizations; a range of *tafsirs* or Qur'an interpretations from classical to contemporary; transcribed sermons from cultures around the world; sayings and deeds of the Prophet Muhammad (*hadith*) and stories from the history of Islamic civilization; legal rulings or opinions (*fatwas*) from *muftis* in many cultures about virtually any topic one might want; political news and activism; personal advice and self-help; how to find mosques, *halal* butchers, and Islamic burial grounds; chat groups and matrimonial sections; times for prayer and calendar converters to and from *hijra* and Gregorian dates; inexpensive travel deals, especially for the pilgrimage to Mecca; and information for new converts on how to conduct themselves according to Islamic standards. And of course one can find a wealth of information about the various meanings of *da'wa* and how it should be conducted and understood.

For young Muslims, as perhaps for young people everywhere, the Internet is a source of both information and comfort. Youth in American high schools who may be feeling isolated because they are alone or virtually alone in wearing Islamic dress in their institution can talk with others who are suffering the same insecurities. Mothers who want to begin homeschooling for their children can find exact instructions on how to begin and proceed. Young men and women who would not be allowed to meet and date by the restrictions of their cultures of family origin can talk with each other, exchange pictures, and share intimate thoughts and feelings in ways never dreamed of by their parents. The competition to represent the voices of American Muslim politics is often best transmitted by the Internet, where young politicos and seasoned academics have an even playing field on which to voice their opinions on new directions in America. Even senior citizens, taking advantage of opportunities to learn how to use the Internet through instruction at Islamic centers or other civic services, can find freedom from the isolation of being home alone and can learn from or talk to others from their faith and culture.

Voices of concern, protest, and mutual support are coming from a wide range of perspectives. "I am a young liberal Muslim Arab," said a Lebanese-born woman in an e-mail message titled "An Arab liberal's anguish." She says that she wears jeans and miniskirts and no veil, watches *Sex and the City* and *The Simpsons*, and plans to pursue a career in international affairs. But venting her frustration about American foreign policy, she says, "I feel deeply estranged from everything the government is trying to do. . . . The U.S. seems not to understand who we are." A young homosexual man finds great comfort in discovering through the Internet that there are other Muslims, like himself, who do not fit into the traditional pattern of what is acceptable as a religious orientation, and they too are struggling to find community in their attempts to reinterpret the Qur'an and traditions to include them. "I feel like I can finally admit who I am, both sexually and religiously, and don't have to feel torn into two parts," he says. Parents who are challenged by new issues in relation to their children, such as whether or not girls should be allowed to date, hear similar concerns from other parents, as well as a quite overwhelming amount of advice from trained or self-styled counselors who are happy to help them solve their problems.

It has often been said that if Islam is going to experience some kind of renewal or revival, post-9/11 America may be the locus of that change. Most certainly the Internet is serving as a vehicle for the exchange of new interpretations, both in the United States itself and between Muslims in America and those overseas. New ideas can be introduced, floated, and tested for their viability. Muslims are in constant communication with each other. Popular as the Internet is, however, it does not satisfy the need for information of all Muslims.

Other new forms of communication engage American Muslims and keep them informed about world events and happenings in the cultures in which they have particular interest. Arabic-speaking Muslims often get their news from such sites as Al-Jazeera, while Lebanese may watch the Lebanese Broadcasting Company and Pakistanis their own channels. Various attempts at establishing national American Muslim TV channels have met with limited results. A new American Muslim organization called Muslim Channels has launched MuslimChannels.tv, a web portal that they claim is an important alternative to such sites as YouTube and MySpace. The founders of the site are attempting to approach online video by combining live 24/7 broadcasts dealing with Islamic affairs from established TV channels around the world with user-generated content (called UGC). Deals involving content supply have been signed with various partners, including Al-Jazeera English; Tehran-based English-language news channel Press TV; U.S. satellite channel Link TV; and international analysis program *Democracy Now!*

as well as such religious programs as Huda TV from Saudi Arabia and the UK-based Islam Channel. The communications director for Muslim Channels hopes that scholars and imams from the more than one thousand Islamic centers across America, as well as members of the user base, will add a great deal of useful content to the programming. No sexual or hate-based videos will be permitted, says communications director Stephanie Khan. Rather, the content will focus on education, clean entertainment, and broader news perspectives—all in one locale.[13]

A number of journals by and for Muslims are now available in the American market, designed also for non-Muslim readership to help propagate a better understanding of Islam. *Azizah*, for Muslim women, has been described in chapter 6. It is joined by such publications as *Elan* (a glossy magazine with a range of contemporary articles), *Islamica* (a quarterly designed to be the *Atlantic Monthly* of the Muslim community, *Muslim Girl* (criticized by some for being too liberal), and others. These publications all reflect the current concern among Muslims to take responsibility for defining themselves rather than allowing the Western media to continue to misrepresent what Islam is and does. Kari Ansari, a convert and the founder of *Muslim Family* magazine in 2003, says, "Our main mission is to encourage integration of the Muslim community into society."[14]

Islamic Music: Is It Acceptable?

Is it really un-Islamic to listen to, play, and enjoy music? All the major Islamic schools of thought prohibit the use of certain kinds of music, which is interpreted by some conservative thinkers to mean that no music of any kind is allowed. But clearly there is room for different points of view on this issue, as there has been on many other issues in the history of Islam. Sufi orders, especially on the Indian subcontinent, have long practiced what is called *qawwali* music, intended to produce in the listener a realization of the presence and oneness of God. Many jazz musicians over the years were Muslim. Yusuf Islam, the former pop singer Cat Stevens, refused to perform for a number of years after his conversion to Islam. Now he suggests that, as in all things, moderation is the key. He believes that songs and singing are Islamically acceptable if the words are appropriate and if praise of God is always the primary intention of one's music. "[Legal prohibition] does not mean that Muslims become melodious-less monks. Muslims have to partake in every aspect of life. . . . So a lot more thought has to go into this . . . because there are songs and singing in Islam, there is melody as well as drums, but it has to be within the limits."[15] Others are less open and tend to condemn music in any Islamic setting.

Yusuf Islam's insistence on the thoughtful inclusion of music in the contemporary activities of Muslims, expressed a decade ago, may be even more relevant in today's American Islam. Numerous musical groups have arisen, many but not all in the African American community, whose offerings are designed to perpetuate the message of Islam in ways that reflect traditional understandings and interpretations in new forms. The style of presentation would not have been recognized by their ancestors, but today's Islamic musicians are passing along, especially to young people, a message of God's oneness and the importance of living a life consonant with the traditional standards of Islamic ethics and morality.

One of the most successful projects of the Muslim Youth in North America (MYNA) organization—providing another kind of Islamic education for youth—is the production of five albums of Islamic songs written by young Muslims from the United States called MYNA RAPS Among its available albums are *The Straight Track*, *The Inner Struggle*, *The Next Level*, and *For the Cause of Allah*. Countering the image of a sterile Islam in which music is not allowed, MYNA RAPS provides energetic, Islamically acceptable ways to celebrate the fun of being Muslim, increase God-consciousness (*taqwa*), and, says the Web site, come closer to Allah. The brothers featured on the MYNA RAPS albums were signed by the Mountain of Light/Jamal Records label associated with Yusuf Islam (Cat Stevens) and now form the group Native Deen (*deen*, or *din*, is Arabic for "religion").

Native Deen, along with other groups like Seven8Six, Noor, and Tyson, perform to sell-out audiences around the world. They are part of a new brand of Islamic music called *nasheed*, which provides a way for contemporary Muslim youth to produce and enjoy pop music while propagating the true principles of Islam. Three of Native Deen's artists—Joshua Salaam, Abdul Malik Ahmad, and Naeem Muhammad, began as solo artists and combined to form this successful group. Native Deen's ambition is to reach as many Muslims as possible; to broaden their appeal they use only traditional percussion instruments. The music is produced on the Mountain of Light label. The group's latest album includes the track "Still Strong," featuring Isam Bachiri of Outlandish.

Nor are these young musicians only men. Kareem Salima, born to Egyptian parents and raised in Oklahoma, combines Islamic music with the country flair characteristic of the American Southwest.

One of the most popular kinds of new Islamic music is American Muslim hip-hop. Singer Mos Def's album *Black on Both Sides*, for example, begins with the *basmalla* or incantation "In the name of God, the Merciful, the Compassionate," which opens every chapter of the Qur'an save one. The link between American Islam and hip-hop music seems to be a natural one, forged around common themes of social justice and cultural empowerment that resonate particularly with African Americans and Latinos/Latinas. Hip-hop began in the 1990s in South Bronx, New York City, created especially to appeal to young men while carrying the message of groups like the Nation of Islam and the Five Percenters (see chapter 4), such as that displayed in the renditions of hip-hop artist B.I.G. A number of musicians, like Mos Def, Q-tip, and Ali Shaheed Muhammad, claim that Sunni Islam is the source of their musical inspiration. Young people, especially in urban areas of the northwestern United States, both contribute to and are deeply influenced by hip-hop music. A Muslim rap group from Los Angeles called Soldiers of Allah was very successful after 9/11 with their album *1924* (a reference to the year in which Ataturk secularized the state of Turkey) and continued to perform raps trying to unify the *umma* and emphasize the importance of the Caliphate. Recently for personal reasons the group's Web site has been shut down and they have disbanded.

Music can also be the vehicle by which some young Muslims try to counter the prejudice that they have experienced many times in their lives, especially since 9/11. "Stop the hate! Stop the hate!" screams vocalist Waqar into the microphone, performing with his band, Diacritical. The son of a Pakistani immigrant, Waqar is a self-styled "punk-rock Muslim." Diacritical is one of some dozen bands that perform around the country under the punk-rock rubric, with provocative names such as Vote Hezbollah, the Kominas ("bastards" in Punjabi), and Al-Thawra (Arabic for "the revolution"). Muslim punk rockers are angry in two directions, and they direct their musical rhetoric toward both: the pain that the American "war on terror" has caused Muslims and the bloodshed caused by Islamic fundamentalists. While they do not claim to be devout Muslims, they call themselves deeply spiritual and are using the language of Islam and of revolution to shock their audiences into an understanding of what they believe to be justice. Most of these "punks" are the American-born children of Muslims who came to the United States in the 1960s, 1970s, and 1980s.[16]

The musical renditions of pop *nasheed*, Muslim hip-hop, and punk rock are far from the more soothing notes of Pakistani Qawwali, but nonetheless claim to fall within the definition of Islamic music. Whether or not such music is acceptable under the Islamic umbrella depends both on the listener and on the time. As in many other things, America may be seen as a place that allows either for innovative leadership or for potentially dangerous forms of unorthodoxy.

Personal Problems and Islamic Solutions

Much has been said already about the concerns that Muslims raise as they try to balance the requirements of their faith and the expectations of American culture. There is no dearth of assistance in helping individuals find answers to their questions through mosques and Islamic centers, the Internet, Muslim journals and newspapers, and many other sources. *The Minaret* magazine, published in Southern California, assures its readers that a *fatwa* (which, technically, is a religious/legal opinion, not a ruling) is only a phone call away, urging that those with concerns call 1–800–95-FATWA for assistance in making important life decisions. "God's Will need not be searched or sought; you need not sweat or pain, you need not reflect or persevere. Instead, you make a phone call."[17] The problem for many Muslims comes in trying to determine what responses are truest to the heart of Islamic law and whether they are applicable or even possible in the American context. Many of the issues that the Muslim community in America faces are being addressed in public presentations by regional and national organizations and institutions. Following are a few of the questions being raised today, along with some of the Islamic responses offered.

• Is it lawful to accept a gift from someone whose money has earned interest in a bank? The conservative response is no, although some would argue that the thought behind the gift matters more than how the money was accumulated.

• Should girls who have not yet reached puberty be allowed, or even encouraged, to wear a scarf to school? The Muslim community is deeply engaged in the issue of dress for girls, and most would argue that they should not be encouraged to wear the scarf at least until puberty. Whatever the girl's decision, it is important for the family to provide a supportive and approving context.

• Can a Muslim attend the funeral of a non-Muslim member of his family? Should he pray for the soul of the dead? Most often the response is yes.

• If an employer does not allow time or space for a Muslim to pray during the workday, is it okay for the worker to skip the prayer? Islam recognizes that prayer can be a hardship as well as a joy, and if at all possible one should try to pray at the appropriate time. If it is absolutely impossible, then the situation falls under what are called the laws of necessity, and the prayer can be made up at another time.

• Should Muslims say prayers over meals, or is this just copying a Christian custom? Although it has not been a traditional Muslim custom (other than saying the *bismallah* invoking the name of God, which is said regularly throughout the day), mealtime prayer is generally acceptable, especially in interfaith gatherings. It is actually gaining popularity in some American Muslim families as well.

As one browses through question-and-answer columns in Muslim journals or joins conversations on the World Wide Web, it is evident that answers are not always clear. Advisors sometimes tend to lean heavily on examples from the past that seem to have little or no relevance to life in contemporary America. Clearly, in some cases such a focus tries to help the believer discover the answer for himself or herself. Many Muslims in American society, for example, wonder if it is acceptable or forbidden to have non-Muslims as friends. While some argue that it is most advisable for Muslims to limit their circle of friends to members of their own faith, others cite the example of the Prophet, who cared deeply even for the polytheists of Mecca and expressed his concern for them, as indicative of the importance of care for non-Muslim neighbors. Interfaith issues have become very important for the Muslim community as a whole, especially after 9/11. Muslims are called on regularly to defend Islam and its place in multi-religious America. Nonetheless, interfaith relations is a confusing idea for many American Muslims, even though they recognize that it will be an important part of their immediate and future agenda.

Women's issues surface regularly. "I am a Muslima who really enjoys exercising," writes one woman. "Although I wear loose clothing and a head covering when I exercise or jog, I have been told that any form of exercising in public by Muslim sisters is forbidden. Do I have to stay in the house to exercise?"[18] This question encompasses concerns for dress, women's public participation, and women's behavior in general, as well as the specific issue of exercise. Clearly, there is no one Muslim answer, but the fact is that girls in schools are often encouraged to participate in sports, especially if their clothing is appropriate. Female Muslim athletes sometimes compete officially in sports and games, occasionally even in the Olympics (in 2008 in Beijing twelve women in *hijab* competed[19] and a Moroccan woman and a Syrian woman won gold medals), and are generally able to modify Islamic dress to meet the requirements of modesty and of the sport itself.

Muslim women commonly raise questions about matters related to their marriages. Sometimes these are rather routine, having to do with the running of the household, such as whether a husband should help with the cleaning and child care. Interestingly, the answer in the American context is almost invariably yes, and many cite examples of the Prophet Muhammad's helping at home. Some wonder if the debts incurred by a woman before marriage should become the responsibility of her new husband, and the answer generally given is that they remain hers, although a responsible and caring husband will want to help. Muslim women whose husbands do not feel it is appropriate for them to work outside the home often seek advice about how to change their husband's mind or how to feel that they are contributing to the community while remaining at home.

Should Muslim women shake hands with men who are not members of their family? The responses vary. More urgent is the question that many ask about whether birth control is Islamically acceptable. A majority of American Muslims now seem to feel that women should be able to use some form of birth control, although there is often disagreement as to which forms are approved. Even more difficult to discuss publicly, although some are courageously doing so, is the presence of HIV in the Muslim community and the importance of honest and early education about this societal menace. "When we first started hearing about the AIDS virus," says the wife of a drug user, "it was a gay thing, then it was a Haitian thing, and then they started finding out that it was affecting IV drug users. For a little while, I kept saying, 'Well I don't use drugs. I'm Muslim. I'm praying five times a day.' But that didn't sit well with me because the fact that you pray does not mean that you are exempt from adversity."[20] This courageous woman, who with her husband did in fact test positive for AIDS, is working to spread information among Muslims about the reality of this disease and urging other Muslims who might be living with the virus to undergo testing, develop support groups, and address those risks that may bring AIDS into the Muslim community.

Those in leadership positions in the American Muslim community urge members to be alert to the various ways of giving an Islamic cast to life's transitional events. They offer advice about how to conduct a ceremony for a new baby. Muslim men who wish to marry Christian women are advised on the appropriate preparations and ceremony and about the importance of meeting the conditions of an Islamic marriage, such as the offer of the bride by the bride's guardian and the acceptance by the groom in front of witnesses. Inheritance laws, carefully articulated in the Qur'an, are being interpreted for American Muslims. Muzammil Siddiqi, former president of the Islamic Society of North America, urges American Muslims to prepare their wills as early as possible, providing guidance according to the stipulations of the Qur'an and *hadith*. "Since one does not know when death may come, one should have a will ready at all times," he says.[21] A "Will Kit" prepared by the ISNA is designed to help ensure the best distribution of one's estate according to Islamic specifications.

Among the many concerns facing Muslims who try to live according to Islamic law and custom is proper disposal of the dead. Traditional practice requires that the body be washed by a person of the same gender, wrapped in a clean shroud to signal the equality of all people, and placed in the ground within twenty-four hours of death. Burial of the body in a simple wooden box has been decreed acceptable because the wood disintegrates quickly into the earth, as does the body. The ritual of washing takes several hours.

In the United States the matter has become rather more complex. Muslims, like other Americans, are expected by law to turn the body of the dead person over to a professional mortician for embalming and providing a casket. When bodies are interred in America they are, of course, subject to U.S. regulations. Virginia recently licensed its first Muslim-owned funeral home, and legislation is under way to allow Muslims who learn the trade to be exempted from having to do embalming. Some have proposed two licensing tracks for morticians, one with embalming training and the other without it.

In a few cases individuals are volunteering to serve Muslim families by washing and preparing the body themselves according to Islamic teachings. Clear guidelines for washing and funeral procedures are available on the ISNA Web site. "I am like a midwife who makes house calls," says one such washer, professing to always have an emergency kit in her car containing the necessary supplies. For wrapping cloths she uses new queen-size bedsheets. Although she does not charge for her services, she does donate any monies offered to a Muslim charitable organization. Some specially trained imams also perform these washing services.

Immigrant Muslims sometimes choose to send the bodies of their loved ones home to the country of family origin to be buried. In America some burial grounds have separate sections for Muslims, and in a few cases whole cemeteries are dedicated for Muslim burial. In 2008 in Bristol, Connecticut, state health officials told the local Muslim community that the dead had to be placed in concrete vaults to protect the safety of existing gravesites. Islamic burial rites, however, insist that the body must be in close contact with the earth. "We looked behind the spirit of the [Islamic] law," said the imam of the Bristol mosque, "and found a compromise." They discovered light-weight plastic containers on the Internet that are in accordance with public health standards. Soil is now spread on the bottom of the vault to serve the Islamic purpose. In other cities acceptable solutions are harder to achieve, and new health regulations sometimes force Muslims to bury their dead in sealed vaults.

Innovation and compromise—key concepts for Muslims trying to live Islamic lives in the context of a Judeo-Christian country that is both secular and increasingly aware of the presence of new religious communities within its borders. It will be for succeeding generations to determine whether the innovations and compromises that seem necessary for the Muslim community as it struggles to find its identity in the West are ultimately acceptable to the body of Islam or are simply too unorthodox to be allowed.

CHAPTER EIGHT

Islam in America Post-9/11

Nothing prepared the Muslim community in America for September 11, 2001. The violence perpetrated on that day shocked and horrified Americans in general, and it is now clear that the event has had devastating consequences not only for the United States but for the world. Americans, Iraqis, Afghans, and many others continue to be killed in the resulting wars. The economy of the Western world has staggered while deficits rise as quickly as oil prices. It is difficult to characterize the consequences of the violent acts of a tiny number of Muslim extremists on that September morning. But none have been affected more directly than the Muslim men and women who live in America and who have had to answer again and again for the decisions of terrorists that they don't even recognize as coreligionists.

Imams and others have been asked countless times since 9/11 why Islam fosters violence, and why no Muslims speak out against acts of terror, and why Muslims hate the West. Answers about the essentially peaceful nature of Islam never seem to suffice, or never seem to be heard, as the American public fixates on each new piece of news at home or abroad that might be viewed as justifying a growing fear of the presence of Muslims in America. Some non-Muslims, of course, have gone out of their way to help Muslims present their case honestly and reasonably, and have spearheaded efforts at better interfaith relations. In the meantime, polls indicate that many Americans still do not understand Islam, still worry that cells teaching and planning for violence against the United States are growing, and still assume at heart that the country would be better off if most of its Muslim population were simply to "go home." African American and other American-born Muslims are in the terrible position of having to defend not only their religion but their rightful identity as Americans who are, in fact, already home.

Some Muslim leaders are now recognizing that to keep responding with the platitude that "Islam means peace" simply will no longer suffice, if it ever did. They are asking themselves, as non-Muslims are asking, whether in fact there might be something within their faith that really *does* allow for violent action, and whether new interpretations of classical texts are essential for Islam to be a viable faith in the twenty-first century. They are looking again at each other, wondering where are the common bonds that render Islam a single faith, albeit with a wide range of possible interpretations and understandings, within the whole complex of multi-faith America. And they are looking at Islam in relation to other religions, analyzing the Qur'an and Sunna for an understanding of how Islam views Judaism, Christianity, and other religions and rethinking that understanding in light of a new world and new mandates to live together harmoniously as fellow citizens.

The reality of a post-9/11 America in which government sanctions still weigh heavily and American public opinion still registers caution and even fear of Muslims frames the context in which both private and public discussion about the future of American Islam must take place. Muslims on a daily basis have to deal with what actually has happened to them since the 2001 invasions.

The U.S. Government and Muslim Civil Rights

Some observers, both Muslim and non-Muslim, have likened the treatment of Muslims and Arabs by the U.S. government since 9/11 to that of Germans during World War I and of Japanese Americans during World War II. Legal protections and civil rights have been taken from many Muslim and Arab American citizens for the reason that they are seen as a direct threat to America and its freedoms. It is ironic that the very president to win the first (and only) Muslim bloc vote because of his promise to protect Muslim civil rights, George W. Bush, should have been the one to preside over the abandonment of those rights and the subjection of Muslims and Arabs to humiliation, deportation, and in some cases forms of torture.

It is an often repeated assumption that when the Soviet Union collapsed, the U.S. government needed a new enemy, and Islam was just right for the job. Such an association, of course, was strongly supported by the Israeli lobby and by American Jewish intellectuals such as Daniel Pipes and Steven

Emerson. A series of measures were taken to "protect" American citizens that have resulted in great difficulty for Muslims and Arabs who also hold citizenship in this country:

1. The USA PATRIOT (Providing Appropriate Tools Required to Intercept and Obstruct Terrorism) Act of October 2001 effectively took away all legal protection of the liberty of American Muslims and Arabs. Numerous civil rights agencies have protested this act and worked to have it lifted, as yet to no avail.

2. The U.S. government has been vigilant in monitoring NGOs, civic, charitable, and religious organizations that might be suspected in some way of harboring terrorism. The assets of some have been frozen. This has served to deprive U.S. Muslims of one of the most important ways in which they can fulfill the obligation of paying *zakat*, through support of charities that give to the poor, widows, and orphans.

3. Government raids on the homes and offices of Muslims in positions of national leadership were carried out shortly after 9/11, particularly in northern Virginia. The raids have been interpreted as part of the government's effort to remove former Islamic leaders and encourage a new kind of leadership that will fit its own definition of "moderate Islam."

"Santa Suspect"   © 2002 MIKE LANE AND POLITICALCARTOONS.COM

4. A few males have been arrested and deported from the country, a real-
    ity that has resulted in some cases in women occupying public positions
    both because the men are gone and also to protect other men from such
    public attention.
5. Other government activities have included profiling, censoring of
    Islamic texts, monitoring mosques, and instituting procedures for search
    and seizure.

Muslims are alarmed at the increased vigilance shown by the American
government since 9/11 in identifying potential terrorists. Measures such as
these have made them fear for themselves, their families, and their communities. In addition, Muslims are suffering from the pain of seeing a few of
their coreligionists act in extremist ways that they strongly disavow, some
even saying that they feel true Islam has been hijacked by those who do violence in the name of the faith.

At the same time that Muslims are rethinking what it means to be Muslim in America, they feel constrained by the reality that their deeds are constantly being observed and their words analyzed. The Muslim community is
clearly still under scrutiny.

Many feel the necessity to restrict their sermons to devotional topics and
to avoid all political conversation. Public discussion of anything having to
do with decisions and policies of the American government is strongly curtailed in some quarters, and Muslims fear that the freedom allowed in the use
of the Internet might result in freedom of speech by some that could lead to
more repressive measures for the community in general.

In addition to scrutiny from the top, Muslims face the constant reality of
anti-Muslim feelings on the part of much of the American public. The term
now most often used to describe those feelings, coined in England in the
early part of this decade, is *Islamophobia*.

Islamophobia

Despite the concerted efforts of Muslims and many non-Muslims to present
an image of Islam as moderate and peaceful, polls as recent as 2008 make
it clear that many Americans continue to be uncomfortable with the presence of Muslims in America. The fact that some of the most prominent U.S.
Christian evangelical leaders have portrayed both the Prophet and his religion in extremely unflattering ways—Muhammad as a wild-eyed fanatic

"Suicide Bomber Barbie"   © 2002 Daryl Cagle and politicalcartoons.com

and a killer, a terrorist, and a demon-possessed pedophile, and Islam as an evil religion—has not helped the cause of better interfaith understanding. The Prophet of Islam serves as a model for Muslim belief and behavior, and for Muslims such images are deeply humiliating, as have been many of the cartoons and other depictions of Arabs and Muslims throughout the twentieth and early twenty-first centuries. Their images changed from fools and knaves to oil-rich sheikhs with beards and huge bellies (and harem girls in the background), and now have evolved into machine-gun-toting terrorists and suicide bombers.

Words and images of hate have sometimes led to acts of violence, and a number of American Muslim mosques and public buildings have been the targets of crime and vandalism. Even before 9/11 Muslims generally identified American prejudice against Islam as the major concern they face in trying to live in the United States. The stakes continue to be raised, and polls consistently show that Americans do not understand the religion of Islam. A majority of Americans report that they are either "somewhat" or "very" worried about radicals within the American Muslim community. While they don't believe that most American Muslims condone violence, they do worry that an increase in the number of Muslims allowed to immigrate may lead to the growth of radical cells or even to advocacy of *shari'a* law. (In fact the government has made it difficult for Muslims to emigrate; only a small number of Iraqis have actually been admitted.) Public voices are still heard on radio, TV, and videos propagating the myth that Muslims indoctrinate their children into a "culture of hatred," as portrayed, for example, in the 2005 documentary film *Obsession: Radical Islam's War Against the West*. More than 28 million copies of the work on DVD have been distributed free of charge. The film, in which radical Islam is equated with Nazism under the convenient label "Islamofascism," ends with a map of the world with a swastika superimposed on it, followed by scenes of carnage caused by "Islamic radicals."

Muslims are particularly concerned about the potential for even greater misinformation and propagation of prejudice with the rapid development of Internet use. Increasingly, schoolchildren and teenagers can access the "Net" for school reports and other projects, and much of what they find is propaganda fostering a negative image of Islam. The threat of Islam is real, warns a book available on the Internet, more than communism was, because Muslims are willing to die for the cause of Islam, spreading their faith through "jihad," or holy war. We must work to stop the spread of Islam before it is too late, warns the author. Those concerned with the easy dissemination of such materials note that Islam is the only monotheistic religion that has become the object of such insults and false accusations. Other instances of anti-Muslim prejudice can be found expressed more informally, but no less effectively, if one accesses Internet chat rooms.

One of the primary tasks of many of the Muslim organizations mentioned in this book is to identify ways in which prejudice against Islam and Muslims continues to be present on the American scene. Consistent efforts are being made to ensure that information about Islam in textbooks and other curricular materials in the public schools is accurate and unbiased. Much work remains to be done. A 2008 review of texts adopted for use in California and available to schools nationwide, for example, revealed that students are still unlikely to get a complete and accurate understanding of contemporary issues in Islam, including terrorism, or of the historical context of the religion. Some organizations work to identify ways in which the public media regularly distort and misrepresent information about Islam in America as well as on the international scene and to call to public attention instances in which U.S. and Canadian Muslims experience prejudicial or unfair treatment in the workplace or other public arenas.

"The New Wall"   © 2003 MONTE WOLVERTON AND POLITICALCARTOONS.COM

Primary among the organizations specifically dedicated to identifying and combating anti-Muslim prejudice in the United States and Canada is the Council on American-Islamic Relations (CAIR) in Washington, D.C. Its American-Muslim Research Center (ARC) documents incidents and events that affect Muslim civil rights in America. Recognizing that most Americans are woefully ignorant and misinformed about Islam, ARC encourages local Muslim communities to reach out and educate other segments of American society through the dissemination of accurate information. CAIR regularly publicizes, on the Internet, incidents in which Muslims in the United States have received unfair or prejudicial treatment. (Anyone may request to join the read-only mailing list of CAIR-NET.) Descriptions of these incidents are often followed by specific information as to where readers may write or be in contact with an appropriate party to influence positive resolution of an issue. Muslim parents who are concerned about the effects of anti-Muslim prejudice on their children can go to the web and find a number of helpful sites. Parents are strongly encouraged to be as candid as possible in discussing prejudice with their children, helping them to realize that they are not alone in their fears and worries and that families and communities can be a strong support.

Not all Muslims living in the United States, of course, are concerned with efforts to protect Muslims from unfair treatment, as not all participate in the various forms of Muslim religious life that are increasingly evident in communities across America. Yet for a growing number of those who consciously identify with Islam and want to live in ways that support their understanding of the faith and its requirements, more and more structures are being put in place. Prejudice against their religion is a reality with which all American Muslims must deal in one way or another, but both Muslim and non-Muslim individuals and organizations are stepping up efforts to identify and address incidents of misrepresentation and unfair treatment. Local and national groups provide instruction and support, and information is available in a variety of forms to help Muslims deal with virtually any concerns. In the meantime, Muslims are finding increasing support in many segments of American society for their efforts to present Islam fairly and reasonably. With the help of colleagues in education, other religious organizations, and even some quarters of the political establishment, they may eventually find that combating anti-Muslim prejudice and offering a picture of a reasonable religious community working for the betterment of American society will become easier to accomplish.

Can There Be an "American *umma*"?

As we have seen, a great range of interpretations of Islam characterizes its faith and practice in the United States. Each group must continue to ask itself if its own interpretation of Islam, and the corresponding implications for how its members choose to live and comport themselves, is indeed relevant in contemporary American society. Will other Americans find it acceptable and if not, to what extent does it matter? Will the youth of their community continue to find it relevant? Those who up to now have tried to lead lives of relative isolation, fearful that too much contact with America will compromise their own faith and culture, now recognize that current generations are finding it necessary to be more open, more receptive to the culture of which they have become a part. And those who choose more "secular" solutions to questions of Islamic identity in the West are sometimes finding that they may have lost some of the clarity and distinctiveness of what it means to be Muslim.

American Muslims have tried for many years to avoid the kind of terminology that polarizes them into "isolationists" on the one hand and "accommodationists" on the other. Neither alternative has been satisfactory to Muslims who are searching for guidelines and principles that can speak to the majority of the members of the complex body that is American Islam. Such potential polarization is less an option in the post-9/11 climate, in which the government and its people are insisting on the emergence of a moderate Islam that avoids the extremes that seem so potentially troublesome. A major task for Muslims now is to clarify what matters are flexible and may be reinterpreted in the Western context and what issues are so clearly part of God's design for human life and response that they cannot be negotiated. What kinds of adjustments to classical interpretations of Sunna and *shari'a* must be made by those living in the United States and how can the limit of flexible interpretation be determined? Which elements of law and custom are mandatory for all faithful Muslims, no matter where they live, and which allow for some reasonable degree of interpretation? What *does* constitute a modern Islam, and how can non-Muslims be made to understand its viability in the America of today? Muslims in all American communities are asking these questions with interest and concern, and advisors representing a range of perspectives, cultures, and interpretations are attempting to provide answers.

Many Muslims living in the United States, both the more recently arrived and members of second- and third-generation Muslim families, do want to assimilate as much as possible into American culture and try not to emphasize elements of their identity that would differentiate them from others. This disinclination to over-identify with Islam has characterized a significant number of American Muslims since the early days of immigrant arrival, fostered, as we have seen, by such factors as the search for employment, intermarriage, dissatisfaction with mosque leadership, and various forms of engagement with American culture. For some, the increase in anti-Muslim prejudice in light of terrorist activities, pro-Israeli sentiment, anti-American rhetoric from many Arab Muslim leaders, and a number of other highly publicized international realities in the last several decades has encouraged this assimilation.

For other members of America's Muslim community, however, these very factors, including the rise in revivalist Islam in many parts of the world, have reinvigorated their religious awareness and responsibility. Encouraged by the challenge that Islam poses internationally to Western secularism and worried about the influences of that secularism on their children in America, they have increasingly looked to and advocated Islam as both a faith and a way of life. Certainly, many first-, second-, and third-generation Muslims do not want to identify themselves too openly in American society for fear of becoming, or having their children become, targets of prejudice and discrimination. Many others, however, are tired of what they see as the biased and unfair representations of Islam and Muslims in the American media and take the opportunity to correct those images by providing in their own lives public examples of what "real Islam" looks like when practiced by conscientious and faithful adherents. For these Muslims—including immigrants, African Americans, and others who have converted to Islam—it is essential to find ways in which to live and express their faith and their Islamic identity at the same time that they acknowledge the necessity of adapting to and participating in American life. They are working out many different modes of participation, and American Islam is now at what many would consider a crucial stage as Muslims attempt to move toward a viable future in the American context.

The search for what, if anything, unifies all Muslims in America is an ongoing concern with a great many dimensions. The question is asked in a great variety of ways: Is there anything that distinguishes American Islam such that there can be an identifiable American *umma*? We have seen in the previous chapters many of the ways in which the quest for such unity is elusive. Immigrants have squabbled over differences in culture and custom. Some newly arrived Pakistanis, for example, may think second- and third-generation Arab Muslims are too liberal in their practice of Islam, and the Arabs in response may resent the "bossy" way in which the Pakistanis tell them how to be Muslim. Many Sunnis vigorously affirm that relations between Sunnis and Shi'ites are wonderful in America, while voices within the Shi'ite community protest that indeed, all is not harmonious. Blacks, Hispanics, Native Americans, and others struggle to find their identity both under the greater umbrella of American Islam and also specifically as members of their respective racial-ethnic groupings. While most national Muslim organizations are predominantly either immigrant or African American, and while there is still lingering resentment among some blacks that they are not directly included in the work of an organization like ISNA, it is also true that a number of coordinating councils now include both immigrant and African American Muslims in positions of leadership. There is no question that continuing the efforts already under way to foster better appreciation, understanding, and cooperation among the different groups that constitute American Islam is an issue extremely high on the agenda for Muslims in the United States.

Almost a decade has now passed since the tragedies of September 11, 2001. While the U.S. government continues to be wary, as do many of its citizens, no violent acts have been perpetrated by Muslims in America, although some arrests have been made. Tensions have eased a bit, though we are still in Code Orange, and Muslims have at least some reason to hope that their constant vigilance in promoting better understanding of Islam, and their responses when injustices have been perpetrated against Muslim Americans, are bearing some fruit. Nevertheless it still is not easy to be a Muslim in America. "I keep my physical and my mental bags packed all the time," says a female Egyptian college professor, "in case anything crazy should happen. Any incident of terror in which a Muslim is implicated, and I'm out of here back to Cairo for good." Many other Muslims of immigrant background feel the same way, while African Americans bear the double burden of being the recipients of both continuing racial prejudice and the knowledge that further Muslim violence in America would leave them nowhere to hide.

Some Muslims would argue, however, that for all the atrocity of 9/11 it may have opened some important doors for them. All indications are that before that time few Americans had much awareness of the presence of Muslims in America. With the attacks Muslims were forced out of anonymity, so to speak, and into the spotlight. Despite the resulting discomfort, and the constant need to have to respond to questions of whether Islam is a religion of violence and why Muslims hate Americans ("If I have to answer those questions one more time I really will scream," said a Muslim called on repeatedly to defend his faith), there came also the opportunity to seriously engage with the issue of Islam as a truly American religion. As Muslims have had to defend their faith, and as they have moved from invisibility to visibility, many have responded with more overt forms of public acknowledgment of Islam. Veiling has increased among women, as have other forms of Islamic dress for men. Attendance at Friday services has increased, more people are observing Ramadan, and the essentially public nature of Islam is no longer hidden but is publicly affirmed.

There is no question that since 9/11 Muslims have rallied, have begun seriously to address tough issues related to living Islamically in America, and—perhaps most importantly—have gathered the courage to seriously ponder their own religion and its roots. It has become a truism to say that if the religion of Islam is to experience any kind of reformation it is most likely that it will happen in the United States, where freedom of religion in general and the absence of state Islam in particular allow more flexibility of interpretation than is true in most other places in the world. It may be that 9/11 was the single most energizing force in encouraging the kind of deep intellectual reflection on Islam that was most evident in the early centuries of the faith.

Tensions in the American House of Islam

Clearly, if there is to be an American *umma* with a sense of integrity and definition, its members must be honest about the differences that cause strain and tension as well as those that give it clarity and commonality. Many rifts exist within American Islam, and the strong attempts at unity expressed in the face of post-9/11 responses may paper them over temporarily but not really solve the issues at stake. On the contrary, it can certainly be argued that part of the task of Muslims in this new twenty-first-century Western location is to be honest about the distinctions that inevitably constitute such a heterodox multicultural Islam and to face up to the fact that all is not entirely happy within the house of American Islam. Following are a few of the potentially contentious arenas:

1. While they may not feel comfortable with the labels, American Muslims are being forced to think in terms of "liberal" and "conservative" in identifying streams of thought in their midst. Are the more conservative voices of Saudi Wahhabism, so influential in immigrant communities, especially in the 1980s, going to be dominant in the American context? A great deal of literature is being developed arguing that this kind of conservative ideology has no place in twenty-first-century America. Are the attempts to stretch Islam into a more liberal position exemplified, for instance, in the mixed-gender worship service led by Amina Wadud or the online defense of gays and lesbians going to be trendsetting for American Muslims? The answer is probably not, evidenced by the fact that the very liberal "Progressive Muslims" movement that appeared to be ascendant only a few years ago has faded from view, replaced by a range of more "moderate" attempts at interpreting Islam and its texts. The American Islamic Congress, for example, promoting tolerance and the exchange of ideas among Muslims and with others, subtitles its Web site "Passionate About Moderation."

2. Throughout the history of Islam, Sunnis and Shi'ites have often experienced severe tensions, generally more for political than theological reasons. That has not been the case in the American context, where until recently the two groups and their subsets have lived together in relative ease. The range of problems that all Muslims encounter in finding their identity in the United States has tended to overshadow internecine difficulties. The American invasion of Iraq and its aftermath, however, seem

to have initiated some significant changes in the Sunni-Shi'ite relationship in the United States. Sectarian tensions in Iraq have been reflected
in some instances in a worsening of mutual attitudes in America, and
in several instances have resulted in Shi'ite mosques being vandalized.
Mohamed Sabur, codirector of the Shi'ite advocacy group called the
Qunoot Foundation, founded in 2007 to address the problem of intra-
faith relations, looks to the destruction in 2006 of the golden dome of
the Al-Askariya Mosque in Samarra, Iraq, as a turning point in rising
sectarian tensions. Even Saddam Hussain himself would not have committed such an attack on one of Shi'ism's holiest shrines, says Sabur.
Some Sunnis in America now condemn Shi'ites as heretics, and Shi'ites
profess themselves increasingly uncomfortable with praying in Sunni
mosques. Shi'ite leaders are becoming more assertive in claiming their
rights within the American Muslim community, a movement that is supported by some Sunni imams who are raising funds to help rebuild the
Samarra shrine. The ultimate course of the Iraq war, still in question at
this writing, may strongly influence the future relationships of Sunnis
and Shi'ites in America.

3. While demographics and the flow of time have blurred the lines between
   what used to be called "immigrant Islam" and "African American Islam,"
   some blacks are becoming more vigilant in calling to the attention of their
   Muslim brothers and sisters the fact that they sometimes still feel left out
   of the conversation. For many years ISNA and the African American
   national conference were held at the same time, thus emphasizing the
   separation. The 2000 presidential election fiasco, in which members of
   the immigrant community chose a candidate for Muslim support without
   checking with their African American coreligionists, opened the door
   for some honest conversation about inclusiveness and racial equality
   within American Islam. A number of black academics have now begun
   to talk and write seriously about the hurt and anger that they have felt at
   being "shut out" and not considered true Muslims by those of immigrant
   descent. This honesty has been jarring within American Islam, but has
   led to serious conversation about trying to bridge the divide often felt
   between blacks and Muslims of other heritage. The efforts of people like
   Imam Siraj Wahaj at Masjid Taqwa in New York, working with youth
   to erase lines of color and culture, may pave the way for better intra-
   communal understanding and appreciation.

4. Another area of tension within American Islam, though one steadfastly
   denied or unacknowledged by most Muslims, is that between men and

women. As we have seen, even Muslim women (or men, of whom there are a very few) who want to adopt the identity of feminist, insist that their feminism is markedly different from that of predominantly white, upper-middle-class non-Muslim American women, and they also assert that men and women enjoy relationships of equity if not absolutely equality within the system of Islam. Nonetheless, voices are increasingly being raised drawing attention to the distinction between the parity enjoyed by men and women as described in the Qur'an and the actual practices of men in relation to women in cultures around the world and, in the case of a few Muslim feminist analysts, also in the American community. Gwendolyn Simmons of the University of Florida offers a straightforward critique of what she sees as the failure of Islam to stand up to its promise of gender equality. "Frankly," she says, "I am tired of the contortions, the bending over backwards, and the justifications for the oppressive, repressive and exclusionary treatment of women in majority Islamic societies as well as in minority Muslim communities in the U.S.A."[1] New feminist interpretations of the Qur'an are contributing to the frank conversation about women in Islam, as are honest descriptions of the treatment that some American Muslim women are beginning to acknowledge does not measure up to the rhetoric about male-female relationships. That story, too, is still in the early stages of its telling.

5. One more area of potential contention for Muslims in America is the complex set of relationships between themselves as residents of a Western country and the individuals and groups who have continued until now to be influential on their thinking and, often, on their well-being. Will the Wahhabis and the Salafis continue through finances or ideology to affect the ways in which Americans interpret Islam? Will young American Muslims who may find themselves attracted to international ideologies such as Al Qaida develop quiet cells of opposition on American soil? Will Shi'ites whose lives are now so deeply indebted to the religious leaders of Iraq, Iran, Lebanon, and other areas of the world continue that dependent relationship, or will they begin to develop forms of American Shi'ite Islam free of such direct guidance? Will American Muslims in the near future be able to develop adequate training facilities for imams and religious leaders so that they do not have to depend on immigrant leadership often ill-equipped to speak English and unfamiliar with the contexts in which Muslims live and work? A great deal of energy today is going into thinking through these kinds of relationships between Muslims in America and the communities of influence in their homes of origin.

Community Relations

If Muslims are being challenged in this post-9/11 environment to look more carefully at relationships within the Islamic community itself, they are also turning outward to establish and cement other kinds of relationships with those outside their immediate circle.

While immigrant Muslims, or those of immigrant heritage, were once reluctant to enter fully into American public life, that situation has obviously changed in recent years, especially since September 11. Although they have not repeated the attempt to establish a national election bloc, Muslims are getting involved in politics at all levels. They are beginning to work through various avenues to exert their influence locally and nationally. While formerly they may have donated money and had it returned because the recipient feared that it would not "look right," Muslims are strategically planning their contributions in such a way that they can be part of the system of influence. They are active on town and city commissions, on local school boards, and in many other venues that allow them to become contributing members of American society. "Concept and Vision—Awareness and Steady Progress" is the motto of the Maryland Muslim Council, for example, as it not only creates grassroots Muslim councils but also works to establish credibility with the larger community and makes plans for the future building of hospitals, shelters, and food banks that will be open to everyone.

Some Muslims who are part of the medical profession are establishing free medical clinics in urban areas. "Caring for Our Neighbors: How Muslim Community-Based Health Organizations Are Bridging the Healthcare Gap in America" is the title of a major new study released by ISPU, the Institute for Social Policy and Understanding. Muslim community-based health organizations, which the study tracks in Los Angeles, Detroit, Houston, and Chicago, are providing an important safety net in health care access for what the report calls the most underserved communities in America. The study helps shed light on the demographic populations served by Muslim health care providers and the growing role of clinics in maintaining American public health and fostering community building. Lance Laird, author of the report, notes the similarity of these Muslim health organizations to Christian and Jewish hospitals established earlier in U.S. history.

The same efforts at connection outside the community are being extended in the realm of religion. As we saw earlier, soon after the Twin Towers destruction Muslims began to try to repair relations with non-Muslims by holding mosque open houses. Many hundreds of mosques invited Christians, Jews, and others to visit with them, see where and how they pray, and hear about an Islam that is nonviolent. While for many years Muslims were the recipients of invitations to participate in interfaith dialogue, increasingly they are themselves becoming the initiators and the hosts of dialogues among Muslims, Jews, and Christians. Sayyid Saeed of the Islamic Society of North America works for better interfaith relations out of his office in Washington, D.C. Saeed, who has received an award for his work on dialogue, has established connections with Jews, Seventh Day Adventists, Lutherans, and others. Muslims and Jews have been participating in local discussions in a number of places under the general rubric "We Refuse to Be Enemies," centering on the hope to reconcile Jews and Palestinians.

Members of the Muslim Student Association are inviting their non-Muslim friends to attend what are known as Fast-a-thons during Ramadan—participants donate the money that they would have spent on food to homeless shelters and soup kitchens. Muslim campus chaplains, who are increasing in number, are regularly providing programming that invites non-Muslims to share in the activities of their Muslim groups. Project Nur, sponsored by the American Islamic Congress, is another example of an initiative designed to help build bridges between Muslim and non-Muslim students on university campuses by promoting coexistence, tolerance, and understanding.[2]

In July 2008 Yale Divinity School hosted the first public dialogue launched by Muslim intellectuals for Christian leaders in the United States. It was a follow-up on what is known as the "A Common Word" document, signed and issued a year earlier by 138 prominent Muslims around the world calling on Christian and Muslim leaders to lead the way in helping to promote peace between Islam and the West. Christians in attendance at Yale were mainly Protestant theologians and church leaders, with some evangelicals, Catholics, and Jews also present. Both Sunni and Shi'ite Muslims came from many international locales to participate. The core of the "A Common Word" project is the affirmation that Islam and Christianity share the common values of love of God and love of neighbor. The group is scheduled to meet with Anglicans in October and Pope Benedict in November. Observers of the July gathering felt that one of its most interesting aspects was the opportunity for Christian evangelicals, whose stated purpose is the conversion of Muslims to Christianity, to talk with representatives of the Islamic faith, for whom conversion is apostasy. For now the project is aimed at Christians and Muslims, although it is anticipated that eventually Jews will be drawn in.

Intellectually, serious efforts have been made since 9/11 to address the question of pluralism in Islam. While Americans who are not Muslim are asking Muslims whether their theology/ideology allows for their full participation in a multi-religious America, Muslims are themselves looking at their texts and their interpretations to understand whether pluralism is actually a viable alternative to Islamic exclusivism. Many of the best Islamic scholars in America are arguing that *pluralism* is the best term to describe the conditions at the time of the Prophet and the revelation of the Qur'an, the history of Islam in its relations with other communities of faith, Islam itself in the contemporary world, and Islam within the culture of the United States. Only a few writers, however, have tried to distinguish between pluralism as a description of multiplicity and pluralism as an attitude affirming that such multiplicity is God's choice for humanity. The bottom line of the discussion, of course, is whether Islam is in fact open to accepting religions such as Judaism and Christianity on their own terms.

Part of the discussion of pluralism tries to prove that Islam is compatible with liberal democracy, and thus belongs in contemporary America. A great deal of discussion has been held showing that Islamic values do promote democracy, human rights, and political pluralism. The discourse is also serving as a vehicle for those who want to argue that the kind of repressive Islam that fostered the ideology behind the 9/11 attacks has no role in genuine Islam, and certainly not in American Islam. Sherman Jackson of the University of Michigan identifies what he calls the "false universal" in Islam, meaning the construction of an Islamic ideology that sounds like Wahhabism and excludes black American Muslims. The reality of 9/11 has made it crucial that a reformed and pluralistic Islam be honed for inclusion in American society, Jackson says. The danger comes when the dominant is equated with the universal, i.e., when primarily imported and traditional interpretations of Islam (as in Wahhabi and Salafi) are offered to the exclusion of others (meaning African Americans). UCLA's Khalid Abou El Fadl in *The Place of Tolerance in Islam* (2002) also argues in defense of an Islam different from that propagated by exclusionary, intolerant Wahhabism.[3]

Others are attempting to come to terms with the fundamental theological question suggested by pluralism: Does Islam accept other religions? For the most part, those who try to respond to this question affirm the commonalities among faiths, at least at the spiritual level, and sometimes they point to the metaphysical unity of all faiths. Judaism and Christianity are accepted as being within the continuity of monotheism, underscoring the unity of the traditions. While most Muslims today, even in America, are reluctant to put any other religion on a par with Islam, some will argue that God has not granted a spiritual monopoly to any one religion, that the Qur'an in fact encourages competition in virtue and goodness among all people of faith, and that Islam is uniquely positioned to serve as a reconciling force among different religions because at its core it promotes tolerance and respect for all. While most of those addressing the question of theological pluralism in Islam affirm that it means acceptance of only Judaism and Christianity, the religions of the Book, as true and acceptable religions, a very few will go even further. The conversation should be extended to include Buddhists, Taoists, and members of other faiths, says Fathi Osman of the Los Angeles Institute for the Study of Islam in the Contemporary World.[4] Isma'ili Harvard scholar Ali Asani seems to take it a step further when he actually moves to expand the "People of the Book" category to include other religious groups such as Hindus and Buddhists, who were encountered by Muslims in the early days of the spread of Islam.[5] Most American Muslims are not willing to make such theological concessions, though many are eager to think more deeply about what it means to affirm the faith of Islam in a culture in which other religions are being practiced and promoted.

The Muslim community in America faces many questions as it looks to the immediate future. How will Muslims, and thus American Islam itself, change as second, third, and fourth generations of immigrants become more distant from their places of origin? Non-Muslim Americans can no longer talk about Islam as "foreign" or even as an "Eastern" religion. Islam has become part of America, and Muslims have become a growing and vital segment of its population. How will this affect both external and internal perceptions of Islam and Muslims? Will the majority of Muslims identify themselves as Americans who happen to be Muslim or as Muslims who happen to live in America? What differences will such identification make in their public and private lives? Will Islam in America achieve its currently stated goal of becoming a significant political force? Is it likely that American resentment and prejudice against Islam will subside as the result of greater contact with Muslims and better understanding of their faith and practices? Who will provide the authoritative voices for American Muslims as they are increasingly able to choose where to go for direction?

The search for an American *umma* distinct from the racial-ethnic identities that have often served to divide and separate rather than unify is high on the agenda of many Muslims today and is particularly important to the youth who will be the new leaders of the community. The coming decades will be crucial as Muslims in the United States become clearer about who they are, what they need, and how they must organize to make their voices heard amid the competing claims of a diverse American society. Whatever patterns of religious, social, and personal life develop, clearly they will have to represent both a continuity with the life and faith of the Prophet and his community and the emergence of a new entity with its own qualities and characteristics—a truly American Islam.

CHRONOLOGY

1492 on	A few Muslims expelled from Spain may have reached American shores
1700s–1800s	Black Africans brought to the Americas via transatlantic slave trade, of whom an estimated 10–20 percent were Muslims
1730–1731	Ayuba Suleiman Diallo (Job Ben Solomon) arrives in Annapolis, Maryland, from Bundu, Senegal, enslaved—writes to his father to free him
1829	Ibrahima supported by U.S. Secretary of State Henry Clay, travels to Liberia
1831	Omar ibn Sayyid pens autobiography (in Arabic) in North Carolina
ca. 1875	Beginning of Muslim immigration, primarily from Syria
early 1900s	First Muslim communities in the Midwest
1907	American Mohammedan Society founded in New York City
1910–1927	Hazrat Inayat Khan teaches Sufi doctrines across America
1913	Moorish American Science Temple established in Newark, New Jersey
1918 on	Second major wave of Muslim immigrants
1920	Mufti Muhammad Sadiq becomes first Ahmadi missionary to America
1920s on	Ford Motor Plant in Dearborn, Michigan, attracts Muslim workers
1924	Islamic Mission of American (popularly called State Street Mosque) founded in New York City
1938	First Canadian mosque built in Edmonton, Alberta

1930s	Federal Writers Project records oral histories of Muslim slaves on islands off Georgia coast
1930s	Third wave of Muslim immigration
1930–1933	Nation of Islam begins
1930–1933	W. D. Fard preaches in Detroit
1932	Elijah Muhammad moves NOI headquarters to Chicago
1934	Completion of "Mother Mosque of America" in Cedar Rapids, Iowa
1935	Arab American Banner Society established in Boston
1947	Malcolm Little joins the NOI while in prison
1947–1960	Muslim immigration from India-Pakistan and Eastern Europe greatly increases
1950	Ahmadiyya headquarters moves to American Fazl Mosque in Washington, D.C.
1952	Federation of Islamic Organizations formed
1952	Malcolm (now X) is released from prison and begins preaching NOI doctrines
1957	Islamic Center in Washington, D.C., completed
late 1950s	Hanafi Madhdhab Center established in Washington, D.C.
1960s	Pir Vilayat Khan emerges as leader of the Sufi order in the West
early 1960s	Darul Islam movement grows up in Brooklyn
1961	Malcolm X founds *Muhammad Speaks* newspaper
1963	Muslim Student Association (MSA) formed at University of Illinois
1964	Allah's Nation of the Five Percenters founded in Harlem
1964	Boxer Cassius Clay becomes Muhammad Ali
1964	Malcolm X makes pilgrimage to Mecca, breaks with the NOI
1964	Malcolm X removed as minister of Temple Number Seven in New York
1965	Malcolm (now El Hajj Malik el-Shabazz) assassinated
1965	Repeal of immigration quotas leads to great increase in Muslim immigration
1968	Islamic Circle of North America (ICNA) founded
1970s	Nimatullahi Order of Sufis in America (Shi'ite) founded in San Francisco
1971	Bawa Muhaiyaddeen Fellowship founded in Philadelphia
1975	Elijah Muhammad dies; Wallace Muhammad becomes leader of NOI
1975	Muslim Student Association headquarters set up in Plainfield, Indiana

1977–1985	Wallace Muhammad brings his followers to orthodox Islam
1978	Louis Farrakhan breaks with Wallace and begins to rebuild the NOI
1980s	Sufism grows among African Americans, especially West African Tijaniyya and Bawa Muhaiyaddeen Fellowship
1980	Wallace Muhammad becomes Warith Deen Mohammed, articulates theories of social change in black America based on Qur'an and Sunna
1981	Islamic Society of North America (ISNA) formed
1983	American Islamic College established in Chicago
1983	Warith Deen declares his followers members of Sunni Islam
mid-1980s	PIEDAD Latino Community and Alianza Islamica founded in New York City
1980s–1990s	Emergence of a number of Muslim political action committees
1980s–1990s	NOI helps fight drug problems in Washington, D.C.
1980s–1990s	Worldwide Muslim immigration for political, social, and economic reasons
1990s	African American Sunni Muslim women form Qur'an study groups, devise grassroots womanist reading of sacred sources
1990s	Islamic hip-hop produced by Five Percenters and Sunni Muslims
1990	American Muslim Council (AMC) organized in Washington, D.C.
1990	Warith Deen Mohammed becomes first Muslim to open the U.S. Senate with prayer
1991	Imam Siraj Wahaj becomes first Muslim to open U.S. House of Representatives with prayer
1993	First Islamic chaplain commissioned in U.S. Army
1993	Islamic Assembly of North America (IANA) founded
1994	Council on American-Islamic Relations (CAIR) established in Washington, D.C.
1994	Junior Association of Muslim Men established at Sing Sing prison
1995	Louis Farrakhan addresses hundreds of thousands as part of Million Man March; calls for interfaith cooperation, spiritual renewal for black men
1996	Denver International Airport first to feature a mosque
1996	First Islamic chaplain commissioned in U.S. Navy
1996	Graduate School of Islamic and Social Sciences (GSISS) begun in Virginia
1997	Muslim symbol displayed on White House ellipse
1998	Pentagon hosts Muslims for Ramadan meal

2000   First attempt at voting a Muslim bloc in the presidential elections

2001   September 11 attacks on New York, Washington, D.C., and Pennsylvania

2002   House of Representatives recognizes Islam as one of world's great religions

2005   Amina Wadud leads mixed-gender congregational prayers in New York City

2006   Council on American-Islamic Relations releases report titled "American Public Opinion About Islam and Muslims"

2006   Ingrid Mattson becomes first female president of Islamic Society of North America

2006   Keith Maurice Ellison becomes first Muslim U.S. congressman

2007   Laleh Bakhtiar becomes first female American translator of the Qur'an

2008   "A Common Word" conference with Muslims and Christians takes place at Yale University

2008   Imam Warith Deen Mohammed dies of heart disease

NOTES

Introduction

1. Lisa Miller, "Islam in America: A Special Report," *Newsweek*, July 30, 2007, online.

2. Brad Braiker, "Americans Are Mixed on U.S. Muslims," *Newsweek*, July 20, 2007, online.

3. Leila Ahmed, *A Border Passage: From Cairo to America—A Woman's Journey* (New York: Farrar, Straus, and Giroux, 1999), 292.

4. Muzammil H. Siddiqi, "Striving for Moral Excellence," *Islamic Horizons*, September/October 1997, 28.

5. Isma'il al Faruqi, "Islamic Ideals in North America," cited by Larry Poston in "The Future of *Da'wa* in North America," *American Journal of Islamic Social Sciences* 8, no. 3 (December 1991): 511.

6. Syed Rifat Mahmoud, "For Your Kind Attention," *United Muslims of America Update* 1, no. 1 (November 1996):1.

1. Muslim Faith and Practice

1. Richard Wormser, *American Islam: Growing Up Muslim in America* (New York: Walker, 1994), 21.

2. http://welinkmuslims.com.

3. Ibid.

4. http://www.cair.com/Zakat.aspx.

5. www.thezakat.org/Zakat-Handbok.aspx.

6. "Ramadan: The Month of Fasting as Observed by Young Muslims," *The Minaret*, January 1997, 25–27.

7. Ibid.

8. Suad Lawrence Islam, "Nector of My Life," *Al Jumuah* (12, 1418 Hijri):30.

9. Michael Wolfe, *The Hadj: An American's Pilgrimage to Mecca* (New York: Grove/Atlantic, 1998).

10. Shahid Athar, *Reflections of an American Muslim* (Chicago: Kazi Publications, 1994), 208.

2. Contributors to the Development of Islam

1. Salmon Rushdie, *The Satanic Verses* (London: Viking, 1988), 394.

2. Cited by W. Montgomery Watt, *The Faith and Practice of al-Ghazali* (London: Grove-Atlantic, 1998).

3. Islam Comes to America

1. See Allan D. Austin, *African Muslims in Antebellum America: A Sourcebook* (New York: Garland, 1984).

2. info@mothermosque.org.

3. Mark Ferris, "To 'Achieve the Pleasure of Allah': Immigrant Muslims in New York City," in Yvonne Yazbeck Haddad and Jane I. Smith, eds., *Muslim Communities in North America* (Albany: State University of New York Press, 1994), 226–227.

4. Asad Husain and Harold Vogelaar, "Activities of the Immigrant Muslim Communities in Chicago," in Haddad and Smith, *Muslim Communities in North America*, 254.

5. M. K. Hermansen, "The Muslims of San Diego," in Haddad and Smith, *Muslim Communities in North America*, 171.

6. Allen E. Richardson, *Islamic Cultures in North America: Patterns of Belief and Devotion of Muslims from Asian Countries in the United States and Canada* (New York: Pilgrim, 1981).

7. Abdulaziz Sachedina, "A Minority Within a Minority: The Case of the Shi'a in North America," in Haddad and Smith, *Muslim Communities in North America*, 3–14.

8. Linda Walbridge, "The Shi'a Mosques and Their Congregations in Dearborn," in Haddad and Smith, *Muslim Communities in North America*, 354.

9. Not to be confused with the *Muslim World* journal produced for nearly a century by Hartford Seminary in Connecticut.

10. *The Message*, February 1997, 29.

11. *The Message*, August 1997, cover.

12. Hazrat Inayat Khan, *The Sufi Message of Hazrat Inayat Khan*, vols. 1–13 (Geneva: International Headquarters Sufi Movement, 1966–1982).

13. Gisela Webb, "Tradition and Innovation in Contemporary American Islamic Spirituality: The Bawa Muhaiyaddeen Fellowship," in Haddad and Smith, *Muslim Communities in North America*, 75–108.

14. Javad Nurbakhsh, *In the Paradise of the Sufis* (New York: Khaniqahi-Nimatullahi Publications, 1979).

4. Islam in the African American Community

1. Alex Haley, *Roots* (Garden City, N.Y.: Doubleday, 1976).

2. Quoted from Albert J. Raboteau, *Slave Religion* (New York: Oxford University Press, 1976), 44–47, in Adib Rashad, *Islam, Black Nationalism, and Slavery* (Beltsville, Md.: Writers Inc., 1995), 45.

3. Quoted by Laleh Bakhtiar, *Sufi Women of America: Angels in the Making* (Chicago: Kazi Publications, 1996), 23.

4. "Noble Drew Ali—A Centennial Remembrance (1986–1986)" (n.p.).

5. See C. Eric Lincoln, *Black Muslims in America*, rev. ed. (Boston: Beacon, 1973).

6. Said during a meeting with Hartford Seminary faculty and mosque members, June 1997.

7. Malcolm X, in Alex Haley, *The Autobiography of Malcolm X* (New York: Ballantine, 1964 [1992]), 97.

8. Malcolm X, "The Truth About the Black Muslims," address at the Boston University School of Theology, May 24, 1960, cited by Lincoln in *Black Muslims in America*, 19.

9. Mattias Gardell, *In the Name of Elijah Muhammad: Louis Farrakhan and the Nation of Islam* (Durham, N.C.: Duke University Press, 1996), 97.

10. Haley, *Autobiography of Malcolm X*, 210.

11. Steven Barboza, *American Jihad: Islam After Malcolm X* (New York: Doubleday, 1994), 104.

12. Ibid., 143.

13. R. Mukhtar Curtis, "Urban Muslims: The Formation of the Dar ul-Islam Movement," in Yvonne Yazbeck Haddad and Jane I. Smith, eds., *Muslim Communities in North America* (Albany: State University of New York Press, 1994), 51–74.

14. Yusuf Nuruddin, "The Five Percenters: A Teenage Nation of Gods and Earths," in Haddad and Smith, *Muslim Communities in North America*, 109–132.

5. The Public Practice of Islam

1. Yahya Emerick, "The Fight for the Soul of Islam in America," in Michael Wolfe, ed., *Taking Back Islam: American Muslims Reclaim Their Faith* (New York: Rodale, 2002), 198.

2. Gulzar Haider, "Muslim Space and the Practice of Architecture," in Barbara Daly Metcalf, ed., *Making Muslim Space in North America and Europe* (Berkeley: University of California Press, 1996), 11.

3. From an advertisement in the *Muslim Magazine*, April 1998, 42.

4. Yvonne Yazbeck Haddad and Adair T. Lummis, *Islamic Values in the United States: A Comparative Study* (New York: Oxford University Press, 1987), 53.

5. Bonne Lovelace, "U.S. Military Designates First Muslim Chaplain," *Islamic Horizons*, May/June 1995, 46.

6. Colbert I. King, "Muslim Converts, Meet the FBI," *Washingtonpost.com*, June 17, 2008.

7. Department of Justice, Office of Justice Programs, Bureau of Justice Statistics, *Prison Statistics*, August 15, 2006.

8. Anna Bowers, "The Search for Justice: Islamic Pedagogy and Inmate Rehabilitation," in Yvonne Y. Haddad, Farid Senzai, and Jane I. Smith, eds., *Educating the Muslims of America* (New York: Oxford University Press, 2009).

9. Omar Afzal, "Beyond Brown, Black, and White: Muslims in North America." *The Message*, July 1997, 21.

6. Women and the Muslim American Family

1. Asma Gull Hasan, *Why I Am a Muslim: An American Odyssey* (London: Element Books, 2004), 167.

2. This remark, made privately to the author, refers particularly to the courageous efforts of pioneers such as Huda Sha'rawi and her colleagues in the early part of the twentieth century, who upon returning to Egypt from a women's conference in Rome defied tradition and threw their veils into the harbor.

3. Asra Nomani, *Standing Alone in Mecca: An American Woman's Struggle for the Soul of Islam* (New York: HarperOne, 2005).

4. Amina Wadud, *Qur'an and Woman: Rereading the Sacred Text from a Woman's Perspective* (New York: Oxford University Press, 1999).

5. Saraji Umm Zaid, "Make Way for the Women! Why Your Mosque Should Be Woman Friendly," *Islam for Today*, online September 4, 2008.

6. Michele Boorstein, "Muslims Try to Balance Traditions, U.S. Culture on Path to Marriage," *Washington Post*, May 27, 2008, online.

7. From a conversation among Christian and Muslim women at Harvard Divinity School in the late 1980s.

8. M. Riaz Khan, "Domestic Violence: American Muslim Families Not Immune," *Islamic Horizons*, July/August 1995, 29.

9. Advice column by Dr. Nashiha al-Sakina in *The Minaret*, August 1996, 43.

10. Yvonne Yazbeck Haddad and Adair T. Lummis, *Islamic Values in the United States: A Comparative Study* (New York: Oxford University Press, 1987), 87.

11. Zaheer Uddin, "Aging Muslims in America," *Islamic Horizons*, July 26, 2008, 37.

12. Dr. Shahid Athar, "Taking Care of the Elderly and the Infants," *The Minaret*, December 1997, 8.

13. Copyright 2007, printed in China.

14. Irshad Manji, *The Trouble with Islam: A Muslim's Call for Reform in Her Faith* (New York: St. Martin's, 2004).

7. Living a Muslim Life in American Society

1. Jameila Al-Hashemi, "The Public School System Versus Islamic School," *Islamic Horizons*, June/July 1997, 55.

2. Mahdi Bray, "School Prayer: The Need for Muslim Proactive Involvement," *Islamic Horizons*, January/February 1995, 18.

3. Alia Amer and Abul Hadi Harman Shah, "Guiding Principles for Islamic Social Behavior," *Al Jumuah* (4–5, 1417 H):23.

4. Jahan-zaib Hassan Gilani, "Muslim Youth in College," *The Message*, November 1997, 34.

5. Nadia Khan, "'Guide Us to the Straight Way': A Look at the Makers of 'Religiously Literate' Young Muslim Americans," in Yvonne Haddad, Farid Senzai, and Jane Smith, eds., *Educating the Muslims of America* (New York: Oxford University Press, 2009).

6. Abdul-Aziz Al-Fazwan, "Fatawa," *Al Jumuah* (7, 1418 H):16.

6. "Multiply Assets Through Investment Clubs," *Islamic Horizons*, March/April 1997, 54.

7. A. Rushdi Siddiqui, "Finances Takes a Chair," *The Message*, November 1997, 42.

8. Judi Muhammad, "Islamic Hospital Care Comes to Detroit," *Islamic Horizons*, September/October 1996, 36.

9. Yvonne Yazbeck Haddad and Adair T. Lummis, *Islamic Values in the United States: A Comparative Study* (New York: Oxford University Press, 1987), 106–107.

10. Vernon Schubel, "The Muharram Majlis: The Role of a Ritual in the Preservation of Shi'a Identity," in Earle H. Waugh, Sharon M. Abu-Laban, and Regula B. Qureshi, eds., *Muslim Families in North America* (Edmonton: University of Alberta Press, 1991), 118.

11. Alexis Kort, "Dar al-Cyber Islam: Women, Domestic Violence, and the Islamic Reformation on the World Wide Web," *Journal of Muslim Minority Affairs* 23, no. 3 (December 2005): 363–383.

12. "You Tube—Muslim Style." You%2otube-Muslim%2ostyle.EML (July 18, 2008).

13. From the online article "Muslim-American Magazines Explore Identity," by Omar Sacirbey, correspondent for the *Christian Science Monitor*, June 23, 2008.

14. Yusuf Islam, "Music: The Good and the Bad," *Islamic Horizons*, September/October 1997, 56.

15. Matthew Philips, "Slam Dancing for Allah," http://msnbc.msn.com.

16. *The Minaret*, October 1997, 43.

17. "Islam Day to Day," *The Message*, March 1996, 41.

18. http://hijabstyle.blogspot.com/2008/.

19. Tarajee Abdur Rahim, "Living with HIV in the Muslim Community," *The Message*, May 1996, 27.

20. Muzammil H. Siddiqi, "Where There's a Will There's a Way," *Islamic Horizons*, July/August 1999, 38.

8. Islam in America Post-9/11

1. Gwendolyn Zohara Simmons, "Are We Up to the Challenge? The Need for a Radical Reordering of the Discourse on Women," in Omid Safi, ed., *Progressive Muslims: On Justice, Gender, and Pluralism* (Oxford: Oneworld, 2003), 235.

2. www.aicongress.org, copyright 2008.

3. Khaled Abou El Fadl, *The Place of Tolerance in Islam* (Boston: Beacon, 2002.

4. Fathi Oslam, "Monotheists and the 'Other': An Islamic Perspective in an Era of Religious Pluralism," *Muslim World Journal* 88 (July–October 1998): 353–363.

5. Ali Asani, "On Pluralism, Intolerance, and the Qur'an," *American Scholar* 1 (Winter 2002): 52–60.

GLOSSARY

The following are terms that have been used throughout this volume, reflecting the concepts and vocabulary relevant to understanding the experience of American Islam. They are given in transliteration from the Arabic with a brief definition.

'abd   Servant, the believer in relation to God

adhan   Call to prayer given five times daily; *mu'adhdhin*—the one to give the call

ahl al-bayt. People of the House, referring to the members of the Prophet's family; descendants of the Prophet's son-in-law 'Ali

ahl al-kitab People of the Book, the Qur'anic reference to Christians, Jews, and others who possess Scripture

arkan   Pillar, referring to the five basic responsibilities incumbent upon all Muslims

'Ashura   The tenth of the month of Muharram, the time when Shi'is remember the martyrdom of Imam Husayn

ayatollah   Literally, "sign of God"; refers to the highest and most learned of Shi'ite clerics

basmallah   Invocation of the name of God

dar al-harb Abode of war, referring to lands outside of Islam (sometimes called *dar al-kufr*, abode of apostasy)

dar al-islam Abode of peace, referring to lands where Islamic law is enforced

da'wa   Call or invitation, summoning others to heed the call of God to Islam; propagation of the faith

dhikr	Remembrance, the congregational Sufi ritual of remembering God
du'a.	Private, personal, nonritualized prayer
'eid	Holiday or festival; *'eid al-fitr*—observance of the end of Ramadan; *'eid al-adha*—observance on the last day of the *hajj* or pilgrimage to Mecca
fiqh	Islamic jurisprudence; codification of the sacred law, or *shari'a*
hadith	Traditions that report the words and deeds of Prophet Muhammad
hajj	Pilgrimage to Mecca prescribed for every Muslim, if possible, once in a lifetime
halal	Legally permissible
hanif	One of the pious believers before Muhammad, not Christians or Jews, who submitted to God's oneness
haram	Unlawful, prohibited
hijab	Head covering worn by women as a sign of piety and Muslim identity
hijra	Emigration of Prophet Muhammad and his followers from Mecca to Medina in 622 c.e.
iftar	Breaking of the daily fast during the month of Ramadan
ijma'	Consensus of the community; one of the four accepted sources of Islamic law
ijtihad	Individual reasoning or interpretation
imam	For Sunnis a religious leader, or one who leads the prayer; for Shi'ites a direct descendant of the Prophet who is the divinely mandated leader of the community
iman	Faith, submission to God through the heart
islam	Personal submission to the will of God through which one enters Islam, the community of the faithful
jahiliyya	The time of ignorance, said to apply to the Arabian society before the revelation of the Qur'an
jihad	Struggle against the lower forces of one's nature or against the enemies of God
Ka'ba	The Holy House, or shrine of Islam, in the Grand Mosque at Mecca
kalam	Word (of God); the speculative theology of Islam
khalifa	Caliph. The one who comes after the Prophet; the titular leader of Muslims until the caliphate was abolished in 1924

khatm	Seal or stamp, referring to the fact that Muhammad is the last of the prophets
kufr	Rejection of the reality and being of God; unbelief
mahdi	The divinely guided leader who will return to establish justice on earth before the resurrection
masjid	Mosque; place where one prostrates oneself before God
mi'raj	The journey taken by Muhammad with the angel Gabriel through the heavens into the presence of God
mufti	Jurisconsult; one who gives a legal opinion (*fatwa*) based on his knowledge of the law
mujaddid	Renewer of the faith, said to come once in each century
nabi	Prophet; a recipient of a communication from God intended for a specific community
niyya	Declaration of intention to carry out a religious responsibility, as in salat, or prayer, in the right spirit of mind and heart
qadi	Judge, one who decides civil and criminal cases according to the *shari'a*
qibla	The direction of prayer facing the Ka'ba in Mecca
qiyas	Reasoning by analogy; one of the four accepted sources of Islamic law
raka'	Bending at the waist in the ritual prayer, followed by prostrations
rasul	Messenger; recipient of a universal message from God
riba	Usury, or interest in excess of the legal rate
salat	The formal or ritual prayer, to be performed five times a day
saum	Fasting during the daylight hours of the month of Ramadan
shahada	Bearing witness that there is no God but God and that Muhammad is his Prophet
shari'a	Islamic sacred law; prescribed conduct for the believer
shaykh	A Sufi master; one who initiates followers into the spiritual and esoteric disciplines (also called *pir* or *murshid*)
Shi'a, Shi'ite	The identifying name for those who are of the party of 'Ali, as distinguished from the majority Sunnis or Sunnites
shirk	The sin of associating anything or anyone with God
shura	The principle of consultation by which decisions in the Islamic community are made

Sufi	One who follows one of the schools of mystical thought in Islam
Sunna	The life example or way of the Prophet Muhammad
Sunni	The identifying name for the great majority of Muslims (generally as distinguished from the Shi'a or Shi'ites)
sura	Chapter of the Qur'an
takbir	Saying "*Allahu akbar*," literally "God is greater," oftens used as a signal of commendation
taqwa	Personal piety
tariqa	Way or path under the leadership of a *shaykh* or *pir*; a Sufi order or brotherhood
taslim	Salutation of peace by which one greets fellow worshipers
tawhid	The essential unity of God; affirmation of God's oneness and consequent human responsibility to live ethically
'ulama'	The learned religious and legal scholars of Islam
umma	The community of all of those who affirm Islam
'umra	The lesser *hajj*, or pilgrimage to Mecca performed at any time of the year
wahy	Revelation, specifically used for the sending down of the message of the Qur'an by God to Prophet Muhammad
wali	A "friend of God," a holy person or saint
wudu'	Ritual washing before performance of the *salat*, or prayer
zakat	Alms payment or welfare tax

RESOURCES FOR THE STUDY
OF ISLAM IN AMERICA

Books

Abd-Allah, Umar F. *A Muslim in Victorian America: The Life of Alexander Russell Webb*. New York: Oxford University Press, 2006. A biography of one of the first and most influential American converts to Islam.

Anway, Carol L. *Daughters of Another Path: Experiences of American Women Choosing Islam*. Baltimore: Yawna Publications, 1996. Interviews of women whose daughters have married Muslims and converted to Islam, sharing both concerns and pleasures.

Athar, Shahid. *Reflections of an American Muslim*. Chicago: Kazi Publications, 1994. A practicing Muslim physician communicates his understanding of Islam to North America.

Austin, Allan D. *African Muslims in Antebellum America: A Sourcebook*. New York: Garland, 1984.

Bakhtiar, Laleh. *Sufi Women of America: Angels in the Making*. Chicago: Kazi Publications, 1996. Interviews with women who have joined Islam through the Naqshbandiyya Sufi movement.

Barboza, Steven. *American Jihad: Islam After Malcolm X*. New York: Doubleday, 1994. Brief biographical sketches of American Muslims, some well known and others not, who have converted to Islam.

Bukhari, Zahid H., Sulayman S. Nyang, Mumtaz Ahmad, and John L. Esposito. *Muslims' Place in the American Public Square: Hopes, Fears, and Aspirations*. Lanham, Md.: AltaMira, 2004. A collection of articles about ways in which Muslims today are participating in politics and other public activities.

Cook, Miriam and Bruce B. Lawrence, eds. *Muslim Networks: From Hajj to Hip Hop*. Chapel Hill: University of North Carolina Press, 2005. Looks at Islam as a series of networks or systems of social affiliation based on shared religious practice.

Curtis, Edward E. IV. *Black Muslim Religion in the Nation of Islam, 1960–1975.* Chapel Hill: University of North Carolina Press, 2006. Practices and beliefs of the Nation of Islam as a unique form of identity influenced by African American culture and Muslim traditions.

——. *The Columbia Sourcebook of Muslims in the United States.* New York: Columbia University Press, 2008. Detailed volume covering history, immigrant and African American relations, gender and sexuality, politics, and religious life.

——. *Islam in Black America.* Albany: State University of New York Press, 2002. Issues of identity, liberation, and difference in African American Islamic thought.

Dannin, Robert. *Black Pilgrimage to Islam.* New York: Oxford University Press, 2002. A sweeping overview of the African American community.

Gardell, Mattias. *In the Name of Elijah Muhammad: Louis Farrakhan and the Nation of Islam.* Durham, N.C.: Duke University Press, 1996. A scholarly and intensive study by a Swedish observer of Nation of Islam ideology and development.

Haddad, Yvonne Yazbeck, ed. *The Muslims of America.* New York: Oxford University Press, 1991. Essays on the history, organization, challenges, responses, outstanding leaders, and future prospects of the Muslim community in the United States and Canada.

Haddad, Yvonne Yazbeck, and John L. Esposito, eds. *Muslims on the Americanization Path?* New York: Oxford University Press, 1998. Essays centered on the question of whether or not Muslims can live faithfully in a non-Muslim country.

Haddad, Yvonne Yazbeck, and Adair T. Lummis. *Islamic Values in the United States: A Comparative Study.* New York: Oxford University Press, 1987.

Haddad, Yvonne Y., Farid Senzai, and Jane I. Smith, eds. *Educating the Muslims of America.* New York: Oxford University Press, 2009. A survey of the state of Muslim education in America in the twenty-first century, including private schools, homeschooling, new forms of Islamic education for youth and adults.

Haddad, Yvonne Yazbeck, and Jane I. Smith. *Mission to America: Five Islamic Sectarian Communities in North America.* Gainesville: University Press of Florida, 1993. A study of five sects whose identity as Muslim is challenged.

——, eds. *Muslim Communities in North America.* Albany: State University of New York Press, 1994. Descriptions and analyses of twenty-two different racial-ethnic and national groupings.

Haddad, Yvonne Y., Jane I. Smith, and Kathleen Moore. *Muslim Women in America: The Challenge of Islamic Identity Today.* New York: Oxford University Press, 2006. A study of the rights and roles of American Muslim women and their contributions in the fields of religious studies, arts and culture, community organizing, and politics.

Haley, Alex. *The Autobiography of Malcolm X.* New York: Ballantine, 1964 (1992). The life of Malcolm told in his own words, from his early days as an East

Coast drug dealer to his prison conversion to his movement out of the Nation of Islam.

Hasan, Asma Gull. *Why I Am a Muslim: An American Odyssey*. London: Element Books, 2004. Description by a young liberal American Muslim woman about how she sees Islam as open, flexible, and fun.

Jackson, Sherman A. *Islam and the Blackamerican: Looking Toward the Third Resurrection*. New York: Oxford University Press, 2005. An erudite and scholarly presentation of Islam, Islamic law, and the role of African Americans in American Islam.

Kahera, Akel Ismail. *Deconstructing the American Mosque: Space, Gender, and Aesthetics*. Austin: University of Texas Press, 2002. History and theory of Muslims' religious aesthetics in the United States since 1950, interpreting forms and meanings of American mosques.

Kepel, Giles. *Allah in the West: Islamic Movements in America and Europe*. Stanford, Calif.: Stanford University Press, 1997. Examines Islam in Britain and France, the birth of black Islam in America, the life of Malcolm X, and the Nation of Islam.

Koszegi, Michael A., and J. Gordon Melton, eds. *Islam in North America: A Sourcebook*. New York: Garland, 1992. Muslim immigrants in North America, sectarian movements, mysticism, and Islamic-Christian relations; useful directory of North American Islamic organizations and centers.

Lee, Martha F. *The Nation of Islam: An American Millenarian Movement*. Syracuse, N.Y.: Syracuse University Press, 1996. Looks at the Nation of Islam as a failed millenarian movement that branched into the American Muslim Mission and the reconstituted Nation.

Leonard, Karen. *Muslims in the United States: The State of Research*. New York: Russell Sage Foundation, 2003. Historical overview of Muslims in the United States, with a focus on contemporary research issues.

Lincoln, C. Eric. *Black Muslims in America*. Rev. ed. Boston: Beacon, 1973. The first significant sociological study of the Nation of Islam before the death of Elijah Muhammad.

Mallon, Elias. *Neighbors: Muslims in North America*. Cincinnati: Friendship Press, 1989. Brief stories told in interview format of American Muslims from a variety of ethnic, cultural, and geographical backgrounds.

Manji, Irshad. *The Trouble with Islam: A Muslim's Call for Reform in Her Faith*. New York: St. Martin's, 2004. A reporter's analysis of what she sees as problems inherent in contemporary Islam.

Marsh, Clifton E. *From Black Muslims to Muslims: The Transition from Separatism to Islam, 1930–1980*. Lanham, Md.: Scarecrow Press, 1984. A treatment of the transition of African American Islam from its earlier separatist ideology to Sunni Islam.

McCloud, Aminah Beverly. *African American Islam*. New York: Routledge, 1995. An introduction to the different expressions of African American Islam, focusing on five early and thirteen contemporary communities.

Metcalf, Barbara Daly, ed. *Making Muslim Space in North America and Europe*. Berkeley: University of California Press, 1996. How Muslims in America and Europe have translated physical and psychological space to fit their needs as Muslims.

Nimer, Mohamed. *The North American Muslim Resource Guide: Muslim Community Life in the United States and Canada*. New York: Routledge, 2002. Survey data and vignettes on population groups with Muslims in America, mosques and Islamic centers, Islamic schools, and Muslim social service agencies.

Nomani, Asra. *Standing Alone in Mecca: An American Woman's Struggle for the Soul of Islam*. New York: HarperOne, 2005. A single mother tells her story of undertaking the pilgrimage alone.

Poston, Larry. *Islamic Da'wah in the West: Muslim Missionary Activity and the Dynamics of Conversion to Islam*. New York: Oxford University Press, 1992. A brief history of *da'wa* in the East and West, including treatment of "paramosque" structures and strategies and the literature of Muslim apologetic.

Qazwini, Hassan. *American Crescent: A Muslim Cleric on the Power of His Faith, the Struggle Against Prejudice, and the Future of Islam and America*. New York: Random House, 2007. An influential Shi'ite cleric in the United States writes about his faith and life through the lens of his migration and his experience of Islam in America.

Rouse, Carolyn Moxley. *Engaged Surrender: African American Women and Islam*. Berkeley: University of California Press, 2004. Moves beyond characterizations of subordinated women in Islam by showing how Islam has proved liberating in the lives of African American converts in Los Angeles.

Safi, Omid, ed. *Progressive Muslims: On Justice, Gender, and Pluralism*. Oxford: Oneworld Publications, 2003. Articles assessing the relationship of Islam to the modern world, dealing with issues of racism, justice, sexuality, and gender.

Schmidt, Garbi. *Islam in Urban America. Sunni Muslims in Chicago*. Philadelphia: Temple University Press, 2004. A very readable description of the various aspects of Islam in Chicago, focusing on young people.

Shaheen, Jack G. *Arab and Muslim Stereotyping in American Popular Culture*. Washington, D.C.: Center for Muslim-Christian Understanding, 1997. Muslims as portrayed on television, in the movies, and in print and broadcast news, contesting the stereotypes.

Smith, Jane I. *Muslims, Christians, and the Challenge of Interfaith Dialogue*. New York: Oxford University Press, 2007. An overview of different contexts of Christian-Muslim dialogue in America, with attention to categories, problems, and theological interpretations.

Turner, Richard Brent. *Islam in the African-American Experience*. 2nd ed. Bloomington: Indiana University Press, 2003. Roots of American Islam overseas and in antebellum America, and the stories of leaders of twentieth-century African American urban Muslim movements.

Wadud, Amina. *Qur'an and Woman: Rereading the Sacred Text from a Woman's Perspective*. New York: Oxford University Press, 1999. Feminist interpretive reading of the Qur'an.

Waugh, Earle H., Baba Abu-Laban, and Regula B. Qureshi, eds. *The Muslim Community in North America*. Edmonton: University of Alberta Press, 1983. Discussion of a range of issues relevant to the lives of Muslims in the United States and Canada.

Waugh, Earle H., Sharon M. Abu-Laban, and Regula B. Qureshi, eds. *Muslim Families in North America*. Edmonton: University of Alberta Press, 1991. Critical issues facing Muslims in the United States and Canada, especially the situation of women, adjustment of families, and strategies for coping in an alien environment.

Wolfe, Michael. *The Hadj. An American's Pilgrimage to Mecca*. New York: Grove/Atlantic, 1998.

_____. *One Thousand Roads to Mecca: Two Centuries of Travelers Writing About the Muslim Pilgrimage*. New York: Grove/Atlantic, 1998.

——, ed. *Taking Back Islam: American Muslims Reclaim Their Faith*. New York: Rodale, 2002. Short and very readable essays about various dimensions of American Islam.

Wormser, Richard. *American Islam: Growing Up Muslim in America*. New York: Walker, 1994. Interviews with Muslim teenagers about everyday concerns.

Muslim Journals and Periodicals

Al Jumuah. Monthly magazine published by the Islamic Revival Association, P.O. Box 5387, Madison, Wis. 53705-5387.

American Journal of Islamic Social Sciences. Association of Muslim Social Scientists, International Institute of Islamic Thought, published simultaneously in Washington, D.C., and Kuala Lumpur, Malaysia.

American Muslim. Quarterly publication of the American Muslim Support Group, P.O. Box 5670, Bel Ridge, Mo. 63121, with the cooperation of Al Ribat al-Islami, P.O. Box 601, La Jolla, Calif. 92038-0601.

Azizah. A magazine committed to being the voice for Muslim women. WOW Publishing, P.O. Box 43410, Atlanta, Ga. 30336-0410.

Elan: Celebrating the Good Life in Northern Virginia. Nearly a decade old, *Elan* chronicles talented northern Virginia artists.

Final Call. Weekly newspaper of Minister Louis Farrakhan, FCN Publishing, 734 W. 79th Street, Chicago, Ill. 60620. Tel: 773-602-1230. Fax: 773-602-1013. Web site: http://www.finalcall.com.

Iqra. Monthly magazine of the South Bay Islamic Association, 3325 N. Third Street, San Jose, Calif. 95112.

Islam in America. Quarterly survey of books, periodicals, and newspapers published by the Alduvai Humanities Library, P.O. Box 2411, Olympia, Wash. 98507-2411.

Islamic Horizons. Bimonthly publication of the Islamic Society of North America (ISNA), P.O. Box 38, Plainfield, Ind. 46168-0038.

Islamica. Quarterly journal that reprints academic journals, especially back and out-of-print issues. Paris: Editions Maisonneuve et Larose.

Journal of Muslim Minority Affairs. Published twice a year as a forum for discussion of issues relating to the life of Muslims in non-Muslim societies. Car-fax Publishing, Ltd., P.O. Box 25, Abingdon, Oxfordshire OX14 3UE, United Kingdom.

The Light and Islamic Review. Lahore Ahmadiyya Movement, 1315 Kingsgate Road, Columbus, Ohio 43221-1504.

The Message. Monthly journal published by the Islamic Circle of North America (ICNA), 166–26 89th Avenue, Jamaica, N.Y. 11432-4254.

The Minaret. Published monthly by the Islamic Center of Southern California, 434 S. Vermont, Los Angeles, Calif. 90020.

Muslim Journal. Weekly newspaper of the ministry of W. D. Muhammad, published by Muslim Journal Enterprises, Inc., 910 W. Van Buren, Suite 100, Chicago, Ill. 60607. Tel: 312-243-7600. Fax: 312-243-9778. E-mail: muslimjrnl@aol.com. Web site: http://www.worldforum.com/muslimj.

Muslim Magazine. Monthly journal started in 1998, designed for both Muslim and non-Muslim readership, with issues focusing on special topics. Editor, 607-A W. Dana Street, Mountain View, Calif. 94041.

Washington Report on Middle East Affairs. Published eight times a year. 1902 18th Street, N.W., Washington, D.C. 20009-1707. Regular sections on Islam in the United States and Canada. Tel: 202-939-6050.

INDEX